Junos® OS

FOR

DUMMIES®

2ND EDITION

Junos® OS FOR DUMMIES®

2ND EDITION

Walter Goralski, Cathy Gadecki, and Michael Bushong

WILEY

John Wiley & Sons, Inc.

Junos® OS For Dummies®, 2nd Edition

Published by
John Wiley & Sons, Inc.
111 River Street
Hoboken, NJ 07030-5774
www.wiley.com

WILEY

About the Authors

Walter Goralski: Walter Goralski is a Senior Staff Engineer and Technical Writer at Juniper Networks, Inc. He has been involved in the networking field for more than forty years. His career has also included fifteen years as an Adjunct Professor at Pace University Graduate School of CS&IS. He is the author of more than ten books on networking topics, including a bestselling book on SONET/SDH. He is currently documenting Juniper Networks' MobileNext line of products.

Cathy Gadecki: Supporting Junos product marketing for over four years at Juniper Networks, Ms. Gadecki has more than 20 years in marketing and product management positions with a focus on creating new markets for network equipment and services, for both startup and established firms. Ms. Gadecki is the co-author of *ATM For Dummies* (John Wiley & Sons, Inc.), which has been reprinted seven times and published in multiple languages. She earned her master's degree in electrical engineering from the Georgia Institute of Technology with a focus on data communications.

Michael Bushong: A Senior Product Manager at Juniper Networks, Michael is tasked with managing Junos software. Michael has spent the past seven years working at Juniper Networks in several capacities. Originally hired to train Junos engineers on architectural, design, and application principles, Michael developed detailed materials covering everything from software architecture to broader applications deployed using Junos software. Michael has since transitioned to product management, where he has focused on the constant evolution of the operating system, spearheading major infrastructure efforts designed to scale the operating system to meet tomorrow's needs. Having majored in mechanical engineering with a specialized focus on advanced fluid mechanics and heat transfer, Michael began his professional career working on research in aerodynamics. He has since spent time with databases at Sybase and, more recently, in ASIC design tools at both Synopsis and Magma Design Automation.

Dedication

Walter Goralski: To my wife Camille, the backbone of support in all my accomplishments.

Cathy Gadecki: To Steve and our five children.

Michael Bushong: To Stacy Prager, now Stacy Bushong, but not when I began writing the book. Thank you, Patrick Ames. And to Chloe and, of course, to Steve and Linda Bushong.

Authors' Acknowledgments

The authors wish to thank the many people who helped bring about this book. Our in-house editor for both editions, Patrick Ames encouraged, guided, and coached us in so many different ways. Jonathan Looney helped with many suggestions and edits for our first edition. Our lead technical editor to the first edition, Mario Puras, tested and confirmed our configurations and output. A large group of Juniper field engineers reviewed the first edition and made invaluable suggestions for improvement: Pedro Cutillas, Christian Graf, Joe Green, Imran Khan, Stefan Lager, and Michael Pergament. On security matters, insight from Barney Sanchez helped us in how to present the new security topics included in the second edition, while Monear Jalal reviewed the first edition. On matters of switching, Yong Kim and David Nguyen helped us in how to present the new switching topics; Kishore Inampudi assisted in the Q-Fabric content; and Lenny Bonsall, Bobby Guhasarkar, Joseph Li, and Michael Peachy shared their expertise for our first edition. Other key subject matter experts checked our work and took our phone calls: Daniel Backman, David Boland, Atif Khan, Kannan Kothandaram, Mike Marshall, Ananth Nagarajan, Brian Pavane, Naren Prabhu, Doug Radcliff, Alan Sardella, and Don Wheeler.

We also wish to thank our John Wiley & Sons, Inc. editors, Katie Feltman, Colleen Totz Diamond, and Melba Hopper.

Publisher's Acknowledgments

We're proud of this book; please send us your comments at http://dummies.custhelp.com. For other comments, please contact our Customer Care Department within the U.S. at 877-762-2974, outside the U.S. at 317-572-3993, or fax 317-572-4002.

Some of the people who helped bring this book to market include the following:

Acquisitions, Editorial

Project Editor: Colleen Totz Diamond

Sr. Acquisitions Editor: Katie Feltman

Copy Editor: Melba Hopper

Technical Editor: Juniper Networks

Editorial Manager: Jodi Jensen

Editorial Assistant: Amanda Graham

Sr. Editorial Assistant: Cherie Case

Cover Photo: © iStockphoto.com / Cary Westfall

Cartoons: Rich Tennant (www.the5thwave.com)

Composition Services

Project Coordinator: Nikki Gee

Layout and Graphics: Corrie Socolovitch

Proofreaders: Melissa Cossell, Evelyn Wellborn

Indexer: BIM Indexing & Proofreading Services

Publishing and Editorial for Technology Dummies

Richard Swadley, Vice President and Executive Group Publisher

Andy Cummings, Vice President and Publisher

Mary Bednarek, Executive Acquisitions Director

Mary C. Corder, Editorial Director

Publishing for Consumer Dummies

Kathy Nebenhaus, Vice President and Executive Publisher

Composition Services

Debbie Stailey, Director of Composition Services

Contents at a Glance

Table of Contents

Part III: Deploying a Device *165*

Chapter 10: Deploying a Router **167**

Chapter 11: Deploying an EX Switch **185**

Introduction

Welcome to *Junos OS For Dummies*. This book provides you with a handy reference for configuring and running Junos software on Juniper Networks products. (We won't bore you with how Junos got here, but you can discover more about Juniper Networks and the evolution of Junos software at www.juniper.net/company.)

More and more, Junos software is being deployed throughout the world running on Juniper Networks platforms designed for switching, routing, and security. You can find it in both the largest and the smallest service provider networks and in the networks at tens of thousands of offices, regional campuses, and data centers of enterprise organizations, as well as in the public sector and on educational campuses.

See whether you can identify with any of the following scenarios:

- **In your branch offices:** You may be updating your branch gateway with an integrated platform, Voice over IP (VoIP), supporting new users, or upgrading older switching, routing, or security infrastructure.

- **In your headquarters or regional office campuses:** You may be adding new users or deploying new or deploying VoIP, new web or upgrading older switching and routing infrastructures, or merging or migrating from other operating systems.

- **In your metropolitan or wide area networks:** You may be transitioning to new optical, Ethernet, or MPLS carrier services; building a new core for your metro, wide area, or data center backbone network; rolling out MPLS; or upgrading an older switching, routing, or security infrastructure.

- **In your data centers:** You may be looking for ways to reduce the power usage of your data center, collapse networking tiers and infrastructure, converge your data centers into fewer sites, deploy networking fabric, scale existing sites, or build out new data centers.

This book can help you with all these scenarios and a whole lot more. We offer this book as a fast and easy way to understand and use the Junos operating system (OS) for all your network needs.

About This Book

We wrote this book thinking that you're probably a lot like us: too many projects, with too little uninterrupted time. So, we created this book to help you do the following:

- ✔ Understand what Junos can do for you and how you can use it in your own network.
- ✔ Quickly use the CLI so that you can configure and change your network using the Junos OS.
- ✔ Deploy any networking device out of the box and onto your network in an hour or two. If it runs Junos, you'll be able to do it.
- ✔ Run, operate, and maintain the Junos OS with high uptime, performance, and security over the long haul.
- ✔ Find easy access to a set of references about the many features and uses of Junos in your network.

Conventions Used in This Book

Junos device output and configuration samples are printed in a monospace font. A bold monospace font within an output snippet indicates something that you, the user, key into the command-line interface (CLI) to launch the command and receive the subsequent output, such as this:

```
user@junos-router> show route
```

By the way, we don't bold configuration samples, however, as the entire configuration would be a bolded series of lines.

This book is based on Junos 11.1. While newer software versions of Junos are always in the works, subsequent release versions don't negate what you find out in this book; they extend the functionality of what you have learned.

Foolish Assumptions

When we wrote this book, we made a few assumptions about you. In essence, we assume that you do, or will, operate or administer a Junos device and need to configure, deploy, maintain, or troubleshoot it. And that means you probably fit within the following:

✔ You are a network professional, although you don't have to be one. Our objective is to get you up and running, so we don't discuss the operations of the protocols in detail.

✔ You may design or operate networks with devices running Junos software — or are about to, are considering it, or are just curious about what the Junos OS is all about.

✔ You may be coming from another network operating system, such as Cisco IOS, in which case, you've found a really good introduction to Junos and the day-to-day administration of the Juniper devices that run it.

✔ You may be a student entering the networking profession.

If you are any of these people, or a hybrid of them all, welcome. You've found the right book.

How This Book Is Organized

This book is divided into five parts with very practical names.

Part I: Discovering Junos OS

This part introduces the Junos OS that is used for switching, routing, MPLS, and security. It also includes a section on migrating from other platforms.

Part II: Setting Up Junos OS

This part helps you set up the basics of your network. You find out how to work with the command-line interface and discover the basic commands for routing, switching, and securing your device.

Part III: Deploying a Device

In this part, we help you set up your router, switch, or security device to your network.

Part IV: Running a Junos Network

In this part, we help you set up additional functionality, including remote management, interfaces, peering, policy, class-of-service, MPLS, and VPNs.

Part V: The Part of Tens

This part offers a quick reference of the ten most helpful commands, the keys to migrating from one network to a Junos network, and other places you can go for more information.

Icons Used in the Book

We use icons throughout this book to key you into time-saving tips, things you really need to know, and the occasional warning or interesting back-grounder. Look for them throughout these pages.

This icon highlights helpful hints that save you time and make your life easier.

Be careful when you see this icon. It marks information that can keep you out of trouble.

Whenever you see this icon, you know that it highlights key information you'll use often.

We mark text that is interesting but that you don't have to read as Technical Stuff. You can skip these items if you're in a hurry or don't want to lose your train of thought. Return to them later or browse through the book some day during lunch and read them at your leisure.

Where to Go from Here

You can go anywhere within your network and deploy or fine-tune the Junos OS with this book in your hands and its content in your head. That's the whole point. We happen to teach and train hundreds of network administrators and engineers about Junos each month, and we work with people just like you who are improving their network response time, traffic handling, or expanding services. We see it all the time — that light bulb that goes off midway through the class or training seminar and the administrators can see their network in a whole new way. That's because there's only one Junos, not variants, and once you learn Junos, you can take that knowledge anywhere on your network and apply it.

Browse through the Table of Contents and consider a starting point and then just dip in. Ramble around a little. Get a feel for the book and then dive in. Remember, you can't get lost with Junos. You can only get better.

Note that we occasionally have updates to our technology books. If this book does have technical updates, they will be posted at

```
dummies.com/go/junosfdupdates
```

Part I
Discovering Junos OS

The 5th Wave — By Rich Tennant

"I guess you could say this is the hub of our network."

In this part . . .

You know that nuclear reactor thingy that Robert Downey in the *Iron Man* movie put in this chest to power his rocket books and extraordinary powers? Well, that's what Junos is to Juniper Networks devices.

This part introduces the Junos OS that is used for switching, routing, MPLS, and security. It also includes a section on migrating from other platforms. You find out all about Junos and how you can power your network at speeds way past the sound barrier.

Chapter 1

Junos Is Everywhere
You Need to Be

· ·

In This Chapter

▶ Understanding the functions of a network operating system

▶ Discovering how Junos OS is different

▶ Looking beyond the operating system to the Junos Platform

· ·

*T*he Junos operating system (Junos OS) is the software that runs networking and security devices from Juniper Networks. Administrators use Junos OS to set up devices and connect them together in a network, and dictate how the devices move, service, and secure traffic across the network. They also use it to monitor and, when necessary, restore the network.

Note: In this book, we use both Junos OS and Junos as one and the same.

This chapter introduces Junos OS by describing the functions of a network operating system and then discussing how they work in Junos. The chapter also explores key differences in how Juniper develops Junos software versus how other vendors create their network operating systems, and introduces additional components of the Junos portfolio.

Functions of a Network OS

Networks consist of specialized devices that pass along traffic from one to another. Each device must know what to do with each arriving bundle of traffic, or *packet,* so that the packet can continue its journey to its destination. The devices perform three primary functions to process each packet:

▰ Controls where the device sends the packets.

▰ Applies services such as prioritization or security.

▰ Forwards the packet to the next connecting device.

These actions are the primary functions of the network operating system that runs on the device. In simplest terms, the *control plane* of the network operating system is the brain of the device with the *forwarding plane* providing the brawn to quickly move packets through the system. Depending on the type of packet, the *services plane* may also provide packet services such as address translation, prioritization, and security.

Control functions

This essential map for connectivity, security, and other orchestrating processes is the function of the network operating system's control plane. The processes and information of the control plane must provide answers to two essential questions:

- ✔ How does the network direct the delivery of packets from one place to another? In other words, what are the routes or paths to establish, how do they change, and how does each device know which route to use for each packet?

- ✔ What does the network do with each of the packets along its journey? In other words, what are the handling rules, or policies, along with the security and services plane established for traffic delivery?

Although the questions can be simply stated, the possible responses are virtually limitless. You can define dozens and dozens of protocols to answer these questions for different types of network maps and all the different types of traffic, not to mention how the control plane monitors and manages everything. The many processes to control the network delivery of packets fill the industry with all those three- and four-letter acronyms that you've somehow managed to file into your memory.

Service functions

The service needs of users grow with new applications triggering new requirements for quality, security, addressing, and content delivery, among others. Applying the specialized processing is the role of the services plane.

For example, as the packets flow through each device, the devices must typically apply a range of filters, policies, and services for protecting the network (and its clients and applications) and assigning priorities for the use of its resources. Visualize watching a YouTube video. Now visualize all your users watching the video all at the same time because some clown in your office passed along an e-mail with the link to everyone. And now think about all the traffic hitting your network all at once, just as your president is on a critical call with your biggest customer. Oofta!

This is just one example of where you may want to define a few of those extra rules that your network can follow in making its packet deliveries. (We provide Chapter 15 to help you set up class of service in your devices.)

Forwarding functions

Along with assembling the intelligence to properly deliver the traffic from one place to another and applying services, the network operating system (and its hardware) must actually deliver packets to the correct destination using this intelligence. Moving packets through a networking device is the function of the network operating system's forwarding plane, also sometimes known as the *data plane*.

Packet forwarding takes care of the handling required to move each packet quickly from its inbound device interface to the proper outbound interface(s). For large networking devices that carry terabits of traffic, this handling must occur at an ultra-über fast rate to maintain the high packet throughput of the machines.

Taking Advantage of One Network OS

Network operating systems have a lot do and can have a big impact on the performance, ease of operations, reliability, and security of your network. Junos OS is different, in that it's one operating system. But why does having one operating system matter?

One operating system means the Juniper engineers build upon the same set of code and then share this code, as appropriate, across all the platforms running Junos. For example, enterprise platforms use the same hardened implementation of the routing protocol Open Shortest Path First (OSPF) that has been running in large service provider networks for many years. It's not a different code set, but the same one. (To set up OSPF, see Chapter 10.)

So, if your responsibilities include administrating the network, you find that many features are configured and managed in the same way on the different platforms, whether they are routers, switches, or security devices. One operating system, therefore, saves you time, potentially lots of it, in everything from training to setup to ongoing operations. Also, if you plan changes in the network, one operating system can save you time there, too. With far less variation to evaluate, test, and deploy, it's less effort for feature roll out, software upgrades, and other network modifications.

Taking a Peek Inside the Junos OS

How engineers design a network operating system impacts the reliability, security, scalability and performance of not just the devices, but also the overall network, particularly in large-scale systems. The operating system must handle the many different processes essential to running today's global networks, while also assuring fair sharing of resources so that no process or service can starve out others.

World-class architecture

The architecture of the Junos operating system cleanly divides the functions of control, services, and forwarding into different planes. The control and services planes include many different processes that run in different modules of the operating system. The explicit division of responsibility allows the software to run on different engines of processing, memory, and other resources. This division of labor is what enables Junos to run all types of platforms in all matter of sizes, from a small box in a home office to the largest boxes in the world handling terabits of data every second.

Figure 1-1 provides a high-level view of the Junos OS software architecture with its three functional processing planes. Shown above the dashed line is the control plane that runs on what is known as the *Routing Engine* (RE) of the Juniper device. Below the dashed line is the packet forwarding plane, which runs on a separate *Packet Forwarding Engine* (PFE) in larger Juniper platforms. The services plane, which provides specialized processing, such as for quality classification and security, is on the right.

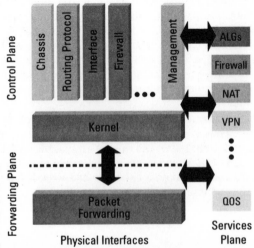

Figure 1-1: Architecture of the Junos OS.

Do you want faster platforms in your network? That's like asking if you'd like to have today off (with pay, of course). Yes, it would be good to have the network go a little faster. Faster, faster, faster is a constant drumbeat for networks. In over ten years of product delivery, Juniper has scaled the throughput of its fastest devices from 40GB per second to multiple terabits per second with a fast expanding set of services. The use of separate processors for the RE, the PFE, and services cards has been the essential architecture element to each performance breakthrough. In particular, separation lets the PFE and services throughput follow in lock-step with the increasing speeds of the custom Application-Specific Integrated Circuits (ASICs) on which the PFE and services run in the largest platforms.

Separating the engines also reduces interdependencies between them. Not only does this separation help preserve the operation of each when another is experiencing problems, it also gives the Juniper engineers more ways to provide system redundancy and failover. For example, you find dual REs in some platforms, whereas the EX Series Ethernet Switches offer a capability called Virtual Chassis to provide redundancy, among other benefits. (See Chapter 11 for the details of this switching feature.)

Plain smart: The planes of Junos OS

Each of the planes of Junos OS provides a critical set of functionality in the operation of the network.

It's all under control

All the functions of the control plane run on the Routing Engine (whether you have a router, switch, or security platform running Junos). Figure 1-1, shown earlier in this chapter, shows the high-level design of the control plane — a set of modules, with clean interfaces between them, and an underlying kernel that controls the modules and manages all the needed communication back and forth among all the components. The kernel also handles the RE communications with the Packet Forwarding Engine and the services. Each of the different modules provides a different control process, such as control for the chassis components, Ethernet switching, routing protocols, interfaces, management, and so on.

The basis of the Junos kernel comes from the FreeBSD UNIX operating system, an open source software system. This mature, general-purpose system provides many of the essential functions of an operating system, such as the scheduling of resources. To transform it into a network operating system, the Juniper engineers extensively modified and hardened the code for the specialized requirements of networking.

You may be wondering if you have a way in Junos OS to protect the control plane itself from a security attack. Yes, you can configure filters and rate-limit the traffic that reaches your RE. (For more on this topic, see Chapter 9.)

Moving forward

The Packet Forwarding Engine is the central processing element of the forwarding plane, systematically moving the packets in and out of the device. In the Junos OS, the PFE has a locally stored *forwarding table*. The forwarding table is a synchronized copy of all the information from the RE that the forwarding plane needs to handle each packet, including outgoing interfaces, addresses, and so on. Storing a local copy of this information allows the PFE to get its job done without going to the control plane every time that it needs to process a packet.

Another benefit to having a local copy is that the PFE can continue forwarding packets, even when a disruption occurs to the control plane, such as when a routing or other process issue happens.

At your service

The services plane provides special handling required by many different types of packets. By separating the processing of services from other functions of the operating systems, Junos OS is able to support a wide variety of different service types in different kinds of platforms.

These services might include prioritizing a packet carrying time-sensitive information, such as a voice call, ahead of others on a congested link; guarding which users can get to what sections or applications of the network; translating addresses where one network meets another; or mediating how the network serves video content.

That's not a problem: The many benefits of modular architecture

Have you ever had a router continually reboot, and when you look on the console, you see that an error occurred in a single nonessential process?

With the Junos OS, you don't see that problem. The modular architecture of Junos OS allows individual control plane processes to run in their own *module* (also sometimes called a *daemon*). Each module has specified processing resources and runs in its own protected memory space, avoiding the processing conflicts that can occur in other platforms. If a malfunction in a module causes an issue, the rest of the system can continue to operate. For example, one module can't disrupt another by scribbling on its memory.

What about a minor hiccup in SNMP bringing down your whole system? That's another misfortune that you won't miss with Junos OS, because its clean separation between control processes helps to isolate small problems so that they can't create worse havoc.

In our many discussions with users, we hear over and over that the stability of Junos OS is the biggest difference that they see after deploying Juniper platforms in their network. They tell us about their boxes running for months and months, even years without interruption. How they popped the device into the rack, set up the configuration, and never looked back. It just keeps going and going and going — oh, that's another company's line.

The modular architecture also eases fault isolation. With each process functioning within its own module, when the occasional problem does occur, pinpointing the exact reason is far less complicated for both you and the Juniper support team. With quick identification and a good understanding of the root cause, you can apply a fix that works, the first time you try.

We have one more benefit to highlight — flexible innovation. The organized structure of the architecture enables deep integration of new capabilities with high functioning interaction with existing processes. For you, this means that native support of new services and features delivers a richness of capability with the high performance that you expect. For example, among the integrations to Junos OS are the security services derived from Juniper's ScreenOS operating system. (You can find out more about some of these features in Chapter 12.)

Developing Junos OS

Software development probably isn't a topic that you expected to find in a networking book. After all, you don't need to build the Junos operating system. Juniper's engineers do that for you.

However, we include a little about this topic because we think it's important. The disciplined development process is an essential reason why Junos OS is different. Unlike most other vendors, Juniper develops new versions of the operating system along a common release path, as shown in Figure 1-2.

Figure 1-2:
Junos
release
path.

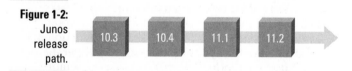

Asking the right questions

Consider reviewing the software development processes of vendors as a part of your evaluation of new network and security equipment, because it can save you time and money down the road. Here are some questions that you can ask vendors about their software development processes:

✔ **Software versions:** Find out how many different software versions exist for the products you are buying, and ask why the different versions exist. Know the differences between versions, and when to use one version versus another. Also, ask about the support and end of life policies for each version.

✔ **New features:** Ask what steps do development engineers follow when adding new features. How do they support changes and fixes to the features in different software versions or release trains? You also want to know how they decide which features to add to which version?

✔ **Fixes:** Ask about the steps for adding fixes to the code. What procedures ensure that a new fix is a part of all releases, including those in the future? In what types of releases are fixes available and how often?

✔ **Testing:** Find out how the vendor tests newly developed features (and fixes). What guidelines determine when a release is ready for customers? How thoroughly is each type of release tested before being released to customers? Ask whether a new release can affect previously working features, and find out whether the vendor's testing includes use-cases to assess how features interact. Ask how the vendor performs performance and scalability testing.

When it's time to upgrade, you simply choose a higher release number, and not only do you get all the newly developed features, you also keep all the important features you've already been using in your network. Also, you're not running a specialized version of software that may be prone to issues; you're running software used by Juniper customers everywhere. (Find out more about Junos release versions and upgrades in Chapter 3.)

Beyond the OS

Since we wrote the first edition of this book, Juniper has expanded its Junos software portfolio beyond the operating system, adding new capabilities to link into the application space as well as client software for mobile and personal computing devices. Together, the Junos operating system, the Junos Space network application platform, and the Junos Pulse client form the Junos Platform. By integrating these software layers of the network into one platform, Juniper is expanding the ways that applications can interact with the network from the cloud out to the end user.

As part of the Junos Platform, Juniper provides a set of programming interfaces and software development kits (SDKs) that developers can use to specify the application interactions. Unlike other platforms that merely enable third parties to interface through APIs, these SDKs give application developers a broad set of development interfaces and tools to build a wide variety of applications richly integrated to the Junos Platform.

The following sections provide a short introduction to these additional components of the Junos portfolio. To learn more about Junos Space and Junos Pulse visit http://www.juniper.net/us/en/products-services/ software/junos-platform.

Junos Space

Junos Space is an open network platform for developing and hosting applications that interact with the network. The Junos Space platform provides multilayered network abstractions and workflows that allow users to automate network operations and increase operator efficiency.

The software includes a scalable runtime environment with multitenant, hotpluggable network application support, a network application development framework, and a Web 2.0 user interface.

Junos Space provides a development environment for fast development of network-aware applications. The application development framework includes a common infrastructure, a software development kit (SDK) with prebuilt core services and widgets to allow easy user-interface prototyping, and standards-based APIs for third-party application integration. Using the Junos Space SDK, developers have the option of creating different classes of applications. These include mashups, customized business process workflows, and native applications.

Junos Pulse

Junos Pulse is an integrated, multi-service network client to secure and control application delivery on mobile and personal computing devices. The client is both identity- and location-aware, enabling seamless migration from one access method to another so that users effortlessly, yet securely, retain access to their applications regardless of their location.

Users can download the Junos Pulse client free of charge from most mobile application stores. In this way, the solution can support not only devices managed by the network provider, but also those managed by the user. Once installed, the client provides secure, authenticated access to corporate networks and resources using SSL VPN technology. Junos Pulse provides a comprehensive mobile security, management, and control solution to protect end devices from viruses, malware, spam, loss, theft, physical compromise, and other threats.

Chapter 2

Jumping Into Junos

*W*hen you first get access to the Junos operating system, you may want to log in and start exploring what you can do with it right away. Perhaps you've heard that running a network with Junos can save you time, and you want to see for yourself what Junos can do. This chapter lays out the basics of how to log in, shares a few of our favorite power tools for operators, gives a guided tour to its two modes of operation, and helps you set up your first configuration.

Jumpstart Instructions

First-time users most typically access the Junos OS running on their device in one of two ways:

✔ **Over a network:** Someone else installed the device and can provide you with the hostname as well as the username and password assigned to you. The device may be on a separate subnet behind a gateway device that protects unauthorized access to it, in which case, you will also need the login credentials of the gateway server.

✔ **In direct connection:** You are directly connected to the device through the console or a management port using a null-modem or rollover cable. The first time you log in to a device that has never been configured, you will be logging in as the root user, and you will not need a password. The *root user* is a super-administrator who can perform any operation, from benign checks such as looking at the status of the device to disruptive operations such as changing the configuration and rebooting the device.

Junos in the Cloud

Junosphere is a cloud-based environment where users can configure and connect virtual devices that are running Junos to support training, network modeling, and other lab activities. The Junosphere services from Juniper Networks enable realistic, large-scale virtual networks, including a means to interoperate the virtual network with physical network elements. Additionally, users can incorporate Junos Space (see Chapter 1), the Junos and Junos Space SDKs (see Chapter 1), virtualized testing equipment and other lab elements into their network. Together these elements enable organizations to create a highly scalable virtual network of devices running the Junos operating system without requiring dedicated lab resources. For more about Junosphere services, turn to Chapter 19.

 To install and access your new device out of the box, check out the *Quick Start Guide* for your product at www.juniper.net/techpubs. Navigate to your specific product to find the guide for your device.

Whichever way you access your Junos device, follow these steps to log in:

1. If you are accessing a previously configured device (otherwise skip this step), use a terminal emulation program, such as Telnet, to open a connection. In this and other examples in the book, we use *netnik* as the hostname:

   ```
   telnet netnik
   ```

2. At the login prompt, enter your username (use the username root if you are logging in for the first time). At the password prompt enter your password (or press Enter if you are logging in for the first time as the root user):

   ```
   netnik (ttyp0)

   login: wiley
   password: ********
   ```

3. If you logged in with the root username (otherwise skip this step), you see a shell, similar to a UNIX shell. Type cli to enter the Junos command-line interface (CLI).

   ```
   root@Amnesiac% cli
   ```

4. You are now in the operational mode of the CLI. You see a command-line prompt, which shows your username followed by an @ sign and the hostname of the device. You can enter a ? anywhere in the command-line and receive a list of possible entries.

   ```
   wiley@netnik> ?
   ```

A few users may access the Junos operating system their first time through one of the Junosphere services available from Juniper Networks. Junosphere offers a virtual network running Junos in a cloud-based delivery model. See the sidebar for more about Junos in the cloud.

Command-Line Essentials

The Junos CLI is the starting point to most operator tasks, providing an intuitive, text-based command shell. If you've used a UNIX-based host, you'll see many similarities.

Most users find the Junos operating system CLI fairly easy to grasp. Many commands are similar to those used by other networking vendors. For example, if you are familiar with the Cisco CLI, you'll find that many Junos CLI commands are the same. The only difference is that you don't need to use the keyword IP.

After looking around the interface for a few minutes, new users begin to find some of the advanced tools provided by the Juniper engineers to make configuring, monitoring, and managing the system easy to do. Some familiar tools include the ?, which provides a list of possible completions, and the Tab key, which provides completion of partially typed commands, saving you many keystrokes.

Among the many intuitive aspects of the CLI are a structured command hierarchy, extensive fail-safe mechanisms that help to catch configuration mistakes and errors, automation tools for speeding and delivering accuracy to your daily operator tasks, and comprehensive online help.

In addition to the CLI, the Junos operating system offers J-Web GUI access. The simplicity of the J-Web interface allows users to quickly and easily deploy many Juniper devices in an enterprise network. J-Web provides a series of quick configuration wizards that simplify device setup and enable real-time network-management service changes and upgrades. See the J-Web sidebar for a brief introduction to the graphical tool with Chapter 5 providing more information.

As J-Web essentially provides a graphical interface and setup wizards for the underlying command-line interface, it's helpful to understand at least the basics about the CLI.

J-Web

The J-Web interface allows you to monitor, configure, troubleshoot, and manage your device by means of an HTTP- or HTTPS-enabled web browser. J-Web provides access to the configuration statements supported by the device, so you can fully configure it without using the CLI editor. For example, in the SRX Series of security gateways, J-Web includes wizards to assist you in configuring firewall policies, NAT, and IPSec VPNs.

A tale of two command modes

A fundamental trait to understand about Junos OS is that it separates the CLI commands into two groups:

- **Operational mode:** A set of commands to manage and monitor device operations. For example, you can monitor the status of the hardware and software and perform maintenance tasks, such as upgrading software or managing device files.

- **Configuration mode:** A set of commands to set up the device and the network. For example, you can configure user access, the system properties, and the device's interfaces, protocols, and services.

The Junos CLI further structures the activities of each mode into a set of hierarchies, as illustrated in Figure 2-1. The hierarchy of each mode is made up of cascading branches of related functions commonly used together where deeper levels are more and more specific.

The structured hierarchy of the CLI brings practical elegance, and it's a favorite trait of long-time Junos users. By logically grouping activities, the Junos CLI provides a familiar, consistent structure for knowing where you are, finding what you want, moving around the interface, and entering commands. Also, when you are setting up a configuration for a particular aspect of the network, such as its protocols, or verifying or troubleshooting the network, everything is in the same place.

The convenient hierarchical structure of Junos means that you don't waste a lot of time scrolling through the entire configuration every time you need to make a change. You simply navigate your way to the necessary section of the command tree.

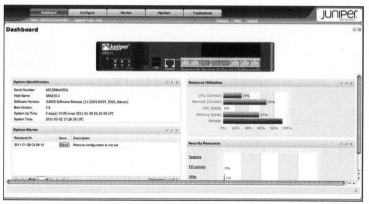

Figure 2-1:
Each Junos
CLI mode
has a hier-
archical
command
structure.

Knowing your location in the CLI

Because of the hierarchy of the Junos CLI, you always know just where you are in the command hierarchy. When you first log into the CLI, Junos places you in operational mode. You enter configuration mode by using the `configure` command:

```
wiley@netnik> configure
Entering configuration mode
[edit]
wiley@netnik#
```

You can identify which mode you are in by the command prompt.

✔ In operational mode, the prompt is a > symbol:

```
wiley@netnik>
```

✔ In configuration mode, the prompt is a # symbol:

```
wiley@netnik#
```

Knowing your place in the hierarchy

In configuration mode, you must apply new commands precisely where they belong — for example, to a specific interface or policy group — so it's impor-tant that you know exactly where you are in the hierarchy. Fortunately, con-figuration mode uses indentation, which helps you recognize its hierarchy. This indentation may remind you of the outline you did in high school for your sophomore research paper.

Before looking at an example of a configuration listing, you may find it helpful to become familiar with two different types of configuration statements:

- ✓ **Container statements:** Contain subordinate levels of the hierarchy.

- ✓ **Leaf statements:** End a hierarchy — that is, they have no subordinate statements.

Now, here's an example configuration listing that shows off the svelte moves of configuration mode:

```
[edit]
system {
  services {
    ftp;
  }
}
```

- ✓ The [edit] banner indicates the starting hierarchical level of the listing.

- ✓ Indentation of each subordinate level shows the configuration hierarchy. Here, ftp is under services, which is under system.

- ✓ The CLI indicates container statements with open and closed curly braces ({ }). Here, system and services are container statements.

- ✓ The CLI indicates leaf statements with a semicolon (;). Here, ftp; is a leaf statement.

Junos ensures that you can easily make your way up and down its configuration interface.

Before moving on to the next section, we want to show you one more smooth move of the CLI. In the preceding example, you find simply the [edit] banner at the very top of the configuration mode. But Junos allows you to look at this same setup from anywhere along its hierarchical path, for example:

```
[edit system services]
ftp;
```

In configuration mode, when you are in deeper levels of the hierarchy, the edit banner always gives you the complete hierarchical path. Here, [edit systems services] indicates that you are in the second level node of system, and then within it, you are in the third level node of services.

When you want to focus on only a small part of the configuration, having the flexibility to work at a specific sublevel of the hierarchy is helpful. Next, you find out how to move up and down the configuration.

Moving through the hierarchy

Configuration mode provides four commands for moving through the hierarchy, and we're confident you will use them again and again.

✔ edit: Jumps you to an exact location that you specify within the hierarchy in which you are currently working. You issue the relative path based on your location in the hierarchy:

```
[edit system]
wiley@netnik# edit syslog host log
```

```
[edit system syslog host log]
wiley@netnik#
```

You can only move up and down a particular hierarchy — not across the hierarchies — with the edit command. To move to another hierarchy, you must first go back to the top of configuration mode to the edit banner.

✔ top: Moves you instantly to the top of the configuration hierarchy.

```
[edit system syslog host log]
wiley@netnik# top
```

```
[edit]
wiley@netnik#
```

Combine top and edit to quickly move to a new hierarchy location:

```
[edit protocols ospf area]
wiley@netnik# top edit system login
```

```
[edit system login]
wiley@netnik#
```

✔ up: Takes you up one level in the configuration hierarchy. You can append a number to specify how many levels, for example, up 4.

✔ exit: Returns you to the hierarchy point prior to the last edit command.

Saving time with typing shortcuts

Many Junos administrators prefer using the CLI rather than a GUI because the CLI generally makes configuring and managing the device quicker for configurations with a lot of customized settings. The downside of using a CLI is that sometimes you have to type long commands or statements. Junos provides two types of shortcuts to minimize your typing: command completion and keyboard sequences.

Using command completion

Command completion is just what the name implies: You type the first few characters of a command or statement, press the spacebar or the Tab key, and Junos completes the word.

You can use either the spacebar or Tab key to complete most command arguments, but only the Tab key completes user-defined variables (such as a firewall filter name).

For example, you can use the `show interfaces` command, which displays the existing configuration for interfaces. With command completion, you can simply type the following:

```
wiley@netnik# show int<spacebar>
```

Junos completes the command, and you see the entire command in the CLI:

```
wiley@netnik# show interfaces
```

If the portion of the command string you're entering is ambiguous, Junos will list the possible options:

```
wiley@netnik# show i<spacebar>
'i' is ambiguous
```

```
Possible completions:
igmp Show Internet Group Management Protocol
ike Show Interface Key Exchange Information
interfaces Show Interface Information
ipsec Show IP Security Information
isis Show Intermediate System-to Intermediate
```

So, type an **n** and press the Enter key to complete:

```
wiley@netnik# show in<spacebar>
wiley@netnik# show interfaces
```

Common abbreviations from other operating systems, such as sh int, are available in JUNOS Software. For example:

```
mike@juniper1> sh<space>ow int<enter>.
```

Benefiting from keyboard sequences

Use the arrow keys or combine a letter with the Ctrl or Esc key for time saving shortcuts. For example, use the arrow keys to scroll through the recent command history to reuse commands, either as you previously typed them or you may modify them. Table 2-1 lists common keyboard shortcuts for the Junos operating system.

Keyboard sequences are particularly useful when you're configuring similar items on the device — for example, numerous interfaces of the same type. Keyboard sequences are also useful when you're debugging a problem on the network and need to reuse the same commands repeatedly.

Table 2-1	Keyboard Sequence Shortcuts
Keyboard Sequence	*Action*
Up arrow (or Ctrl+P) and down arrow (or Ctrl+N)	Move backward and forward through the most recently executed commands.
Left arrow (or Ctrl+B) and right arrow (or Ctrl+F)	Move the cursor, character by character, through the text on the command line.
Esc+B	Move back one word.
Esc+F	Move forward one word.
Ctrl+A	Move to beginning of command line.
Ctrl+E	Move to end of command line.
Ctrl+K	Delete all text from cursor to end of command line.
Esc+D	Delete the word after the cursor.
Esc+Backspace	Delete the word before the cursor.
Ctrl+Y	Paste the deleted text at the cursor.

Getting help

The question mark (?) is always ready and waiting to help you out. You can enter a ? at any prompt, or even within commands, to find the possible valid command entries or command completions at that particular point.

For example, entering **help?** at the top of configuration mode, as shown in Listing 2-1, provides a listing of available help commands. These help commands provide access to the Junos technical documentation directly from the command-line interface. Juniper loads the documentation on new devices and also includes it as a part of upgrade builds.

Listing 2-1: Using ? to View Help Commands

```
[edit]
wiley@netnik# help ?
Possible completions:
  <[Enter]>           Execute this command
  Apropos             Find help information about a topic
  reference           Reference material
```

(continued)

Listing 2-1 *(continued)*

```
syslog              System log error messages
tip                 Tip for the day
topic               Help for high level topics
|                   Pipe through a command
```

The help commands are available in both operational and configuration modes. For example, under this command in configuration mode, you can use the help topic command to provide usage guidelines and the help reference command to lookup command syntax descriptions for configuration statements.

Defining How You Want Devices to Work

Configuration mode is all about setting up how your device works in your network. When you configure your device, you define its settings for the specifics of your network operations. This process includes specifying the addresses to use, configuring the management console, setting up user accounts and permissions, applying routing and switching protocols, and implementing security measures. Each statement configures different functions of the device that direct the particular properties of device operation.

The following sections describe the configuration process; introduce the commands to set up, change, and delete configuration statements; and explain two ways to make these statements active in your device.

Understanding the configuration process

Perhaps you're among the unfortunate with a story to tell about your worst configuration nightmare, how during a bleary-eyed 3 a.m. trouble-call, you made matters worse with some fat-thumb move. Or maybe it's about the time you mixed up the exact order of your line-by-line command entries and found yourself with more to clean up. (Ever remember adding security to a remote box from a tradeshow, only to find that the new firewall locked you out of the very interface that you were using to get into the box?)

Whatever your story, you're not alone. Many different studies show that more than 60 percent of network downtime can be attributed to human factors (*a.k.a.*, absent-minded errors).

Fortunately, the Juniper engineers worked closely with early customers in designing the Junos CLI, and those early users requested a wealth of smart features. Today, Junos can help you avoid a great deal of hassle and headache, too.

Figure 2-2 outlines the configuration process of the Junos OS. The essential difference between using Junos and many other network operating systems is that you don't make changes to the actual configuration on the device, but to a *candidate configuration* that you can later check and commit to.

You can think of the candidate configuration as your scratch pad for entering your device configuration and making any needed changes, additions or deletions. While you always enter your configuration or its changes as a candidate file, the candidate doesn't actually run your device. When you are ready to make your candidate the running configuration of your device, you can compare and test the candidate and then activate it as the new running configuration, all at once, with the *commit* step.

TOP LEVEL
NODE

2nd LEVEL
NODES

Figure 2-2:
The Junos
OS configu-
ration steps.

3rd LEVEL
NODES

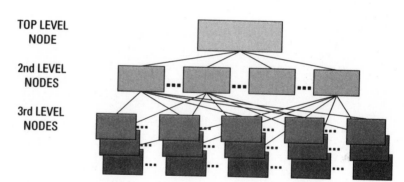

So, how can the Junos CLI help you avoid being "3 a.m. stupid," any time of the day? Here's a short list of command-line features that can help in that regard (the sections that follow provide the details on how to use them):

- ✔ `show | compare`: Use to see the exact changes you made and to look for typos or omissions. For example, if you copy a portion of the configuration to a new interface, `show | compare` highlights the changes so that you can detect whether you've left anything out.

- ✔ `commit check`: When your changes are ready (or any time while entering changes), use `commit check` to find out whether the CLI understands everything you've entered. The system verifies the logic and completeness of your new configuration entries without activating any changes. If the CLI finds a problem, it lets you know.

✔ `commit confirmed`: When you're ready to activate your candidate as the active configuration, you have two options: `commit` and `commit confirmed`. `commit confirmed` is the better choice because it saves you from requiring physical access to the box in case your changes accidently isolate your device. Remember that if you don't confirm your changes (by entering `commit` or `commit check`) within ten minutes of activation (or another interval that you can set), the device reverts back to the prior configuration.

✔ `rollback`: The Junos CLI gives you one last safety feature that not only helps protect you, but also makes changes easier. `rollback` lets you restore the rescue or any of the prior 50 configurations (the rescue configuration is a user-predefined, known working configuration). Using `rollback` is much quicker than undoing one command at a time in the command-line interface.

The `confirmed` command is there to help you. We've heard stories about folks who didn't bother using this option — and then later were stuck trying to figure out how to fix what they had just done that isolated a remote site. Get in the habit of taking the little extra step to `commit confirmed`.

Creating and editing the configuration

You set up or change your device's configuration in the configuration mode of the Junos CLI. To enter configuration mode, use the `configure` command at the operational mode prompt:

```
wiley@netnik> configure
Entering configuration mode
```

```
[edit]
wiley@netnik#
```

You are now ready to create or edit the candidate configuration. Enter `set ?` after the configuration mode prompt to see the complete list of top-level configuration statements that are available for the set up of your device, as shown next in Listing 2-2. These top-level groups organize all Junos configuration statements into hierarchies of related commands.

Listing 2-2:   Using `set` `?` to View Statements

```
[edit]
wiley@netnik# set ?
Possible completions:
> chassis             Chassis configuration
> class-of-service    Class-of-service configuration
> firewall            Define a firewall configuration
```

```
> forwarding-options   Configure options to control packet forwarding
> interfaces           Interface configuration
> policy-options       Routing policy option configuration
> protocols            Routing protocol configuration
> routing-instances    Routing instance configuration
> routing-options      Protocol-independent routing option
        configuration
> snmp                 Simple Network Management Protocol configuration
> system               System parameters
```

You use these top-level commands and their underlying hierarchies to set up the various properties of your device. You can enter them into the candidate configuration line by line, copy them as text, or import them from a file. Part II of this book provides the details on the various commands and the ways to enter them. For now, as a simple example, here's how you would add a new Gigabit Ethernet interface by directly entering the appropriate set command via the CLI:

```
[edit]
wiley@netnik# set interfaces ge-1/1/0 unit 0 family inet
        address 192.168.0.1/24
```

You can use Junos automation to strictly guide users in making changes to a configuration. By creating an *op script* for the device, users can perform controlled configuration changes based on supplied input from command-line arguments, interactive prompts, or Junos show commands. The advantage of this approach is that you can code the structure of the change into the script itself. This mitigates human error and lets users with less expertise change the configuration in controlled ways. See Chapter 3 for an introduction to Junos automation.

Committing your configuration

The candidate configuration file is only the "proposed" configuration; your device does not use any of this configuration until you activate this candidate configuration using the commit command, but first you'll want to check your work.

Checking your work

While editing your candidate configuration you can make as many changes as you want, in any order that you want. You can be interrupted numerous times, and when you are done, check your work to make sure you didn't miss anything.

For example, in configuration mode, Junos OS checks for omitted statements required at a particular hierarchy level whenever you attempt to move from that hierarchy level or when you issue the `show` command:

```
[edit protocols]
wiley@netnik# show
pim {
  interface so-0/0/0 {
    priority 4;
    version 2;
    # Warning: missing mandatory statement(s): 'mode'
  }
}
<snip>
```

You can use the `show` command at the top of configuration mode to view the entire candidate configuration or within any sub-hierarchy to see the configuration from that hierarchical level and below.

The `show` command displays all the statements in a configuration, one screen at a time. To see the next screen, press Enter or the spacebar.

The `commit check` command validates the logic and completeness of the candidate without activating any changes. These are the same validations that run when you commit the candidate configuration. If the Junos operating system finds a problem in the candidate, Junos lets you know:

```
[edit]
wiley@netnik# commit check
[edit interfaces lo0 unit 0 family inet]
    'address 192.168.69.1/24'
        Loopback addresses' prefix must be 32 bits
error: configuration check-out failed
```

Saving your work

When you've made all your changes and done all your checks and are ready to make your candidate the active configuration running the device, enter the `commit` command:

```
[edit]
wiley@netnik# commit
```

As part of the commit process, Junos checks basic syntax and semantics. For example, the software makes sure that a policy has been defined before it is referenced. If any syntax or semantic problems are found, the `commit` command returns an error:

```
[edit]
wiley@netnik# commit
error: Policy error: Policy my-policy referenced but not
      defined
error: BGP: export list not applied
error: configuration check-out failed
```

You must fix all mistakes before the candidate (or any part of the candidate) can become active.

When the activation is done, you see the `commit complete` message, which indicates that all the configuration statements of your candidate are now operating as the active configuration of your device:

```
[edit]
wiley@netnik# commit
commit complete
```

Junos activation is a batch process — all the device configuration statements start operating only after you enter a `commit` statement, and all at the same time. In other systems, you might have to carefully consider the order in which you enter commands, because each command becomes immediately active as soon as you press Enter. You don't have this constraint with Junos. All configuration statements start to run at the same time without any delays.

Confirming before you commit

Having a Junos candidate configuration activate all at once might seem a bit nerve-wracking. What happens if the configuration starts going haywire and network performance starts deteriorating? Worse, what happens if the configuration you committed locks you out of the device so that you can no longer log in?

Junos provides a path for the timid and the cautious user alike. You can try out a candidate configuration. If you don't like it, Junos returns to the previous version of the configuration automatically. This approach is an easy way to get out of a jam. To try out a candidate configuration, instead of using the `commit` command, use `commit confirmed`:

```
[edit]
wiley@netnik# commit confirmed
commit confirmed will be automatically rolled back in 10
      minutes unless confirmed
commit complete
```

The default wait is ten minutes, and you have to explicitly accept the commitment, either by typing the `commit` command again or by typing the `commit check` command. Then you see the `commit complete` message.

If ten minutes is too long to wait in your functional network, use a shorter delay, such as one minute, to tell whether the configuration is working:

```
[edit]
wiley@netnik# commit confirmed 1
commit confirmed will be automatically rolled back in 1
        minutes unless confirmed
commit complete
```

If the device operation isn't correct, don't worry. When the confirm time expires, Junos automatically returns to the previous configuration, which you know is a working configuration:

```
Broadcast Message from root@netnik (no tty) at 16:36 PDT…
Commit was not confirmed; automatic rollback complete.
```

Even the most experienced Junos engineers and administrators use the `commit confirmed` command as an insurance policy on their own work. Doing so can sometimes save hours lost sending someone to a remote site so that they can physically access a device which has become inadvertently isolated from the rest of the network through a configuration misstep.

Going Back to a Prior Configuration

When you activate a new configuration, the Junos operating system automatically keeps an archive of the previous active configuration. This automatic backup mechanism lets you return quickly to a previous configuration. You have several different options when you use the `rollback` command as discussed in this section.

Rolling back to a past configuration

To return to a configuration that Junos has automatically archived, use the `rollback` command in configuration mode:

```
[edit]
wiley@netnik# rollback 1
load complete
```

This `rollback` command loads the previous configuration but stops short of activating it. If you need to change what's in the configuration, you can modify and review it, and then when you are ready to make the configuration active, enter the `commit` command.

In addition to archiving the last version of the configuration, Junos stores the last 50 active configurations. These files are on the device's flash and hard disk drives, so you can restore the configuration saved in a particular file.

Use the ? query with the `rollback` command to list the full archive:

```
[edit]
wiley@netnik# rollback ?
Possible completions:
  <[Enter]>                  Execute this command
    0            2011-09-01 12:34:56 PST by wiley via cli
    1            2011-09-01 12:30:03 PST by wiley via cli
    2            2011-09-01 14:23:44 PST by wiley via cli
    ...
2011-08-03 08:00:12 PST by root via cli
2011-08-03 07:45:21 PST by root via cli
  |                          Pipe through a command
```

Pick the configuration by date and time and specify the number in the `roll-back` command to load that configuration:

```
[edit]
wiley@netnik# rollback 2
load complete
```

To reset the candidate configuration to the currently active configuration use the `rollback` (or `rollback 0`) command.

As another option of restoring configurations, Chapter 5 shows you how to copy the currently active configuration or a previous one from the device to a file server on the network, as well as how to reload a configuration file onto the device.

Verifying the restored configuration

Verify that the configuration is what you want with the `show` command, or if you aren't sure what differences exist between the active (running) configuration and a rollback file, investigate with the `show | compare` command:

```
[edit interfaces]
wiley@netnik# show | compare rollback 2
[edit interfaces]
- fe-3/0/1 {
-     vlan-tagging;
-     unit 240 {
-         vlan-id 240;
-         family inet {
-             address 10.14.250.1/28;
-             address 10.14.250.17/28
-             {
-                 preferred;
```

```
-           }
-           address 10.14.250.33/28;
-           address 10.14.250.49/28;
-           address 10.14.250.65/28;
-       }
-   }
- }
```

The recently deleted statements are listed with a minus sign (–) as the first character, whereas recently added statements are noted with an addition sign (+).

This Way to the Exit

Most people remember to log out when they complete their work, but even when you walk away from your desk for just a few moments, make it a habit to log out to prevent others from accessing the device.

You can log out with this simple operational mode command:

```
wiley@netnik> exit
```

If you're in configuration mode, use the exit or quit commands to return to operational mode first. If you're not at the top level of the configuration, use one of the following command sequences to get there:

```
[edit protocols bgp group isp-group]
wiley@netnik# top
```

```
[edit]
wiley@netnik# exit
Exiting configuration mode
```

```
wiley@netnik>
```

or

```
[edit protocols bgp group isp-group]
wiley@netnik# exit configuration-mode
Exiting configuration mode
```

```
wiley@netnik>
```

When you're ready to learn more about how to set up the basics of your device, head to Chapter 5 for the next steps.

Power Tools

You find lots of help tools intuitively integrated into the Junos CLI. For example, this chapter introduces `help`, `show | compare`, `command completion`, `commit check`, and `rollback`. Other powerful tools that you'll find particularly helpful when setting up your configuration include the following list.

✔ **Syntax checking:** Checks for small errors as you're typing at the command-line. The CLI immediately lets you know if an entered line doesn't conform to valid syntax and offers tips for correcting it.

✔ **Annotations:** Use `annotate` followed by your notes when you want to leave comments for other team members. If something goes wrong, your operations teams will have critical information immediately at hand on the device, instead of trying to hunt down design guides that may have been lost long ago.

✔ **Rename and replace:** Change the contents of a configuration variable with the `rename` or `replace` command. Use `rename` to change a specific statement and `replace` to change a character string anywhere that the string occurs in the configuration. Chapter 5 shows you how to use these commands.

✔ **Rescue configuration:** Enter the `rollback rescue` command to quickly return to the saved configuration designated as the rescue configuration.

✔ **Predefined changes and installs:** You can set up configurations for new cards ahead of insertion. If the card is not yet installed, Junos just ignores that part of the configuration. Use `deactivate` when you want

to input configuration changes and leave them inactive until needed or schedule the specific time with the `commit at` command. These power tools are handy if one team installs the hardware and another configures the software, or you want to have everything ready in advance for a scheduled maintenance window.

✔ **Restrict access permissions:** Set authorization privileges for different users. You can use predefined user classes, as well as customize who can access what command hierarchy, or even specific individual commands. For example, you can set up your user groups so that only a small number of your operational staff, with expert experience in your deployment procedures and change management, have the needed permissions to commit new changes. See Chapter 6 to learn more about setting up user permissions.

✔ **Junos automation:** Enables you to automate, in your own way, the commands of the CLI, in both configuration and operational modes, and also lets you set up custom event policies. Using Junos automation not only saves time, but also can reduce downtime by preventing configuration errors and speeding problem resolution and restoration. Chapter 3 further introduces Junos automation.

Chapter 3 also introduces the keyword `run` as another power tool of configuration mode; this keyword lets you run any operational mode command while you are in configuration mode. Also, discover a few of the powerful ways that you can use the pipe (|) command to filter or direct output in Chapter 3.

Chapter 3

Operating Your Network with Junos

● ●

In This Chapter

▶ Exploring the operational mode of the Junos CLI

▶ Displaying output just as you like it

▶ Monitoring and supporting your device and your network

▶ Using Junos Space applications to automate operations

▶ Managing and maintaining the system software

● ●

*T*he Junos OS provides many tools to help you in the daily activities of running your network operations. You find lots of these tools in the operational mode of the Junos CLI. Others, such as monitoring and logging, are set up in the device configuration, while a few more are applications running on Junos Space (see Chapter 1). Wherever you find them, this chapter introduces you to the tools you'll turn to again and again in your routing, switching, and security devices to operate your network.

Exploring Operational Mode

After setting up the Junos device in configuration mode, you use operational mode to operate your device in the network. Operational mode commands run the device and keep an eye on what the device software and hardware are doing, along with giving you helpful views into the current operations of your overall network.

Understanding the command hierarchy

Even with all the Junos OS commands split between operational and configuration mode, each mode still has hundreds of possible commands. If the CLI showed them all in a single list, it would fill many screens and be difficult to use. So the Junos OS software arranges them into hierarchies that group together related commands (refer to Chapter 2).

Among the most commonly used of the operational hierarchies are the show and clear commands. You use the show command to display status and statistics for just about everything on the device, from the network interfaces (show interfaces) to the hardware (show chassis hardware) to the routing protocols (show ospf, show bgp, and so on). You use the clear command to clear, or zero, statistics collected by the device.

Figure 3-1 shows a sample of hierarchies under the clear and show commands of the operational mode. Notice that both top-level commands have bgp, interfaces, and system commands. Then the next level down has different options in the hierarchies. From these hierarchies, some of the commands available are clear bgp neighbor *neighbor-name*, show bgp neighbor *neighbor-name*, and show interfaces.

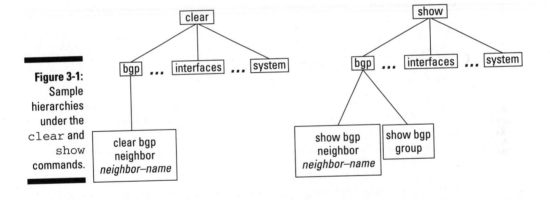

Figure 3-1: Sample hierarchies under the clear and show commands.

Switching between modes

If you are in configuration mode, you can move to operational mode by entering the exit configuration-mode command, or even shorter, the exit command. Remember, if you've made changes in the configuration, enter a commit command, or your changes are lost.

To get back into configuration mode, you can simply enter co. Because no other command starts with those two letters, the CLI recognizes the command and autofills to completion the rest of the configuration command.

When you first log in to the device, you are in operational mode. By typing a
? at the command prompt, you can view a list of all the top-level operational
commands for your device. Listing 3-1 shows a subset of the commands,
where the command name is on the left and a description is on the right.

Listing 3-1:   A Sampling of the Operational Mode Command Hierarchy

```
wiley@netnik> ?
Possible completions:
  clear              Clear information in the system
  configure          Manipulate software configuration information
  file               Perform file operations
  help               Provide help information
  monitor            Show real-time debugging information
  ping               Ping remote target
  quit               Exit the management session
  request            Make system-level requests
  restart            Restart software process
  set                Set CLI properties, date/time, craft interface message
  show               Show system information
  ssh                Start secure shell on another host
  telnet             Telnet to another host
  traceroute         Trace route to remote host
```

If you have experience using Cisco IOS software, be aware that the Junos OS
does not use the keyword IP in its commands. Understand that small difference, and you notice that many of the operations commands are otherwise
the same. For example, the IOS command show ip route simply becomes
show route in Junos.

If you peek under each command, you see the next level in the hierarchy.
Listing 3-2 illustrates a truncated list of the different varieties of the show
commands.

Listing 3-2:   A Truncated List of the show Commands

```
wiley@netnik> show ?
Possible completions:
  accounting         Show accounting profiles and records
  aps                Show Automatic Protection Switching information
  arp                Show system Address Resolution Protocol table entries
  as-path            Show table of known autonomous system paths
  bfd                Show Bidirectional Forwarding Detection information
  bgp                Show Border Gateway Protocol information
  chassis            Show chassis information
  class-of-service   Show class-of-service (CoS) information
  cli                Show command-line interface settings
  configuration      Show current configuration
```

Using ? allows you to see the subordinate commands in the next level of the hierarchy. Drill down one more level of the hierarchy, into the show chassis hierarchy, and you see

```
wiley@netnik> show chassis ?
Possible completions:
  alarms           Show alarm status
  environment      Show component status, temperature, cooling system speeds
  firmware         Show firmware and operating system version for components
  fpc              Show Flexible PIC Concentrator status
  hardware         Show installed hardware components
  location         Show physical location of chassis
  mac-addresses    Show media access control addresses
  pic              Show Physical Interface Card state, type, and uptime
  routing-engine   Show Routing Engine status
```

Where does the hierarchy for a command end? When you see Enter as one of the possible command completions, such as shown here:

```
wiley@netnik> show chassis hardware ?
Possible completions:
  <[Enter]>        Execute this command
  detail           Include RAM and disk information in output
  extensive        Display ID EEPROM information
  models           Display serial number and model number for orderable FRUs
  |                Pipe through a command
```

So, when you finally reach the end of the hierarchy, press Enter to see output data, as shown in Listing 3-3.

Listing 3-3: The Output Data at the End of a Hierarchy

```
wiley@netnik> show chassis hardware
Hardware inventory:
Item             Version  Part number  Serial number  Description
Chassis                                25708          M20
Backplane        REV 03   710-002334   BB9738         M20 Backplane
Power Supply A   REV 06   740-001465   005234         AC Power Supply
Display          REV 04   710-001519   BA4681         M20 FPM Board
Routing Engine 0 REV 06   740-003239   1000224893     RE-2.0
Routing Engine 1 REV 06   740-003239   9000022146     RE-2.0
SSB 0            REV 02   710-001951   AZ8112         Internet Processor IIv1
SSB 1            N/A      N/A          N/A            Backup
FPC 0            REV 03   710-003308   BD8455         E-FPC
  PIC 0          REV 08   750-002303   AZ5310         4x F/E, 100 BASE-TX
  PIC 1          REV 07   750-004745   BC9368         2x CT3-NxDS0
  PIC 2          REV 03   750-002965   HC9279         4x CT3
Fan Tray 0                                            Front Upper Fan Tray
Fan Tray 1                                            Front Middle Fan Tray
Fan Tray 2                                            Front Bottom Fan Tray
Fan Tray 3                                            Rear Fan Tray
```

Another tool in your toolbox: the run keyword

You can execute an operational mode command from within configuration mode using the keyword run. Simply add the keyword run before any operational mode command, such as run show interfaces. run is particularly handy when you want to run operational commands that let you verify a newly committed configuration. With the run keyword, you can check any operational aspect of your device without having to switch modes.

The output of the show commands in operational mode is different from the output of the show commands in configuration mode. Operational mode has a large group of show commands to display status and statistics for just about everything on the device. In configuration mode the command outputs a listing of the candidate configuration.

Recognizing common utility commands

Junos supports standard network utilities and remote access for management. You may recognize a few of these fundamental commands from UNIX and other operating systems:

- ✔ ping: Is the standard IP command to test whether other devices, interface cards, or nodes are reachable on the network.
- ✔ traceroute: Reports the path taken by packets from your device to a destination on an IP network.
- ✔ ssh: Is the standard UNIX secure shell program for opening a user shell on another device or host on the network.
- ✔ telnet: Opens a terminal connection to another device or host on the network.

Displaying Output

The Junos CLI offers you a great deal of flexibility in displaying output. For example, you can request output in different formats, specify how to show more, and pipe (|) the output to display exactly what you want.

Choosing your format

The Junos operational mode show commands commonly include these display options: terse, brief, detail, and extensive (where the commands are listed from the least to the most displayed output). You can use these options to adjust the show output listings according to what you need.

For example, compare the output when adding terse and brief to the following show interfaces command:

```
wiley@netnik> show interfaces fe-1/1/1 terse
Interface Admin Link Proto Local Remote
fe-1/1/1 up up
at-1/3/0.0 up up inet 1.0.0.1 --> 1.0.0.2
iso
```

```
wiley@netnik> show interfaces fe-1/1/1 brief
Physical interface: fe-1/1/1 Enabled, Physic link is Down
Link-level type:Ethernet, MTU: 1514, Spped: 100mbps, Loopback:
Disabled, Source filtering: Disabled
Flow control : Enabled
Device flags : Present Running Down
Interface flags: Hardware-Down SNMP-Traps Internal: 0x4000
Link flags : None
```

Tell me more

The Junos CLI display screen automatically paginates output, including the <more> prompt as the last line. Press the h key at any <more> prompt to ask for help and list the options, such as moving forward and backward in the output, searching, and saving. Listing 3-4 shows an example of using the <more> prompt.

Listing 3-4: Options for Responding to a <more> Prompt

```
wiley@netnik> show ethernet-switching interfaces detail
Interface: ge-0/0/0.0 Index: 64
  State: down
  VLANs:
    default              untagged              blocked - blocked by STP

<snip of output to shorten the example>

Interface: ge-0/0/12.0 Index: 76
  State: down
  VLANs:
    default              untagged              blocked - blocked by STP
---<more>--- h
```

```
---(Help for CLI automore)---
Clear all match and except strings:                              c or C
Display all line matching a regexp:                         m or M <string>
Display all lines except those matching a regexp:  e or E <string>
Display this help text:                                              h
Don't hold in automore at bottom of output:         N
Hold in automore at bottom of output:               H
Move down half display:                                   TAB, d, or ^D
Move down one line:                                        Enter, j, ^N,
          ^X, ^Z, or Down-Arrow
Move down one page:                                        Space, f, ^F,
               or Right-Arrow
Move to bottom of output:                                 G, ^E, or End
Move to top of output:                                     g, ^A, or
               Home
Move up half display:                                      u or ^U
Move up one line:                                           k, Delete,
          Backspace, ^P, or Up-Arrow
Move up one page:                                          b, ^B, or
               Left-Arrow
Quit automore:                                             q, Q, ^K
Redraw display:                                           ^L or ^R
Repeat a keystroke command 1 to 9 times:   Meta-1..9
Repeat last search:                                              n
Save output to a file:                                        s or S
               <filename/url>
Search backwards thru the output:            ?<string>
Search forwards thru the output:             /<string>
---(End of Help)---
```

Using the pipe command tool

Pipe (|) is among the most powerful command tools in Junos. With this command tool, you can select a specific subset of output in a single command step. Become familiar with using pipe, and you'll save yourself hours of tedium reading and parsing through long lists of output. Let Junos do the work by giving you just the output you want. In Junos, both operational and configuration mode commands include options for using pipe to modify the output.

The key to understanding pipe is to remember that the output of the command to the left of the pipe symbol serves as input to the command (or file) to the right of the pipe.

The power of pipe to combine commands creates its superb utility. You can query the CLI to find valid ways to pipe a command, as shown in the operational mode in Listing 3-5.

Listing 3-5: Options to Combine show route and the Pipe Symbol

```
wiley@netnik> show route | ?
Possible completions:
count          Count occurrences
display        Show additional kinds of information
except         Show only text that does not match a pattern
find           Search for first occurrence of pattern
hold           Hold text without exiting the --More-- prompt
last           Display end of output only
match          Show only text that matches a pattern
no-more        Don't paginate output
request        Make system-level requests
resolve        Resolve IP addresses
save           Save output text to file
trim           Trim specified number of columns from start of line
```

A few examples from a configured device are the best way to learn about pipe in operational mode. (Turn to Chapter 5 for a clever trick on how to use pipe to copy a series of set commands using the show | display set command.)

Limiting the output

The most common ways to use the pipe (|) symbol is to constrain the output using match, except, find, or last:

✔ | match: Specifies exactly what you want to display:

```
wiley@netnik > show configuration | match at-
2/1/0 {
at-2/1/1 {
at-2/2/0 {
at-5/2/0 {
        at-5/3/0 {
```

✔ | except: Displays output that ignores a specific string:

```
wiley@netnik> show system users | except root
8:28PM up 1 day, 13:59, 2 users, load averages:
0.01, 0.01, 0.00
USER TTY FROM LOGIN@ IDLE WHAT
wiley.netnik 7:25PM - cli
```

✔ | find: Displays output starting at the first occurrence of the matching text:

```
wiley@netnik> show ethernet-switching interfaces detail | find "Index: 80"
Interface: ge-0/0/16.0 Index: 80
```

✔ | last: Displays only the last screen of the listing:

```
wiley@netnik> show ethernet-switching interfaces detail | last
Interface: ge-0/0/16.0 Index: 80
```

Counting lines and more

You can also use pipe with show commands to change the type of output. For example, | count gives the number of lines in the output:

```
wiley@netnik> show interfaces terse | count
Count: 27 lines
```

You can use more than one pipe character in a single command. The Junos OS views the multiple pipes as a logical AND; it displays the output that matches all the pipes. For example, you can determine the total number of configured Fast Ethernet interfaces with the following command:

```
wiley@netnik> show interfaces terse | match fe- | count
Count: 14 lines
```

Filtering output to a file

Using pipe, you can also create a file that stores the output of a command, for example:

```
wiley@netnik> request support information | save <filename>
Wrote 1143 lines of output to 'filename'
```

See Chapter 5 for more on archiving to a server and how to access a file.

Using Onboard Instrumentation Tools

In addition to the commands available in the operational mode of the CLI, Junos provides an extensive set of onboard instrumentation tools to help you keep things running smoothly.

Onboard instrumentation enables you to proactively gather information from the Junos OS, thereby receiving advance notification of issues before they create service-impacting havoc. You set up these monitoring and logging tools in configuration mode (see Chapter 7) so that you have the operational data you need — whether it's to know that things are A-OK or to provide the details needed to resolve some issue in your network.

These tools gather critical operational status, statistics, and other information. Handling these functions onboard a network device speeds problem-solving. (Chapter 17 outlines how to use these and other tools in troubleshooting your network.)

Monitoring the operations of your network

Self-monitoring allows continuous feedback, capturing network-wide on down to highly granular views into device operations. This capability not only can alert you to issues, but also enables you to save a great deal of time when diagnosing network problems, as needed details are already available. You won't lose precious troubleshooting minutes just to gather basic data that you need to analyze what the problem might be.

You can use these tools to automate network monitoring in the Junos OS:

- **Real-time performance monitoring (RPM):** Measures the performance of traffic as it travels between network devices so that you can continuously monitor its delay. The RPM probes can collect round-trip time minimums, averages, maximums, jitter, and other data on both a per-destination and per-application basis.

- **Flow accounting:** Provides a method for collecting traffic flow statistics, enabling operations teams to track utilization of links for capacity planning, security analysis, fault isolation, billing, and more. You can gather statistics on an individual physical device, logical device, interface, or subinterface.

- **Health monitor:** Notifies your network management system (NMS) when something requires attention. Health monitor extends the Remote Network Monitoring (RMON) alarm infrastructure of Junos OS (with minimum user configuration requirements) by providing predefined monitoring of the operating system processes and device hardware — for example, file system usage, CPU usage, and memory usage.

Logging and tracing events

The logging and tracing operations of Junos OS allow you to find out about events that occur in your device — normal operations, as well as error conditions. For fast resolution, use the following tools to trace and analyze the sequence of events leading to network or device issues:

- **System logging:** Generates system log messages (syslog messages) for recording events that occur on the device, including hardware and processes in the operating system. Events include any change in the system, whether they are planned, expected, or indicate a problem. A few examples — among the thousands we could cite — are an interface start up, login failure, or hardware failure conditions.

- **Trace logging (tracing options):** Provides a wide range of variables for observing network and system events of protocol operations. Examples include BGP state changes, graceful restart events, and even tracking SNMP operations and statistics. Trace logging is a valuable tool when you need to find out what's going on in a device running Junos.

For the most efficient debugging, it's good practice to set the appropriate `traceoptions` parameters in the configuration ahead of time and leave them disabled. Then, when you need them, they're ready, and you can quickly start finding out what's going on.

Applying onboard automation

Junos automation is a broad suite of tools for automating the methods and procedures of operating a network. Automation can not only save your team time, it also helps to assure high performance in the operation of the network. In addition, it helps you manage greater scale in the network by simplifying complex tasks.

The toolsets enable you to automate a majority of the commands used within the Junos command line, further control the commit process, and automate the response to defined events. Table 3-1 provides a summary of what you can do with Junos automation.

Table 3-1	Junos Automation Summary	
Automation Function	*Automation Trigger*	*Automation Activity*
Operations Automation	Instructs Junos as prompted by the command line and other scripts.	Creates custom commands for specific solution/user needs.
		Combines a series of iterative steps to diagnose network problems.
		Automates configuration changes.
Event Automation	Instructs Junos of actions to take in response to events on the device or in the network.	Gathers relevant troubleshooting info and correlates events from leading indicators.
		Automates event responses with a set of actions.
		Automates time-of-day configuration changes.
Configuration Automation	Instructs Junos during the commit process.	Abstracts complex configuration into a simple set of variable-based commands. Provides change management to avert and correct misconfiguration. Enforces best practices and business rules.

The Juniper website offers a wealth of resources and tools that you can use to get started with Junos automation, including a library of templates to customize and run on your device. To find the library, training, and recommended reading, visit www.juniper.net/automation. Be sure to look for the "Day One" series on Junos automation to learn more about automating the methods and procedures of your network. The books provide step-by-step instructions and lots of examples, whether you are automating operations or configuration or want to set up event policies. Then head over to the Junos Automation community page to find experts who share the latest tips and can answer your questions: www.juniper.net/us/en/community/junos/script-automation/.

Exploring Junos Space

Junos Space (refer to Chapter 1) provides multiple applications for operating your network. Among these are three tools specifically designed to automate and ease troubleshooting and maintenance activities for high network uptime.

- ✔ **Service Now:** Automates diagnostics to speed up resolution of problems and increase operation efficiency.

- ✔ **Service Insight:** Enables proactive network maintenance with targeted, network intelligence.

- ✔ **Route Insight:** Enables rapid planning, troubleshooting, and change simulation.

Service Now

Junos Space Service Now enables Service Automation as a part of Juniper Technical Services for support. This service automation is available to all organizations with a support contract and can speed detection, diagnosis, and remediation of issues requiring Juniper support assistance.

Service Now uses onboard automation and event policies defined by engineers in the Juniper Networks Technical Assistance Center (JTAC), the Juniper group that provides customer support. These automation tools perform the first steps that a JTAC engineer would use to help you resolve issues in your network. For example, the tools detect issues on devices, collect troubleshooting and diagnostic information, and send an indication to the Service Now application. You can optionally choose for your systems to send collected data securely and directly to JTAC, saving you significant time and effort, particularly beneficial when every minute counts during the event of a problem.

Service Insight

Junos Space Service Insight provides data and analysis essential to proactive maintenance of the network. Service Insight uses periodic health data collected via Service Now to provide analysis that lets you take action specific to your implementation — for example, proactive bug and End of Life/End of Service notifications. This service is particularly useful if you maintain numerous devices.

Route Insight

Junos Space Route Insight provides real-time visibility into the dynamic routing operation of the entire network by peering with your devices to create an accurate, up-to-date routed topology map. Route Insight provides real-time alerts of IP-layer network changes and lets network operators record and replay complete network event history in order to understand all application traffic paths. This historical perspective on route changes can speed up the process of identifying and resolving network problems that often are hard to diagnose. This application can also help you model and simulate network changes, thus enabling you to better understand their potential impact.

Using the System Software

A key part of operating your device is managing and maintaining the system software itself, including the upgrade to new Junos OS releases.

Restarting and requesting system-wide functions

Operational mode provides commands for restarting and resetting individual processes as well as rebooting the device and upgrading its system software.

✔ **Restart:** Allows you to restart most Junos processes within operational mode. Junos is a modular operating system (see Chapter 1) whereby independent processes run in their own protected memory space. As such, these processes (called *daemons*) can be independently managed.

✔ **Request:** A set of commands that you can use to perform system-wide functions such as rebooting, upgrading, and shutting down the device. This group also provides you with the ability to put individual components online, take them offline, and restart them without having to reboot the entire device.

Although a process runs independently in the operating system, take special care when using the `restart` command. For example, a restart of the SNMP process is only disruptive to SNMP, but a restart of routing could have drastic consequences in your network by disrupting and resetting its routing paths.

To restart a specific routing protocol, such as OSPF (see Chapter 10), you can deactivate and then reactivate it in configuration mode. When a problem exists with only one protocol, this approach is better than restarting the entire routing daemon of Junos, which affects all the routing protocols.

Upgrading to new releases

A topic essential to operating your network is software upgrades. The delivery model of new Junos releases simplifies the process of upgrading compared to other networking systems. (For more on this topic, see Chapter 1.)

The algorithm for selecting which new version to use is straightforward: Choose a release with a higher number, and you receive the existing capabilities of your device along with the new functionality available up through to that release version. Any organization with a valid support contract can freely download new releases of the Junos OS from the Juniper support site.

About new releases and numbers

Juniper frequently ships new major versions of the Junos OS to deliver new features and functionality to its customers. The company recently announced the transition to a development schedule that supports the delivery of three releases per year.

Maintenance and service releases

Following the availability of any major Junos OS version, Juniper also issues maintenance and service releases to deliver needed fixes to that shipping version throughout its support life (see below for more about the Junos OS support life).

- ✔ **Maintenance releases:** Standard releases to provide fixes in shipped and supported version releases. The software download page links to the latest revision available for each currently supported Junos OS version.

- ✔ **Service releases:** Targeted releases to provide more timely delivery of critical fixes to meet customer needs. Service releases may be limited to specific platforms or use cases. Juniper constrains the scope of the fixes to only critical fixes. The service releases are available through JTAC.

TIP

Understanding release numbers

Starting in 2010, Junos releases are numbered according to a year.sequence convention. For example, the last release of 2011 is 11.4 and the first release in 2012 will be 12.1.

You can determine the release version from the release package name. For example:

```
jinstall-ex-4200-11.2R2.4-domestic-
         signed.tgz
```

✔ **jinstall-ex-4200** is the descriptor of the release platform, in this example the EX4200.

✔ **11.2** is the major version number (the second release of the year in 2011).

✔ **R** is the type of release. In this example, the R designates a shipped release. Other

types are S for service release and B for a Beta release.

✔ **2** is the revision number — that is, the numbered sequence of the maintenance releases, where the First Release Shipment (FRS) is always R1.

✔ **4** is the build number (also known as the spin number) of the release. The spin number indicates the specific software build of the release and may be requested by JTAC during service discussions.

✔ **domestic-signed** indicates that the software is for use in the U.S. and Canada. The other type is worldwide, designated by export-signed.

About engineering support

Similar to other networking vendors, Juniper supports the Junos operating system in two phases, as shown in Figure 3-2.

✔ During *engineering support* of a release, the engineering teams create updated releases (maintenance and service) to address any coding issues. Juniper describes the end of engineering support as End of Engineering (EOE).

✔ During the time of only *JTAC support*, the JTAC engineers help to resolve issues with solutions and workarounds that don't require changes in the release code. Juniper describes the end of JTAC support as the End of Life (EOL).

Juniper provides a six-month notice of the EOL for each of the version releases. When the release reaches EOL, Juniper removes the software images from its site, and JTAC provides support on a reasonable commercial basis.

The last release of the year is known as an Extended End of Life (EEOL) release and provides active engineering support for three years, followed by six months of JTAC support.

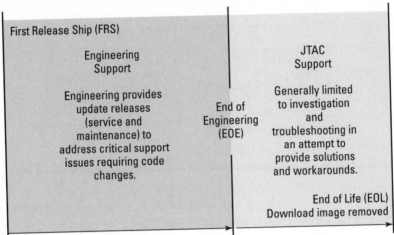

Figure 3-2:
Junos sup-
port phases.

First Release Ship (FRS)

Engineering
Support

Engineering provides
update releases
(service and
maintenance) to
address critical support
issues requiring code
changes.

End of
Engineering
(EOE)

JTAC
Support

Generally limited
to investigation
and
troubleshooting in
an attempt to
provide solutions
and workarounds.

End of Life (EOL)
Download image removed

Downloading new releases

You can find the latest supported releases of the Junos OS on Juniper's down-load site. Navigate to www.juniper.net/customers/csc/software.

Find the image for the particular platform that you're upgrading. Choose between the domestic image, which is for use in the United States and Canada, and a worldwide image (export). The technical documentation for each platform is freely available in multiple formats.

Although they don't necessarily need to, many users routinely upgrade the version of the Junos OS running on their devices. Regular upgrades ensure that they have ready access to the latest features. If their network requires a new feature, it's already a part of the software on their devices, and they simply activate it in their deployed release whenever they're ready to use it.

The online technical documentation, *Junos Installation and Upgrade Guide*, pro-vides details about upgrading the software version of your device.

Chapter 4

Migrating to Junos

*O*rganizations with new requirements to update or modernize their networks — to meet new needs of cloud services and mobility or to enhance the security, reliability, performance, and cost-effectiveness of their existing applications — discover many benefits in migrating to solutions running Junos. Available solutions include ways to scale and consolidate data centers, update campus and branch networks, and integrate and virtualize security infrastructure.

This chapter introduces a few of the ways that organizations migrate their networks to Junos and also summarizes the portfolio of devices running the Junos OS. Chapter 19 covers the most commonly used tools and resources for migrating to Junos.

Collapsing Switching Layers

If your organization is consolidating or redesigning data centers, even building a new one, or modernizing your campus network, you may be thinking about new ways to optimize the switching infrastructure. Certainly, high availability, performance, operational simplicity, and cost remain key considerations. However, scalability and power consumption may be top of mind as the challenges you most want to solve.

Mountains of gear

In the data center or campus network, the access layer provides the physical connections to servers, storage, security, and other IP devices. In a typical configuration, aggregation switches interconnect these access switches, while a core layer provides connectivity between the aggregation layer and the gateway routers that link to the Internet and/or the WAN that interconnects all your sites.

While this three-layer breakout allowed new devices and switches to be added without requiring a major overhaul to the existing network, in many data centers, more than 50 percent of available switching ports are now used to connect to other switches. The compounding complexity of scaling across three layers not only adds wiring but also can increase the risk of failure and the effort to manage the infrastructure. Also, the power and space needed to run all those switches can further strain energy and financial budgets.

For many organizations, the challenges are only growing with not only more and more traffic but new requirements driven by cloud-based services and virtualization. For example, virtualization adds the need to move much of the traffic across servers in the data center, requiring far more flexibility than when the network simply had to move the traffic in/out of dedicated application server farms.

If your applications and traffic needs are changing, you may be looking at design alternatives for your data center and campus networks. New switching solutions with higher port densities, faster interface speeds, and more flexible ways to expand ports offer new options for optimizing your network for growth.

Collapsing to a two-layer network

A design option that you may be considering to optimize your data center or campus network is reducing the number of switching layers. The availability of high-density switches with many high-speed 10 Gigabit Ethernet interfaces allow you to consider collapsing the aggregation and core layers of your network(s). In this design, your access switches can directly connect to the core over wire-speed 10 Gigabit Ethernet links.

By reducing the number of switches, the design can save not only capital cost but also reduce power, cooling, and space requirements. Additionally, collapsing layers removes potential points of failure and simplifies network operations — including OS upgrades; moves, adds, changes; and troubleshooting.

If you are upgrading your switching infrastructure, you may begin your migration to Junos by deploying new switches that can eliminate the aggregation layer of your network.

Virtual Chassis technology for collapsing layers

The Juniper solution provides a way for a group of interconnected switches to operate as a single, logical device with a single IP address. The key enabling capability is known as Virtual Chassis technology. When deployed in a Virtual Chassis configuration, the switches are also monitored and managed in Junos OS as one device, enabling organizations to separate physical topology from logical groupings of endpoints and allowing more efficient resource utilization.

Virtual Chassis technology not only reduces the number of individual devices to manage, it also allows network tiers to be consolidated, further simplifying the network. A single Virtual Chassis configuration can also span multiple nodes, reducing the need for uplinks and limiting the need for larger, more expensive nodes on superior tiers. (The next section further discusses the benefits of Virtual Chassis, and Chapter 11 helps you set up the solution.)

Scaling the Access Switching Layer

You may be looking for new ways to scale the access switching layer of your data center to support more servers. If so, you may find that migrating to Juniper Networks access switching solutions is not only cost-effective, but also provides greater flexibility in your network. You can deploy Juniper switches in a variety of access architectures, including top-of-rack or end-of-row, or an innovative combination of both. In the upcoming section, "Speeding Up the Data Center Network," we discuss the option to upgrade the connections of your access layer to 10 Gigabit Ethernet ports.

Top or end of row

Perhaps you locate your access switches in your data center at the top of the rack (TOR) because it simplifies wiring, keeping more cables within the rack. Yet, many of the small, fixed-configuration switches used in these TOR designs have limited features and functionality. Additionally, administrators must manage each switch individually, increasing operational demands.

Perhaps the access switches in your data center are at the end of the row (EOR) where you can justify larger chassis switches with greater functionality. However, cables must run from all the boxes on the network to the end of the row. If each row doesn't require all the ports of the large chassis switch, port utilization is low. Also, even a partially configured chassis can have significant space, power, and cooling requirements.

Best of both design options

Ideally, you want an architecture that delivers the benefits of each design option, without their drawbacks. If you had a platform that distributed the ports of a chassis solution across the row or, alternatively, allowed you to incrementally grow at the end of the row as needed, these could be attractive alternatives to your existing design.

Virtual Chassis technology for scaling data center networks

Virtual Chassis technology, available on many Juniper Networks switches (and introduced in the earlier section, "Virtual Chassis technology for collapsing layers"), enables both of these alternative designs, as shown in Figure 4-1.

Figure 4-1: Top of the rack and end of the row designs with Virtual Chassis technology.

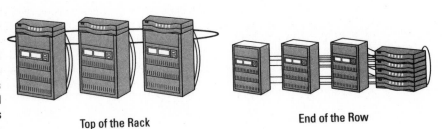

Top of the Rack   End of the Row

For example, the technology enables up to ten Juniper Networks EX4200 Ethernet Switches to interconnect over a 128 Gbps backplane and act as a single logical device sharing a common configuration file. It's also possible to connect switches located on different floors or in different buildings, using the front-panel 10 Gigabit Ethernet fiber uplink ports.

Deploying Virtual Chassis technology as a part of the access layer solution offers some distinct advantages:

✔ **Pay-as-you-grow scalability:** Expand port densities only as you need, so you can begin economically with a single switch (1 RU) and avoid the up-front investment of chassis-based solutions.

✔ **Reduced power, cooling, and space needs:** Each switch uses far less power and generates far less heat than chassis-based systems, and because you can incrementally add new platforms as you need, you don't have to pay to power and cool capacity that you aren't using, or take up valuable rack space with a largely empty chassis.

✔ **High availability:** Interconnect the switches to automatically leverage the multiple Routing Engines to help preserve availability in the rare event of a master switch failure.

✔ **Location independence:** Distribute switches beyond one rack to wiring closets, other floors, and even different buildings, giving you more configuration flexibility. The only distance limitation becomes that of the physical media.

✔ **Ease of management:** Manage and operate up to ten switches as though they were a single physical chassis, simplifying configuration, maintenance, upgrading, and troubleshooting.

Speeding Up the Data Center Network

Beyond the steps to collapse and scale your switching network in the data center, you may also be considering how to speed the connections to your servers and converge your LAN with your storage area network (SAN) infrastructure in a single, fast, and flexible backbone. If these items are on your new initiatives list, you should ask Juniper about their solution migration path that ultimately leads to a high-performance fabric running your data center network as a single switching layer.

A need for speed

In a move to a two-layer network in your data center, you may also be considering the option of a speed upgrade to 10 Gigabit Ethernet (10 GbE) ports [from 1 Gigabit Ethernet (1 GbE)], not only for your network uplinks, but also to connect your servers. If your traffic is growing extremely rapidly, moving now to 10 Gigabit Ethernet to connect some or all of your servers can help you in staying ahead of user demand.

When upgrading the speed of your server connections, you can also eliminate redundant LAN and SAN interface connections on servers to consolidate storage and Ethernet traffic on common 10 GbE connections. Look for a solution that offers storage and I/O convergence yet preserves existing investments in SAN and LAN infrastructure and reduces management complexity. Storage and I/O convergence require low latency and lossless 10 GbE technologies at the access layer to support Fibre Channel over Ethernet (FCoE) and Fiber Channel (FC) interfaces.

Wouldn't it be sweet if you could find a way to connect all your servers at 10 Gigabit Ethernet speed and converge your LAN and SAN infrastructure, and it all actually worked without busting your budget?

Collapsing to a single layer network

With the latest announcement of the QFabric architecture and QFX Series components, Juniper Networks offers a solution to create a single-tier network that can be operated and managed like a single Ethernet switch. What is essential to understanding the design is that the QFabric architecture is not a network. It is a switch.

The benefits of running the data center backbone as a single switch that can connect both servers and storage infrastructure include any-to-any connectivity with single-hop latency for all data flows, while also eliminating the challenges of managing the physical locality of processing and data. The ability to manage the fabric as a single, logical entity without the need to run multi-link protocols such as Spanning Tree or TRILL is almost too good to be true.

QFabric as a one layer backbone

You can make the move to a single layer fabric in a series of steps that starts with deploying a QF/Node, such as the QFX3500, as a 10 Gigabit Ethernet switch. Optionally, you can include Fibre Channel over Ethernet (FCoE) and Fiber Channel (FC) interfaces to connect your storage devices. The QFX3500 supports standards-based FCoE and Data Center Bridging (DCB) features and can operate as a Fibre Channel Transit Switch or Fibre Channel Gateway to support your storage traffic.

When your needs scale beyond a few switches, you can then move to the fabric architecture. The QFX3500 switch requires no hardware modifications to transform into a QFabric QF/Node device. You can think of the QF/Node as the line cards of the fabric. To complete the deployment of QFabric as a single switching layer, you add the QF/Interconnect, which you can think of as the backplane of the fabric, and the QF/Director, which you can think of as the control plane of the fabric. Further, you can connect existing racks running other 10 GbE/1 GbE switches into the QFabric through the QF/Node.

When you run Junos, the QFabric components operate as a large distributed switch. As when you operate a switch, you don't have to configure or fuss with what's happening on the inside. While unlike any switch that has come before — faster, more distributed, and more scalable than any Ethernet chassis — QFabric retains the operational simplicity of a switch. You operate your data center backbone as a single switching layer, providing ultra fast, any-to-any connectivity between the interconnected devices.

Securing the Infrastructure

The security needs of networks are also continuously changing as new threats emerge and as data is shared across many different users and applications. Staying ahead of both the new threats and business needs means frequent assessment as to whether the current security infrastructure adequately meets the full set of demands from the organization, or whether it makes sense to migrate to a new solution.

Inbound and outbound threats

As the network attack landscape continues to evolve, IT managers must guard against the many different types of attacks that could affect their network.

Relatively simple network level attacks have morphed into more complex attacks that use both network and application-level components to achieve their malicious goals. With end-users directly accessing the Web and casually surfing sites that are known malware download sources, they may be unknowingly revealing personal or corporate private data via e-mail scams or hidden background programs that collect and forward data. This means that an IT manager must not only stop attacks at each layer of the network, for each application and for all types of content, but they also need to stop both inbound and outbound threats.

✔ **Inbound threats:** Are those that originate from outside the corporate network, for example, from an attacker on the Internet who intends to penetrate the corporation's perimeter defenses. These threats include virtually all types of attacks from worms to viruses to spyware to phishing e-mails.

✔ **Outbound threats:** Are those that originate from someone inside, such as an employee of the company who has a machine that has been unknowingly compromised and is propagating a worm or virus throughout the corporate network. Other examples of outbound attacks are users who respond to phishing attacks by entering their personal data on a malicious web site, and spyware which is resident on an employee's machine that quietly sends sensitive corporate information to a malicious party on the Internet.

Meeting new security needs

Stopping all inbound and outbound attacks requires a concerted, multilayered solution to prevent damage to the network, company assets, and end users.

While bi-directional protection is a critical component, it is equally critical to implement solution components that target specific types of attacks. No single solution component will stop the long list of network-level, application-level, and content-based attacks.

For example, viruses are embedded within files, such as an attachment or an executable. To ensure maximum protection against viruses, IT managers should implement a true, file-based antivirus offering that deconstructs the payload, decodes the file or script, evaluates it for potential viruses and then reconstructs it, sending it on its way.

To protect the network against application-level attacks via the network such as targeting software vulnerabilities — which includes most network worms, or sending sensitive credit card data from a spyware infected system — an Intrusion Prevention System (IPS) is the recommended solution. An IPS should look deep into the application layer traffic to detect attacks. It is important to choose a solution that does more than merely inspect the packets at the network layer or that decodes only a few protocols at Layer 7. The solution should understand and inspect application traffic of all types, fully understand the details of each protocol, and use a combination of methods such as application level stateful inspection, anomaly detection, and other heuristics to stop threats.

An often overlooked attack protection element is the ability to control access to known malware download sites. By assembling an attack protection solution that incorporates web filtering to block access to known malicious web sites, IT managers can reduce the number of malicious downloads that are brought into the network. Another mechanism that can help reduce the number of incoming attacks is to implement a gateway antispam solution that can act as a preliminary filter by blocking known spam and phishing sources.

Juniper security solutions

To provide protection against inbound and outbound attacks at all levels, Juniper Networks integrates a complete set of best-in-class content security software features (commonly referred to as Unified Threat Management, or UTM, features) into the secure router and firewall/VPN line of platforms. By leveraging the development, support, and market expertise of many leading content security partners, Juniper is able to deliver a set of best-in-class UTM features.

Integrated on Juniper Networks branch firewall/VPN platforms is the Deep Inspection firewall, a proven IPS solution that builds on the strengths of stateful inspection and integrates stateful signatures and protocol anomaly detection mechanisms to provide both network and application-level attack protection at the perimeter. Using policy-based management, administrators can pick and choose which protocols to inspect with protocol anomaly detection and/or stateful signatures, what types of attacks to look for, and which action to take if an attack is discovered.

Integrated partner solutions provide antivirus, web filtering, and inbound spam and phishing attacks. The partner-based antivirus solution detects and protects against the most dangerous and virulent viruses, worms, malicious backdoors, dialers, keyboard loggers, password stealers, trojans, and other malicious code. Included in the joint solution is a best-of-class detection of spyware, adware, and other malware-related programs.

To block access to malicious web sites, an administrator can assemble an appropriate web-use policy based on 54 different categories encompassing over 25 million URLs (and growing every day). The branch and regional office platforms provide antispam features to help slow the flood of unwanted e-mail and the potential attacks they carry.

About the Devices Running Junos

Juniper offers routing, switching, and security platforms running Junos for branch and regional offices, corporate sites and data centers, along with the metro, edge, and core sites of service provider networks. The decision of what platform to use depends on where you're deploying it, and thereby, the required throughput and feature set. You find out how to install different platforms running Junos in Chapter 5.

For the very latest on the Juniper products running Junos visit `juniper. net/products_and_services`.

Routers

Juniper Networks routing platforms meet a full range of networking needs from small branch offices to the largest TeraPop sites in the world. Table 4-1 outlines the different types of platforms. Chapter 10 helps you in deploying the routing platforms in your network.

The routing platforms support IPv4 and IPv6 addressing, all standard routing protocols, routing policy, multicast (traffic from one point that must go to many points), and MPLS VPNs. Additionally, the platforms offer stateful firewall, many types of tunneling and other security features, classification and accounting of traffic, and other services that require rich packet processing along with many High Availability features.

Table 4-1	Juniper Networks Routing Platforms
Routing Series	*General Usage Tips*
J Series	Branch and regional offices requiring routing, security, application optimization, voice capabilities, and a variety of WAN interfaces in a single remotely manageable platform
M Series	Network gateway points in large office, campus, and data center sites that require IP/MPLS capabilities with added security and networking services
MX Series	Ethernet LAN and data center aggregation, data center core, metro Ethernet aggregation and core, and Ethernet services edge networks requiring high capacity routing, high port density, and a rich set of security and networking services
T Series	Core backbones of high availability service provider networks, as well as the core routing of businesses, schools, and governments that require multi-Terabit throughput rates

Switches

Juniper offers a broad portfolio of switches running Junos to meet needs from the branch to the campus to the data center.

EX Series

The Juniper Networks EX Series Ethernet Switches come in a range of high performance and high port density platforms for the access, aggregation, and core layers of the network, as detailed in Table 4-2. Chapter 11 provides the steps for deploying the switching platforms in your network.

The EX Series switches meet today's most advanced switching requirements for security and unified communications with integrated access control policy enforcement and extensive quality of service (QoS) features. Juniper's Virtual Chassis technology, available with the EX4200, EX4500, and EX8200 Ethernet Switches, enables multiple interconnected switches to operate as a single, logical device, reducing the number of switches and interconnections to manage.

Table 4-2	Juniper Networks EX Series Ethernet Switches
EX Series	*General Usage Tips*
EX2200	Access-layer deployments in branch offices and campus networks requiring a level of functionality and performance typically associated with higher-cost Ethernet switches
EX3200	Low-density access deployments in the wiring closets of remote offices and small LANs in large office buildings that require a high-performance standalone solution
EX4200	Data center and campus environments that require both the reliability of modular systems and the economics and flexibility of stackable switches in one high-performance, scalable solution
EX4500	High-density 10 gigabit per second (Gbps) data center, campus, and service provider deployments requiring a scalable, compact, high-performance platform
EX8200	Data center and campus core environments that require the flexibility of modular platforms for high port densities, scalability, and high availability

QFX Series

Juniper's QFabric enables a revolutionary data center design by creating a single tier network that operates like a single Ethernet switch. In designing QFabric, Juniper has essentially taken the three basic components of a self-contained switch fabric — linecards, backplane, and Routing Engines — and broken them out into independent, stand-alone devices — the QF/Node, the QF/Interconnect, and the QF/Director, respectively. The total solution provides a quantum leap forward in the scale and performance of the data center backbone. Table 4-3 introduces the current components of the QFX Series.

Table 4-3	Juniper Networks QFX Series
QFX Series	*General Usage Tips*
QFX3500	High performance and high-density 10 Gbps data center deployments requiring compact, ultra-low latency, feature-rich Layer 2 and Layer 3 switch with Fibre Channel I/O convergence capabilities. QFX3500 is also a fabric-ready solution and transitions into a QF/Node edge device in a QFabric architecture.
QFabric Components: QF/Node, QF/Interconnect, and QF/Director	Modern data center network architectures that require support for virtualization, convergence, and cloud computing. QFabric scales elegantly and eliminates operational expenses and complexity of today's hierarchical architecture.

Security Devices

Juniper Networks SRX Series Services Gateways meet the network and security requirements of data center consolidation and cloud offerings, branch integration projects, rapid managed services deployments, and aggregation of security solutions. Table 4-4 summarizes the array of choices. Turn to Chapter 12 to find out how to deploy the security platforms in your network.

The SRX Series Services Gateways pack high port density, advanced security, rich routing, and flexible connectivity into a single, easily managed platform that supports highly available data center and branch operations. Hardware and OS consolidation, operational flexibility, and unmatched performance simplify deployment and operations for lower costs of operations.

Table 4-4	Juniper Networks SRX Series Services Gateways
SRX Series	*General Usage Tips*
SRX100, SRX210, SRX220, and SRX240	Small to medium stand-alone and distributed enterprise locations that require a combination of firewall, IPsec VPN, and unified threat management (UTM). The SRX 210/220/240 support a variety of WAN interfaces through expansion slots.
SRX650	Regional distributed enterprise locations requiring firewall, IPsec VPN, and unified threat management (UTM) with higher throughput than available in the smallest SRX Series platforms
SRX1400	Small to mid-size data centers and 10 gigabit per second (Gbps) Ethernet network environments requiring consolidated functionality, high performance, and services integration
SRX3400 and SRX3600	Data centers requiring segmentation or other environments requiring a way to integrate security functionality and enforce unique per-zone security policies in small to midsize server farms and hosting sites
SRX5600 and SRX5800	Large enterprise data centers, hosted or co-located data centers, and service provider infrastructure requiring a full range of integrated security features in a platform that can be flexibly expanded over time as traffic volume grows

Part II
Setting Up Junos OS

The 5th Wave   By Rich Tennant

"I'm not saying I believe in anything. All I know is since it's been there our server is running 50% faster."

In this part . . .

Have you ever tried to bake something without a recipe? You really need the right proportions, or your breakfast ends up tasting like your dog's chewy bone. Think of this part as the recipe for setting up the basics of your network. You find out how to work with the command-line interface and discover the basic commands for routing, switching, and securing your device.

Chapter 5

Configuring the Device with the CLI and J-Web

● ●

In This Chapter

▶ Installing the hardware and software for various devices

▶ Configuring devices with the CLI

▶ Returning to a backed-up version of the configuration

▶ Configuring device with J-Web

● ●

*T*he first step in using any network device involves installing the hardware and software necessary for its operation. Then you can configure the device to perform the tasks needed to fit its role in the network. You can save configuration for later use, and you can configure the device using typed-in commands or a more user-friendly point-and-click interface. This chapter covers both methods.

This chapter covers installation of hardware and software for a typical Junos OS device. You see how to set up access to the device for users authorized to perform configuration and get an overview of the 18 common steps to configure any Junos OS device. Then we handle various ways to save and work with configuration files. Finally, we show you how to accomplish the same thing with J-Web.

Installing the Hardware and Software

Devices that run the Junos OS vary in size and shape from very small (switches with only a few ports that run on regular office current) to massive large (multi-rack core routers that require multiple experienced installer and mechanical lifts). So creating a unified hardware configuration section is impossible. Nevertheless, some general rules are valid for hardware installation of Junos OS devices of all sizes and shapes. In this section, we show you the small MX80 and the large MX960 as examples, but only for illustration purposes.

TIP

Practicing safety

The importance of following safety protocols can't be overstated. If proper precautions are not taken, severe harm to personnel or the device can result. Follow these guidelines to ensure your safety and protect the device from damage. Always be alert and exercise good judgment. *Note:* Only trained and qualified personnel should install the device.

✔ **Use the *Getting Started Guide.*** Perform only the procedures described in the *Getting Started Guide* that came with your device. Otherwise, the device might not work as intended.

✔ **Keep the work area clean.** Keep the area around the chassis clear and free before, during, and after installation. Do not wear loose clothing or jewelry that could be caught in the chassis.

✔ **Wear safety glasses.** If you are working under any conditions that could be hazardous to your eyes, wear safety glasses.

✔ **Get help lifting heavy objects.** Never attempt to lift an object that is too heavy for one person to handle.

✔ **Respect electricity.** Don't risk electrical shock. Do not perform wiring tasks during electrical storms or operate the router unless it is properly grounded.

✔ **Avoid other shock risks.** Don't open or remove the chassis covers unless instructed, don't insert objects into openings, avoid spilling liquids, and don't touch exposed wires or terminals.

Installing hardware for the MX80

After you have read the instructions, cleared the site, and assembled the necessary safety equipment for the size of device you are installing, you are ready to install the hardware. Note, however, that the details for doing so vary depending on the size of the chassis. For example, the MX80 is compact and weighs only about 30 pounds (13.6 kg), whereas the MX960 is much heavier (up to 350 pounds, or 158.8 kg). For the MX960, Juniper recommends the use of a mechanical lift for the installation.

Here is the procedure you follow to install the hardware for the smaller MX80:

1. **Follow the device-specific site preparation checklist.**

2. **Review the safety guidelines.**

3. **Unpack the router and verify the parts received.**

4. **Install the mounting hardware.**

5. **Lift the router into the rack and secure the brackets (usually, two people can do this with ease).**

6. Connect the grounding cables.

7. Turn on the router (most smaller Junos OS devices have power cords and plugs).

8. Perform initial software configuration (which is the same as for all Junos OS devices).

Installing hardware for the MX960

The installation for a large router, in this case the MX960, is similar to smaller routers like the MX80 but differs in the details. Be sure the steps you follow are the correct ones for the specific device you are using.

To install the hardware for the MX960, you follow the same steps as you did for the MX80, but you use a mechanical lift to position the router in the rack and secure the mounting hardware. Then you do the following:

1. Connect the grounding cables.

2. Connect power to the router (larger Junos OS devices have direct AC or DC connections).

3. Perform initial software configuration (which is the same as for all Junos OS devices).

Installing software for your network

In addition to Junos OS, only basic factory-default configuration is installed on the device. Therefore, you must configure Junos OS software to work with your specific network. You can restore the basic configuration if you want. However, the features active in this basic configuration vary based on the hardware capabilities of different devices.

The content of the factory-default configuration file may vary across the Junos OS product families, but they all have a factory-default configuration:

- ✔ **M, T, and MX routers:** The factory-default configurations for these routers includes only a root user account and simple logging settings.

- ✔ **EX switches:** The factory-default configuration for EX switches is more elaborate. On EX switches, all ports are in Layer 2 mode, and the Rapid Spanning Tree Protocol (RSTP) and Link Layer Discovery Protocol (LLDP) are enabled, as well as Power over Ethernet (PoE).

✔ **SRX Services Gateways:** The factory-default configuration for SRX Services Gateways changes with the model. Smaller SRX devices have Layer 2 and Layer 3 ports, but larger SRXs all have Layer 3 ports. Dynamic Host Configuration Protocol (DHCP) is enabled, and an IP address is configured for management purposes on some SRX devices. But, as expected for security devices, all SRXs have rudimentary security policies in place. (See Chapter 12 for more details on SRX setup and configuration.)

Regardless of which factory-default configuration is included on the device, you can restore a Junos OS device to the factory-default settings with the `load factory-default` command. Here is an example from an MX series router:

```
[edit]
root@mx# load factory-default
warning: activating factory configuration

[edit]
root@mx# show
#Last changed: 2011-02-14 11:55:41 UTC
system {
    syslog {
        user * {
            any emergency;
        }
        file messages {
            any notice;
            authorization info;
        }
        file interactive-commands {
            interactive commands;
        }
    }
    ## Warning: missing mandatory statement(s): 'root-authentication'
}
```

As you can see, loading the factory-default configuration results in a `missing mandatory statement` warning. You must configure a password for the root account before you can commit the factory-default configuration.

Connecting to the Junos OS

After you install the hardware, you are ready to configure the Junos OS beyond the factory-default settings (which are not really adequate for real-world situations). To do this, you have to connect to the Junos OS running on the device.

Generally, here are the three ways to connect to the Junos OS:

✔ Via the console

✔ Via the CLI interface

✔ Via the J-Web interface

Each of the three methods listed above can be used to do almost any configuration task. However, most people use the console connection initially and then switch to either the CLI or J-Web for more detailed configurations, as we'll see.

Console connection

All Junos OS devices have an RJ-45 console port labeled CONSOLE. You can connect from a laptop or other computer using a direct crossover serial connector or through a console server. The console port does not require previous configuration, and there are no restrictions on what can be configured. Only a terminal emulation program is needed on a laptop or computer.

Although powerful, the console connection configuration method requires a person to be physically close to the device. The device could be located on a mountaintop, in the middle of a remote desert, or locked in a closet in the cell block of a maximum-security prison.

CLI interface

The RJ-45 console port is *not* the same as the CLI port used for remote TCP/IP access (often labeled ETHERNET). Physically, they look the same, but you must configure the IP address and mask for the CLI port before using it, usually through the serial console interface. Once established, the dedicated management port (usually simply called *fxp0*) can be connected to a complete management LAN for management purposes, or through a router for global access.

J-Web interface

J-Web is not a separate port, but an interface that lets you manage the Junos OS based on a graphical interface inside a web browser. Although J-Web is limited when it comes to debugging operations like traceoptions, J-Web is a nice way to assess overall health of a system quickly (people interpret graphics much more quickly than they can read and understand words).

Most users make sure they are familiar with both the CLI and J-Web interfaces. Vendors make heavy use of graphical management interfaces, but support staff often work with the CLI. Avoid frustration: Learn them both.

Configuring Junos OS Devices with the CLI

Remember, you can configure all devices running the Junos OS three ways: the console, the CLI interface, and J-Web. Note that because the SRX is a security device, it's a bit special. Even so, the initial configuration steps in this section apply to it, as well.

The Junos OS features two modes, configuration mode and operational mode — you configure the device with configuration mode and operate (monitor) its functions with operational mode (refer to Chapter 2 for more on this major division). Most configuration actions begin with set, and most operation commands begin with show. In the following sections, you first use configuration mode to configure the device and then you see how operation commands are used to watch the device perform.

All Junos OS devices come with almost the same bare-bones factory-default configuration when you turn them on. You use the same basic steps to complete the configuration, which we show you in the upcoming section, "Configuring the device."

There are three copies (or images) of the software on Junos OS devices. One of these copies is on a CompactFlash card in the Routing Engine (see Chapter 3 for an overview of the Junos OS hardware). Another copy is on a rotating hard drive in the Routing Engine. The third copy is on a USB flash drive (on smaller devices such as the MX80) or a PC Card (on larger devices such as the T1600 core router) that can be inserted into a slot on the Routing Engine faceplate.

When the device boots, it first attempts to load the software image on the USB flash drive or PC Card. If a flash drive or PC Card is not present, or if the attempt to load the software fails, the device tries the image on the CompactFlash card. Finally, the image (or copy) of the software of the hard drive is tried.

When the device boots successfully, you are ready to tackle the initial configuration.

Getting the configuration information

Before configuring the device, you need to determine the following:

- ✔ The name the device will use on the network (such as Router1)
- ✔ The Domain name that the device will use (such as example.com)
- ✔ The IP address and prefix length for the ETHERNET (CLI) interface
- ✔ The IP address of the default router for the Ethernet management network
- ✔ The IP address of a DNS server (to resolve the device name)
- ✔ The Password for the root user

Not all of this information needs to be configured — for example, the domain name and DNS server. However, most network operators require these pieces of information and nothing is gained by omitting them.

Once you have established this information, you are ready to configure the device.

Configuring the device

You will follow the same basic steps for configuring all Junos OS devices, as shown in this section. However, the steps shown here do not achieve a complete device configuration. In other words, if the device is a router, the basic configuration will not allow the router to forward packets. There is no routing protocol configuration in the list in this section. But these basic steps will allow you to use the CLI port to complete the router configuration.

1. **Verify that the router is powered on and displaying the root prompt.**

2. **Log in as the** root **user. There is no password yet.**

3. **Start the CLI.**

   ```
   root# cli
   root@>
   ```

4. **Enter configuration mode. Note the change in the prompt from > to #.**

   We cover operational mode (>) and configuration mode (#) in more detail later in this chapter.

   ```
   cli> configure
   [edit]
   root@#
   ```

5. **Configure the name of the device. If the name includes spaces, enclose the name in double quotation marks (" "). Use the generic** *host-name* **here.**

```
[edit]
root@# set system host-name host-name
```

6. **Create a management console user account. Use the generic** *password* **rather than an actual password.**

```
[edit]
root@# set system login user user-name authentication plain-text-password
New password: password
Retype new password: password
```

Don't worry about the `plain-text-password`. Your password is not stored as plain text. This item just means you'll be entering the password as plain text and not as a special sequence of digits from a security device or other form.

7. **Set the user account to** `super-user`.

A super user can create and grant root and admin permissions, as well as save the world.

```
[edit]
root@# set system login user user-name class super-user
```

8. **Configure the device's domain name. Use the generic** *domain-name* **instead of an actual domain name like juniper.net.**

```
[edit]
root@# set system domain-name domain-name
```

9. **Configure the IP address and prefix length for the device's Ethernet interface. Use the generic** *address/prefix-length* **rather than an actual IPv4 (inet) or IPv6 (inet6) address. Here you use an IPv4 address.**

```
[edit]
root@# set interface fxp0 unit 0 family inet address address/prefix-length
```

10. **Configure the host IP address of a backup router.**

This router is used only while the routing protocol is not running on the router you are configuring.

```
[edit]
root@# set system backup-router address
```

11. **Configure the host IP address of a DNS server.**

    This step allows you to see names rather than IP addresses in later command output.

    ```
    [edit]
    root@# set system name-server address
    ```

12. **Configure the root authentication password by entering either a clear-text password, an encrypted password, or an SSH public key string (as with Digital Signature Algorithm (DSA) or Rivest-Shamir-Adelman (RSA).**

    This router is used only while the routing protocol is not running on the router you are configuring.

    You can use plain text password authentication:

    ```
    [edit]
    root@# set system root-authentication plain-text-password
    New password: password
    Retype new password: password
    ```

    Or you can use encrypted password authentication:

    ```
    [edit]
    root@# set system root-authentication encrypted-password
         encrypted-password
    ```

    Or you can use SSH DSA public key authentication:

    ```
    [edit]
    root@# set system root-authentication ssh-dsa public-key
    ```

    Or you can use SSH RSA public key authentication:

    ```
    [edit]
    root@# set system root-authentication ssh-rsa public-key
    ```

    Remember, plain-text-password just means the way you enter the plain text password, not the way it is stored or used by the system.

13. **(Optional) Configure the static routes to remote subnets that have access to the management port (usually fxp0). To access the management port from the remote subnet, add a static route to that subnet in the routing table.**

    The retain keyword ensures that the static route remains in the table at all times, and the no-readvertise keyword provides some security by making sure the route to the management subnet is never shared with other routers.

    ```
    [edit]
    root@# set routing-options static route remote-subnet next-hop
         destination-IP retain no-readvertise
    ```

14. **(Optional) Configure the telnet service at the** `[edit system ser-vices]` **hierarchy level.**

    If you do not configure this service, no one can use Telnet to access the device (some operators choose to deny Telnet).

    ```
    [edit]
    root@# set system services telnet
    ```

15. **Display your configuration with an operational mode command to verify that it is correct.**

    ```
    [edit]
    root@# show
    system {
        host-name host-name;
        domain-name domain-name;
        backup-router address;
        root-authentication {
            authentication-method (password | public-key);
        }
        name-server {
            address;
        }
    }
    interfaces {
        fxp0 {
            unit 0 {
                family inet {
                    address address/prefix-length;
                }
            }
        }
    }
    ```

Sometimes it's best not to configure too much during one session. In this way, you can more easily pinpoint areas of concern if the device does not behave as expected.

Commit the configuration to activate it on the device.

```
[edit]
root@# commit
```

16. **(Optional) Configure additional properties by adding the necessary configuration statement. Then commit the changes to activate them on the device. (However, you can do this later, after you verify that what you have done is functioning as expected.)**

    ```
    [edit]
    root@host-name# commit
    ```

Note that the device now has a name: host-name in this case. You can also use commit confirmed to restore the previous configuration after a 10-minute interval, unless you type **commit** or **commit check** in that interval. You can alter the wait period by adding the time in minutes to the command (for example, commit confirmed 5 sets the window to 5 minutes).

17. When you finish configuring the device, exit configuration mode.

```
[edit]
root@host-name# exit
root@host-name>
```

If you need to reinstall the Junos OS, boot the device from the removable media. But make sure you don't insert the removable media during normal operations. The device might not behave as expected when booted from the removable media.

The main configuration file is stored as juniper.conf. On many Junos OS devices, when the device boots from the storage media (in the order outlined previously), it expands its search in the /config directory in the following order:

- ✔ The main configuration file juniper.conf
- ✔ The rescue configuration file rescue.conf
- ✔ The archived rollback configuration file (more on these later in this chapter) juniper.conf.1

When the search finds the first configuration file that can load correctly, the configuration loads and the search process ends. If no configuration can be loaded correctly, the device does not function properly. If the device boots from an alternate boot device, the Junos OS displays a message when you log on to the device.

Displaying set Commands

You configure the Junos OS device with the set commands. You use them to either initially configure the device or change an existing configuration. But if you display a configuration with the show operational command, it does not display the list of show commands used to create the display. However, there is a way to display the set commands, as we'll see in this section.

Most configuration actions begin with set, and most operation commands begin with show.

One reason this book focuses on the Junos CLI is because it is filled with different ways to do the same thing. Once you get the hang of the options, you start finding all the shortcuts and expressway on ramps. One of the most frequently used and easiest configuration shortcuts is to display an existing set of commands known to work and then reuse it somewhere else, as shown here:

```
root@host-name> show configuration interfaces ge-0/0/1 | display set
set interfaces ge-0/0/1 unit 0 family inet address 192.168.100.1/30
```

You can use the command to display the whole configuration or just a portion, as just shown.

In the displayed listing, look for the set command that you want to reuse and copy it using an available copy command, such as the common keyboard command, Ctrl+C. Then move your cursor to where you want to reuse the command and paste it (by pressing Ctrl+V). You can cut and paste the entire output (the returns are embedded at the end of each line). Before pressing Enter, you can make any other changes needed in the command lines, such as changing the IP address.

You can combine the top command with other commands to enter new statements at the top of the hierarchy, regardless of where you are currently working in the configuration — for example:

```
top set interfaces ge-0/0/1 unit 0 family inet address 192.168.100.1/30
```

Making Changes to the Junos OS Configuration . . . Faster

Networks are complex, dynamic systems that must often be changed in order to meet new business demands, needs, or mergers. Think about it: A minor organization changes, but it cascades into headaches because you have to change every single network device to accommodate the reorganization. Well, the Junos OS has many helpful commands to shorten the time it takes to make changes in the existing configuration — that is, renaming, copying, replacing, and inserting, which I cover in the following sections.

Renaming a section of the configuration

Sometimes you may want to rename a section of the Junos configuration, for example, to alter an older naming convention to adhere to a new policy. Assume that you want to rename ge-0/0/0 to the new naming convention of ge-1/0/0. Here is the current configuration snippet:

```
root@host-name# show interfaces ge-0/0/0
unit 0 {
    family inet {
        address 100.100.100.1/24;
    }
}
```

You can rename the interface in one step with the `rename` command:

```
root@host-name# rename interfaces ge-0/0/0 to ge-1/0/0
```

Now, use the `show` command to check that the change occurred:

```
root@host-name# show interfaces ge-1/0/0
unit 0 {
    family inet {
        address 100.100.100.1/24;
    }
}
```

Copying parts of the configuration

Junos also allows you to make copies of parts of the configuration by using the `copy` command. For example, assume that you create a template for a local user called `logintemplate`, and you want to make a copy for a new user named `joe` who has recently joined your team:

```
root@host-name# show system login user
user logintemplate {
    full-name "Generate network operations user";
    class netops;
    authentication {
        encrypted-password "$1$Naeta3Iw$./sgTTPKONoHOPJdsXvP6."; ## SECRET-DATA
    }
}
```

You can make a copy of this template for the new user, `joe`, by using the `copy` command:

```
root@host-name# edit system login
root@host-name# copy user logintemplate to user joe
```

And, again, check to confirm that Junos created the new local user:

```
root@host-name# show
user logintemplate {
    full-name "Generate network operations user";
    class netops;
    authentication {
        encrypted-password "$1$Naeta3Iw$./sgTTPK0NoH0PJdsXvP6."; ## SECRET-DATA
    }
}
user joe {
    full-name "network operations user";
    class netops;
    authentication {
        encrypted-password "$1$Naeta3Iw$./sgTTPK0NoH0PJdsXvP6."; ## SECRET-DATA
    }
}
```

To complete the setup of joe, you can modify his password, and he's ready to go.

Replacing a part of the configuration

Another useful command is replace, which changes a given character string throughout the configuration to something else. For example, assume that interface ge-0/0/0 is referenced in the protocols branch of the configuration, because you configured OSPF on it, as shown here:

```
root@host-name# show interfaces ge-0/0/0
unit 0 {
    family inet {
        address 100.100.100.1/24;
    }
}
root@host-name# show protocols ospf
area 0.0.0.0 {
    interface ge-0/0/0.0;
}
```

In this example, you can use the replace command to rename the interface to the new naming convention throughout the entire configuration:

```
root@host-name# replace pattern ge-0/0/0 with ge-1/0/0
```

You can use show interfaces to view the configuration, and you can see that the name changes in both the interfaces and the protocols:

```
root@host-name# show interfaces ge-1/0/0
unit 0 {
    family inet {
        address 100.100.100.1/24;
    }
}

root@host-name# show protocols ospf
area 0.0.0.0 {
    interface ge-1/0/0.0;
}
```

Inserting a configuration statement

Finally, the `insert` command allows you to insert a configuration statement either before or after an item in an ordered sequence. This command is especially useful if you are configuring firewall filters and routing policies and need to change the ordering of terms, as shown in this example:

```
[edit policy-options policy-statement multiterm]
jadmin@juniper1# insert term accept before term reject
```

Here, you are inserting the `accept` term before the `reject` term, which in a routing policing, can save you hours upon hours of midnight troubleshooting. See Chapter 14 for more information about policies and the insert command. Just remember that like `copy`, `replace`, and `rename`, the `insert` command can save you time and effort when you are configuring your Junos device.

Archiving Configurations

When you activate a new configuration, the Junos OS software automatically keeps an archive of the previous active configuration. This automatic backup mechanism lets you return quickly to a previous configuration using the `rollback` command. In addition, you can copy the currently active configuration or a previous configuration from the router to a file server on the network, and if you need to return to a backed-up version, you can manually reload and restore the configuration file onto the router.

Using the rollback command

To return to a configuration that the Junos OS software has automatically archived, use the `rollback` command in configuration mode:

```
[edit]
user@host-name# rollback 1
load complete
```

This `rollback` command loads the previous configuration but stops short of activating it. If you need to change what's in the configuration, you can modify it. To see what statements are in the configuration, use the configuration mode `show` command:

```
[edit]
user@host-name# show
```

The `show` command displays all the statements in a configuration one screen at a time. To see the next screen, press Enter or the spacebar.

When you're ready to activate the configuration, use the `commit` command:

```
[edit]
user@host-name# commit
commit complete
```

Restoring the full archive

In addition to archiving the last version of the configuration, the Junos OS software stores the last 50 active configurations. These files are on the router's flash and hard disks, so you can restore the configuration saved in a particular file.

Use help with the `rollback` command to list the full archive:

```
[edit]
user@host-name# rollback ?
Possible completions:
  <[Enter]>              Execute this command
  0                      2007-10-31 12:34:56 PST by fred via cli
  1                      2007-10-31 12:30:03 PST by fred via cli
  2                      2007-10-30 14:23:44 PST by fred via cli
  ...
  48                     2007-09-03 08:00:03 PST by root via cli
  49                     2007-09-03 07:45:21 PST by root via cli
  |                      Pipe through a command
```

Pick the configuration by date and time and specify the number in the `rollback` command to load that configuration:

```
[edit]
user@host-name# rollback 2
load complete
```

Verify that the change is what you want by using the show command, and then activate it with the commit command:

```
[edit]
user@host-name# show
...

[edit]
user@host-name# commit
commit complete
```

Archiving manually from a server

You can manually archive configuration files by copying them to a file server on your network, by following these steps:

1. **Use the Junos OS** file copy **operational mode command to copy the active configuration, the file** juniper.conf.gz, **in the router's /** config **directory:**

   ```
   user@host-name> file copy /config/juniper.conf.gz server1:/homes/fred/tmp
   user@server's password:
   juniper.conf.gz                            100% 2127      2.1KB/s   00:00
   ```

2. **Once the file is on the server, rename it so that the next time you copy the active configuration, you don't overwrite the previous one — for example:**

   ```
   user@host-name> mv juniper.conf.gz juniper.conf.gz-20071031
   ```

3. **If you need to return to that active configuration, copy it back to the router by using the** file copy **command again to put it back in your home directory on the router:**

   ```
   user@host-name> file copy server1:/homes/fred/tmp/juniper.conf.gz-20071031
   user@server's password:
   juniper.conf.gz-20071031                   100% 2127      2.1KB/s   00:00
   ```

4. **After the copy operation completes, look at the files in your home directory to make sure the file arrived safely:**

   ```
   user@host-name> file list
   juniper.conf.gz-20071031
   ```

5. **Change from operational mode to configuration mode by using the** configure **command, load the configuration file with the** load **command, and review it with the** show **command.**

6. **Finally, activate the configuration file using the** `commit` **command:**

```
user@host-name> configure
Entering configuration mode
```

```
[edit]
user@host-name# load juniper.conf.gz-20071031
load complete
```

```
[edit]
user@host-name# show
...
```

```
[edit]
user@host-name# commit
commit complete
```

Creating and saving configurations

When you add new equipment or customers to your network, change the design of the network and its services, or install new network cards or hardware in the router, you need to modify the router's configuration to define and activate the new features. You can modify the configuration when you're rolling out the new equipment or services, or you can modify it beforehand, in anticipation of the hardware arrival or the service start date, and then flip the activation switch at the appropriate time.

As you become more familiar with Junos software, creating configurations in advance — when you're not under deadline pressure — can be a very useful technique for managing time and reducing stress.

Configuring Junos OS Devices with J-Web

The last section in this chapter is a bit misleading. Not misleading in the sense that you can't configure the device with J-Web; you certainly can. It's a bit misleading in the sense that everything done in this chapter since the hardware install with the CLI can also be done with J-Web. So, although J-Web is a different configuration tool — a graphical user interface (GUI) and network management tool, not a CLI — the result is the same.

You may be asking: If the end result of using J-Web is the same as when using the CLI, why care about J-Web? The answer is shown in the following list, which shows some benefits of using J-Web rather than CLI:

✔ Many users prefer to work with GUIs rather than command lines because a GUI is their usual operating environment, so they are familiar with it.

✔ You can complete more configuration steps at once on a single page.

✔ Multifunction devices (such as switches that route and perform firewall functions, act as a DHCP server, and so on) are rendered more understandable when features are presented as functional sections.

✔ The J-Web GUI is easier to understand and use than commands and modes are.

All in all, J-Web can make configuration of Junos OS devices, especially low-end devices, simpler and more compartmentalized.

Figure 5-1 shows the login page for the SRX 100 Services Gateway (note that the interface may look slightly different depending on which version you are working on). Just connect the device to your network, connect your laptop or computer to the SRX device with an Ethernet cable, and open a browser on your laptop or computer. Type http://192.168.1.1, and you see the login page. The process is like connecting to and configuring a DSL router in your home.

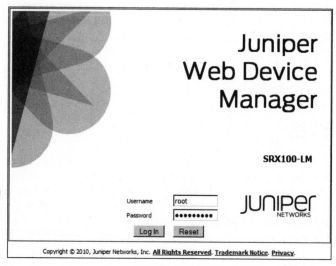

Figure 5-1: Logging in to J-Web.

After you configure the SRX, a system identification page launches as part of the Setup Wizard (see Figure 5-2). The wizard has about 10 screens, and in each screen, you simply fill in the information. You must fill in the fields with asterisks to move to the next screen. In about 15 minutes, you have a basic configuration, and the device is working.

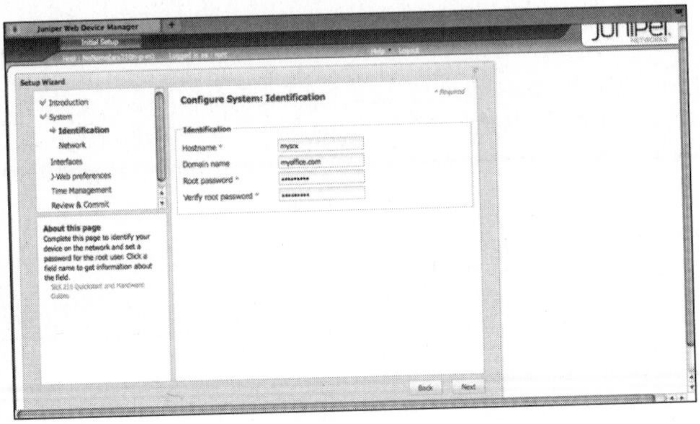

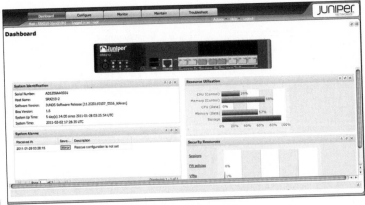

Figure 5-2: Starting the Setup Wizard.

After you configure J-Web, you see the J-Web Dashboard whenever you log in (refer to Figure 5-1). The Dashboard, shown in Figure 5-3, immediately shows you a chassis view, the system identification, resource utilization, and security resources. Tabs at the top of the Dashboard let you configure, monitor, maintain, and troubleshoot the device all in a web-page manner. There's no CLI, just fields, buttons, and help screens.

Figure 5-3: The Dashboard of a SRX100.

Why you need to know CLI

So why isn't this book about Junos J-Web? The simple answer is that you wouldn't get to know the Junos OS by focusing on J-Web; you'd see how to use the J-Web interface. This book shows you all about how to set up and deploy Junos networks, and for that, the CLI is the best teacher around. It's like watching a video of French cooking versus spending the day cooking a four-course French meal.

If all you have is an SRX100 doing all your office's routing and firewalling, J-Web is for you. If you have anything more complicated, use J-Web as a time-saving device for quick fixes, or use it to monitor your device's health.

Juniper Networks is always tweaking the J-Web interface, so it's worth checking it out often, even if you don't use it. At some point, you might just say, "Wow, I didn't know I could do that on J-Web."

Chapter 6

Setting Up Junos Devices

• •

In This Chapter

▶ Setting up options for more complete router operation

▶ Configuring user accounts with different capabilities

▶ Configuring the management and loopback interfaces for non-user traffic

▶ Configuring network interfaces for user traffic

▶ Configuring other options, such as time zones

• •

A network device needs more than a basic "the device can start itself up" software configuration to perform its role as a router connecting IP subnets or a switch connecting LANs. In a sense, this entire book is about configuring the Junos OS to do what is necessary for a specific situation.

In this chapter, we take the configuration another large step forward. You see how to set up options such as system logging and configure user accounts and network interfaces for user traffic. You even see how to configure options such as time zones and banners for login.

By the time you finish the chapter, you will know how to complete the configuration of the Junos OS in terms of access and other essentials.

Understanding the Initial Configuration

The initial configuration on Junos OS devices can be summarized as follows:

✔ M, T, and MX routers have

  • Single root account with no password

  • Simple logging settings

✔ EX switches have

- All ports in Layer 2 mode
- Rapid Spanning Tree Protocol (RSTP) enabled
- Link Layer Discovery Protocol (LLDP) enabled
- Power over Ethernet (PoE) enabled

✔ SRX Services Gateways have

- Layer 2 and Layer 3 ports (smaller SRX devices)
- Layer 3 ports only (larger SRX devices)
- Some security policies (all SRC devices)

In addition to the standard three ways to access a device for configuration — via the console, CLI interface, or J-Web interface — SRX devices allow access through the Network and Security Manager (NSM). The NSM is a Juniper Networks management platform for SRX platforms. NSM is not limited to SRX firewalls, but is most often used there. (See Chapter 12 for more about NSM in the SRX.)

Setting Up System Options

Junos OS devices can be located almost anywhere: in general office space, on a rack in an equipment room, or as part of a large "farm" of related devices, sometimes the size of a factory. But in all these environments, the Junos OS device typically hums merrily along with no one watching it. But what if the hum turns into the software equivalent of grinding brakes on an automobile or of a weird *ka-chunk* whenever you shift gears? In that case, it's very important to be able to know when the problem started and what else might have gone on during the same timeframe, along with having various other details available if needed.

In other words, you need *logging*. As you probably know, logging is how the system keeps track of what it's doing in a human-friendly way.

You can set up two types of logging on a Junos OS device to record events as they happen:

✔ System logging (*syslog*), which records device-wide events of importance

✔ Trace logging (*tracing*), which zooms in on events relating to a specific area such as a routing protocol operation

Although you may be tempted, you don't really want to watch and record *everything* with maximum syslogs and every possible tracing function (because much of what happens on a network is, thankfully, relatively boring and repetitive). Instead, you really need to look for events that indicate things may be going haywire, and then focus on just the areas that might be the cause.

For this reason, a lot of operators set up syslog files to capture anything that might be going wrong, and then use the tracing process to look at that particular area. You can look at the device operation in real time, but that's usually not a great idea because this monitoring process can cause operational issues (as in s-l-o-w).

Logging is an excellent way to monitor the operation of your router. This chapter covers only the logging and tracing basics. Chapter 7 covers the international standard for device management, the Simple Network Monitoring Protocol (SNMP).

The following sections set up some basic logging capabilities for a Junos OS device, followed by how to use tracing to zoom in on an area suspected of being a problem.

Configuring syslogs

Configuring syslog is straightforward: You configure the file in which to store the logs, the type of events you want to track, and the event *severity*. The severity is just a measure of how bad you want the condition to be before you record it. To use the automobile analogy, do you want to know every time the fuel efficiency dips below a certain level? (If so, get ready for a lot of logs whenever you hit a stop light.) Or do you just need to know when it's time to change the oil? (Probably a better idea for day-to-day operations.) So, in terms of the syslog, you want to know when an event happens that potentially requires action soon.

Here's a configuration example that stores logs of all events that have a severity level of `warning` (or more severe) in a file named `log-messages`:

```
[edit system]
user@host-device# set syslog file log-messages any warning
```

In this configuration, `any warning` indicates the event (`any`) and severity level (`warning`). Tables 6-1 and 6-2 provide different types of logging events and severity levels you can use in collecting syslog messages, such as `authorization error` or `change-log notice` to chart activity on the router that might be suspicious and damaging to the current router setup. To look at the syslog messages in the file on the router, use the `show log` command, followed by the name of the log file:

```
user@host-device> show log log-messages
```

Table 6-1	**Types of Logging Events**
Configuration Option	*Type of Event*
Any	Any device event
authoriza-tion	Authentication and authorization attempts
change-log	Changes to the device's configuration
conflict-log	Changes to the device's configuration that are inappropriate for the device hardware
daemon	Relating to the Junos OS software processes
firewall	Packet filtering performed by firewall filters
ftp	File transfers done with FTP
interactive-commands	Commands typed at the command-line interface or by a JUNOScript client application
kernel	Relating to the Junos OS kernel
Pfe	Packet forwarding software
User	User processes

Table 6-2		**Logging Severity Levels**
Name	*Number*	*Description*
Any	---	All severity levels (in other words, include all events)
None	---	No severity levels (in other words, discard all events)
Debug	7	Debugging information
Info	6	General device operation
Notice	5	General device operational events of more interest than "info"
Warning	4	General warnings
Error	3	General errors
Critical	2	Critical errors that might affect device operation
Alert	1	Errors requiring immediate attention
Emergency	0	Errors that cause the device to stop operating

Tracing routing events

In addition to the syslog feature, you can use the `traceoptions` feature to get more detailed information about a particular operational area. (This process provides information similar to that produced by the `debug` feature on some other companies' devices.) For example, you may want to keep an eye on routing protocol operation. When you do, you can turn tracing on for all routing protocols or for an individual routing protocol.

To get an idea of the general routing protocol operation on the router, configure a file in which to store the operational events and a list of flags that define the types of events you want to record. The following configuration collects information about all events (flags) in the file `trace-events`:

```
[edit]
user@junos-router# set routing-options traceoptions file trace-events
     world-readable

[edit]
user@junos-router# set routing-options traceoptions flag all
```

The flags that are available vary from device to device and from area to area. In the preceding code, `world-readable` means that any user who can validly access the device can read the trace file, which is a good idea in many cases (no one wants to mess around with user permissions during a crisis). However, the default condition is the `no-world-readable` option, which limits trace file access to a limited pool of users.

Configuring User Accounts

In the previous section, a trace file was set up that was "world-readable" so that anyone who managed to log in to the device successfully could read the file. However, by default, only a certain set of users can view trace files (if you put all users into this user set, of course, then all users who access the devices can read the trace files). In this section, you find out how users can be set up to have a greater or lesser number of capabilities, or *privileges*.

Sets of users with their privileges are called *classes*, and four standard login privilege classes exist on a Junos OS device, as shown in Table 6-3.

Table 6-3	Standard Login Privilege Classes	
Name	*Description*	*Usage Recommendation*
Super-user	A `super-user` can perform any and all operations on the device.	Reserve this privilege level for the key people who monitor and maintain all aspects of your devices.
Operator	An `operator` is allowed to work in operational mode to check the status of the device and the routing protocols, clear statistics, and perform reset operations, including restarting routing processes and rebooting the device.	This class can look at the device configuration, but can't modify it. This privilege level is for the network operations team that is responsible for monitoring your devices.
Read-only	Someone with `read-only` privilege can only monitor the status of the device and routing protocols.	Give to low-level watchers of the network who must get an engineer or administrator when they see something amiss.
Unauthorized	`unauthorized` is a class with no privileges at all on the device.	When users in this class log in, the Junos OS software immediately logs them out. It sounds odd, but this class can be useful if these users *do* have privileges on other devices.

You may be tempted to put every valid user into the `super-user` class and be done with it, but doing so is usually a big mistake. Super-users can do literally *everything*, including granting super-user privileges to other users. One well-known trick is to quickly log in as a super-user and create an innocent-looking user ID ("guest-1") that also just happens to have super-user privileges and log out again. But the damage is done.

Everyone will claim they can't do their job unless they have super-user privileges. This is nonsense, and a bit like saying you can't write a book unless you have superpowers and a red cape (then again, that would be really neat). Save your super-user class for people who really need it.

If you have a small group of devices, setting up individual accounts is a straightforward way to provide access for network administrators. Although you'll need to manually configure the account information on each device, if the number of devices is minimal and you don't have to modify the information very often, this method is the way to go. For larger networks, however, using a centralized authentication server is much easier because you can store all account information in one place, and you update it only once when changes occur.

Local user configuration

We'll show you the local user configuration method first. When you create an account on a device for an individual user, you assign a login name, password, and privileges, and you provide information about the user. This process is very similar to what you did for the initial device setup. Here's an example that sets up a super-user account for a user named Mike (I know Mike, and he's indeed a super-user):

```
[edit system login]
user@junos-device# set user mike class super-user

[edit system login]
user@junos-device# set user mike full-name "Mike Bushong"

[edit system login]
user@junos-device# set user mike authentication plain-text-password
New password:********
Retype new password:********
```

The first command defines an account for the user Mike and gives him super-user privileges (shown earlier in Table 6-3), which allow him to perform all operations on the router. The second command defines his full name. And the third command creates a password for Mike. Even though the command says it's a plain-text-password (ASCII), the Junos OS software encrypts the password, as you can see when you display the configuration:

```
[edit system login]
user@junos-device# show
user mike {
  uid 2001;
  class super-user;
  authentication {
    encrypted-password "$1$BmFLXWlx$sYKMY7XrTRHv40AD3/Z7U1"; ## SECRET-DATA
  }
}
```

No, we didn't enter the user ID (uid); the system did. The system assigns that ID just as a concise way to keep track of user information.

Authentication server user configuration

Larger organizations generally centralize the authentication process, setting up RADIUS (or TACACS+) servers on the network. (Here, we talk about RADIUS, which is the Remote Authentication Dial-In User Service.) All account information — username, password, and privilege class — is stored on the server. When a user attempts to log in to the router, the router queries the RADIUS server to validate the user.

Here's how you set up centralized authentication:

1. **Enter configuration mode and configure the IP address and password (which RADIUS calls a "secret") of the RADIUS server:**

   ```
   [edit system]
   user@junos-device# set radius-server 192.168.10.1 secret 123456
   ```

   ```
   [edit system]
   user@junos-device# show
   radius-server {
      192.168.10.1 secret "$9$ZQUk.fTz6Ct5TcyevLX"; ## SECRET-DATA
   }
   ```

   Again, when you display the RADIUS server configuration, note that the password is encrypted.

2. **Make RADIUS the primary authentication method:**

   ```
   [edit system]
   user@junos-device# set authentication-order [ radius password ]
   ```

With this configuration, when a user tries to log in to the router, the Junos OS software first attempts to authenticate the user against the RADIUS database. If this step succeeds and the user's credentials match those on the server, the user is allowed to log in. If it fails, or if the RADIUS server is down, the software checks for accounts configured locally on the router. If the user has a local account and the credentials match, the user can log in. Otherwise, access to the router is denied.

Using a RADIUS server for authentication also lets you set up a single account for a group of users. Instead of setting up lots of individual accounts for people who have the same job responsibilities, you can create a shared account for the entire group. On the router, create the group account as follows:

```
[edit system login]
user@junos-device# set user architects class super-user
```

```
[edit system login]
user@junos-device# set user architects full-name "Network design team"
```

Your next step is to map the user on the RADIUS server to the group account name you just gave the user on the router. How you do this step depends on which RADIUS software you're using on the server.

User configuration and permissions

Regardless of where you configure them, user permissions are an important part of user parameters. The privilege classes are just a convenient way to gather a collection of permissions together for common purposes. But you don't have to do that. You can grant individual permissions outside of the privilege class structure.

For example, you can explicitly create a class called `configurators` who are explicitly granted permission to edit a configuration file but nothing else. Realistic? Maybe not. But it does work.

```
[edit system login]
user@junos-device# set class configurators permissions configure
```

This, of course, is the answer to where users can be set up to read `no-world-readable` trace files (and nothing else, if you like). If you grant `trace` permission to a user class, you let users in this class view trace files and trace file settings. Many of the predefined user classes include this permission (and many others).

Configuring the Management and Loopback Interfaces

The major characteristic of network devices is that they have network interfaces, and usually more than one. Routers can have literally hundreds and so can large switches.

The Junos OS supports many types of interfaces, including these:

- ✔ The Ethernet family (Fast Ethernet, Gigabit Ethernet, and so on)
- ✔ Serial interfaces
- ✔ Public transport interfaces, such as T1/E1, SONET/SDH, and others
- ✔ Public network interfaces, such as frame relay or ATM
- ✔ Multicast interfaces

✔ ADSL

✔ Tunnel interfaces

✔ Loopback interface (`lo0`)

✔ Management interface (`fxp0`)

This section looks at configuring the last two interface types on the list: the management interface (usually `fxp0`) and the loopback interface (`lo0`, short for "loopback 0"). Both of these interfaces, `lo0` and `fxp0`, are critical to get right for correct device operation. But, first, take a look at the physical and logical properties that must be set for any interface.

Knowing the physical and logical interface properties

The first thing that pops into your mind when you think about interfaces is probably the IP address. IP addresses are assigned to individual interfaces, and those addresses are used by protocols and other routing features to control traffic within the router and within the network to which that router is connected.

However, nothing about an interface says that it must have a specific IP address assigned to it. In fact, you can assign the same address to an Ethernet interface and then delete it and assign the exact same address to a SONET/SDH serial interface. The address is really a logical property of the link, not inherently associated with any of the physical characteristics of the line.

Physical interface properties

Physical characteristics of links dictate how bits are sent over a link. These properties include *encapsulation* (how the bits are structured inside a transmission frame), *clocking* (how individual bits are distinguished at the line level), *encryption* (how the bits conceal their true meaning), and so on.

Physical interface properties differ from logical properties in that they generally have to be configured identically on both ends of the link to ensure that the two end devices are speaking the same language. In Junos, physical properties are configured at the highest interface level, for example [edit interfaces lo0].

Logical interface properties

Logical interface properties are the parameters not intrinsically linked to the physical interface. Logical properties govern how the interface behaves, but they don't affect whether the underlying connection on that link can be made. The IP address is the prototypical logical interface parameter.

In addition to the IP address, other logical properties include the types of protocol families (MPLS, ISO, and so on) supported, as well as the type of IP address (IPv4 or IPv6). In the Junos OS, logical properties are configured at the "unit" level, for example [edit interfaces lo0 unit 0].

Configuring the management interface

One interface you need to set up on the router is the router's management interface, which is called fxp0 on many Junos OS devices. You use this interface for out-of-band (meaning "not over the same network the user data travels") access to the device. Unlike other network interfaces on the device, which receive and transmit traffic flowing between different network interfaces on the device (*transit traffic*), the out-of-band management interface accepts traffic only to and from the router itself.

Using a separate, dedicated interface for managing the router is good for two reasons:

- ✔ It doesn't interfere with network traffic.
- ✔ The interface is available even if other network interfaces go down.

The fxp0 interface is an Ethernet interface running IPv4, so you configure it like this:

```
[edit interfaces]
user@junos-device# set fxp0 unit 0 family inet address 192.168.50.2/24
```

Here, the default physical interface values for the fxp interface type are accepted and assigned the IPv4 address (family inet), a logical property, at the unit 0 level. And, yes, there can be other units with other addresses, or even more than one address on unit 0!

Configuring the loopback interface

Oddly, the device's loopback address is not used to loop traffic back to the sender. However, it is a stable address for the device that can be used whether or not a particular physical interface is down. Once each network interface has an address, it can send and receive traffic. However, if the interface goes down or if you need to remove it from the router for some reason, the router may no longer be reachable on the network by applications such as SNMP that monitor the router. To prevent this issue, you assign an address to the router by configuring the router's loopback interface:

```
[edit interfaces]
user@junos-device# set lo0 unit 0 family inet address 192.168.10.1/32
```

The loopback address is a special internal interface within the router and is not associated with any physical hardware, so you don't need to specify an FPC or PIC slot or a port number.

Configuring Network Interfaces

Once the management and loopback interfaces are complete, you can finish configuring the network interfaces on the device. The Junos OS supports a lot of different interface types that are configured with a two-letter text identifier. Many (but not all) interface identifiers are listed in Table 6-4.

Table 6-4   Common Interface Types and Their Identifiers

Interface Type	Interface Text Identifier
ATM over SONET/SDH	At
Encryption Services	Es
Fast Ethernet	Fe
Gigabit Ethernet	Ge
Loopback	lo0
Router internal interface for out-of-band management	fxp0
Router interface for internal management	fxp1
Serial	Se
Services for ES and AS PICs	Sp
SONET/SDH	So
T1	t1

Note that in Table 6-4, `fxpo0` and `lo0`, which are non-user-traffic interfaces, are on the list.

The simplest way to tell which interfaces are actually installed on your device is by using the `show interfaces terse` command:

```
fred@junos-router# show interfaces terse
Interface               Admin Link Proto Local            Remote
fe-0/0/0                up    up
fe-0/0/0.0              up    up   inet  192.168.10.2/24
fe-1/1/0                up    up
fe-1/1/0.0              up    up   inet  192.168.10.41/24
ge-1/2/0                up    up
```

```
ge-1/2/0.0                    up    up    inet  10.0.0.1/24
ge-1/3/0                      up    up
ge-1/3/0.0                    up    up    inet6 3001::2/64
                                          iso
lo0                           up    up
lo0.0                         up    up    inet  192.168.10.1/32
```

The `Local` column in the output lists the interface addresses. Let's look at the numbers after the two-letter type and see what the "Proto" column means.

You set the protocol supported on the interface with the family keyword, and the protocol can be one or more of the more common families such as these (this is not an exhaustive list):

✔ `inet`: For IPv4. Specify a 32-bit IPv4 prefix, followed by a slash and the prefix length (as shown in this section).

✔ `inet6`: For IPv6. Specify a 64-bit IPv6 prefix, followed by a slash and the prefix length.

✔ `iso`: For interfaces that need to support CLNS, which is the ISO network layer service protocol that is used by IS-IS. You also need to configure one or more addresses on the router's loopback (`lo0`) interface, which IS-IS uses for its interface addresses.

✔ `mpls`: For interfaces that need to send and receive Multiprotocol Label Switching traffic. You don't need to configure an address for this protocol.

The "family" refers to the type of frame content that the (logical) interface must look for when deciding how to process the bits. What looks like an IPv4 packet with an error, for example, may be a perfectly valid MPLS data unit.

The numbers following the interface type (such as `ge-`) refer to the chassis slot, processor, and port on which the interface is sending and receiving bits. In the original Junos OS, these numbers were called the Flexible PIC Concentrator (FPC), the PIC (which had no official expansion), and the connector port respectively. But although the meanings have changed, the CLI still configures interfaces by these three numbers.

You assign an IPv4 address to a Gigabit Ethernet interface, as follows:

```
[edit]
user@junos-device# set interfaces ge-1/2/0 unit 0 family inet address
                192.168.10.40/24
```

It's worth seeing how the address displays in the configuration file because this configuration snippet visually shows the different sections of the interface configuration by the layers of indentation:

```
[edit]
user@junos-device# show
interfaces {
  ge-1/2/0 {
    unit 0 {
      family inet {
        address 192.168.10.40/24
      }
    }
  }
}
```

In this example, the IPv4 address 192.168.10.40/24 is assigned to the first connector on the third processor of the board in the third chassis slot (1/2/0 — computers always start counting with 0, as though the first day of the month were October 0).

Configuring other Gigabit Ethernet properties

For an interface such as Gigabit Ethernet, you can usually leave all other properties at their default values. Properties such as whether the link should use flow control can be set, but usually the default (no flow control) is fine.

However, one additional physical interface property (meaning it is set at the ge-1/2/0 level) is important: the maximum transmission unit (MTU) size. This property is the maximum size of the information field that can be packed inside an Ethernet frame. The MTU is important because there is no sub-unit to a frame. All frames are processed immediately upon receipt. If an IPv4 packet stuffed into the frame exceeds the MTU size, the overflow bits are not sent, and the received frame will have an error. Even if the IP packet fits, if the additional fields (MPLS tags, VLAN tags, and so on) cause the frame to exceed the MTU size, there will be an error at the receiver.

For Gigabit Ethernet interfaces (all interfaces have default and maximum sizes), the MTU size of the IP packet is 1500 bytes (which is usually not a problem). The MTU size for the link (Layer 2) is 1514 bytes, meaning that the link allows no more than 14 bytes of overhead in the frame header and trailer. For Gigabit Ethernet, if you intend to send more, you can increase the MTU size up to a maximum of 9018 bytes (some interface boards support only 9014 bytes).

Most people ignore the MTU size until it causes an issue and traffic on an otherwise functioning link suddenly disappears. Many network operators' first challenge is to track down and figure out an MTU issue!

You can change the Gigabit Ethernet MTU size on `ge-1/2/0` to 9000 bytes (larger MTUs are more efficient) as follows:

```
[edit]
user@junos-device# set interfaces ge-1/2/0 mtu 9000
```

Remember, physical interface properties must match at both ends of link.

Configuring Other Options

Any self-respecting Junos OS device will include other things, such as the banner and time and time zone, which you configure in this section.

Configuring a banner for login

When you log in to the Junos OS device, you're immediately placed into the CLI and can start working. The prompt shows the username you used to log in and the name of the device:

```
user@junos-device>
```

Because the device is shared on a network, you may want to send a message to all the other users who log in. One way to do so is to display a message on the screen each time someone logs in. This *banner* containing the message displays before or after the login prompt, depending on which command you use.

After entering configuration mode, use the banner command `set system login message` to place your message before the login prompt. The `\n` puts one blank line (a new line) after the text and before the login prompt:

```
[edit]
user@junos-device# set system login message "Junos OS device managed by the
       4Dummies Network team\n"
```

The following banner appears each time someone logs in to the router:

```
user@remote-host# ssh junos-device
Junos OS device managed by the 4Dummies Network team
```

```
junos-device (ttyp0)
login:
```

If your company has legal requirements in place to limit access to key network devices, such as routers, you can use the login banner to warn that only certain people are allowed to work on the router. Be sure to use the specific language the legal department provides for the banner.

Never welcome or otherwise encourage people to use the device in text you include in a banner.

Here's an example of a warning login message:

```
[edit]
user@junos-device# set system login message "--------------------------------
-----\nWARNING: Unauthorized access is prohibited.\n-----------
--------------------------"
```

Here's what the login message looks like:

```
user@remote-host# ssh junos-device
---------------------------------------------
WARNING: Unauthorized access is prohibited.
---------------------------------------------

junos-device (ttyp0)
login:
```

To make announcements for such things as network or router down time or for a scheduled network maintenance window, use the set system announcement command:

```
[edit]
user@junos-device# set system announcement "Network maintenance will occur
        Saturday night from 2000 to 2300; please log out before then"
```

Announcement command banners show up *after* the user logs in — so that you don't broadcast sensitive things to anyone and everyone, such as maintenance schedules:

```
junos-device (ttyp0)

login: user
password: ********

--- Junos OS 11.3R1.8 built 2011-08-22 19:51:10 UTC
Network maintenance will occur Saturday night from 2000 to 2300; please log
        out before then
user@junos-device>
```

Setting the time and time zone

To accurately know what (and when) events happen on a single device, it needs to have the correct time and time zone. On a whole network, all the devices must have the same time, especially when you're trying to track events and problems. Otherwise, you'll have difficulty tracking sequences of events and determining what went wrong and exactly when.

With Junos, you set the time much like you do when setting a watch. This task is reasonably easy to do in a small network. Simply set the time in operational mode, as follows:

```
user@junos-device> set date 200802121646
Tue Aug 22 17:45:00 UTC 2011
```

The time the router displays is not the local time (unless you're in the United Kingdom in winter); rather, it's UTC (Universal Coordinated Time, once called Greenwich Mean Time, or GMT). If you want to use the local time zone instead, set the time zone for the device in configuration mode. For the western United States, set the local time zone with this configuration (this is for standard time):

```
[edit system]
user@junos-device# set time-zone GMT-7
```

If you operate a larger network or have networks with devices in different time zones, use UTC across the entire network. Today, networks generally also have a centralized time server of some kind, and you use the Network Time Protocol (NTP) on the device to have it automatically synchronize itself to the time server. If it knows the IP address of the NTP server, the device can synchronize its time whenever it boots:

```
[edit system]
user@junos-device# set ntp boot-server 192.168.10.20
```

In a stable network, you don't reboot devices very often, but the time on the router can slowly drift. You can have the router periodically synchronize its time with the NTP server by leaving out the `boot-server` option:

```
[edit system]
user@junos-device# set ntp server 192.168.10.20
```

Logging Out

Whenever you finish working on the device, don't just walk away from your terminal session. Log out! This prevents anyone from randomly walking up to your terminal or PC and accessing the device. If you're working in operational command mode, you can log out with a simple `exit` command:

```
user@junos-device> exit
logout
Connection closed by foreign host.
user@remote-server#
```

Because you can log out only from operational command mode, when working in configuration mode, you must finish your configuration session and return to operational mode:

```
[edit system]
user@junos-device# exit configuration-mode
Exiting configuration mode
```

```
user@junos-device> exit
logout
Connection closed by foreign host.
user@remote-server#
```

Chapter 7

Managing Your Network with Junos OS

*I*magine that you've spent a lot of time getting your Junos OS device up and running and part of a larger network, and now you want to take a break. However, before you can take that break and "safely" leave your device, you must set it up so that you can access and manage it remotely.

This chapter describes how to access the device remotely, explaining everything from the physical interface to the different monitoring tools. You pick a management interface, access the device, set up management with SNMP, and come up with a more complete scheme for system logging.

Note: Before continuing, if you need a refresher on the basics for enhancing the initial configuration of the Junos OS and working with the management interface, basic logging events, and tracing, please refer to Chapter 6.

Choosing a Management Interface

To manage the Junos OS without being physically present, your fundamental requirement is to create an interface through which you can communicate. Although you may think the question is *which* interface to use, the question is actually which interface *can* you use. You have a couple of choices, depending on how you want to manage your networked devices. Of course, you have choices depending on your management requirements and the type of device you're using.

Making these choices boils down to answering two decisions: determining whether you want to use your network-facing in-band interfaces or a specialized management interface (out-of-band management), and determining whether you need to access the router with root permissions (in-band management). To make the decision, you need to know the differences between the two options.

- ✔ **Out-of-band management:** Identifies remote management through a network that is separate from the traffic-carrying network on which the device is deployed. Put simply, out-of-band management uses an interface that carries only management traffic, whereas the other interfaces on the router carry LAN/WAN traffic. (In Chapter 6, you configure the management interface as part of your initial device configuration, but that doesn't mean you must use it for all management!)

- ✔ **In-band management:** Is remote management where one of the LAN/WAN interfaces is used to manage the router. That is to say that you use the network to carry both network traffic and management traffic across the same links.

Generally speaking, most Junos OS administrators find it safer and more reliable to separate the traffic-bearing network from the management network, because when you have network issues, you want to guarantee access to your devices. Using the troubled network to resolve those issues makes you vulnerable. If you can't access the device during these times, your ability to remotely troubleshoot — and ultimately resolve — problems can be compromised. On the other hand, smaller organizations may not have the resources to construct what amounts to a *second* network to manage the first.

The ports on any device are prime real estate, like USB ports on a PC. Using up one of those ports to handle management traffic reduces the ports available for network traffic. A device with only a few ports or one whose ports are all in use can become an issue.

As mentioned, using in-band management can be a budget issue, because the benefits of an out-of-band management network come with a corresponding cost. It's expensive (sometimes prohibitively so) to have a separate network infrastructure to handle only management traffic. Such a management network requires the deployment of terminal servers and switches to pass management traffic, and those devices incur their own set of support costs, in terms of both dollars and personnel.

The decision between out-of-band and in-band management is really one of cost: Do you have the resources to set up and maintain a separate management network? If you do, we recommend using the out-of-band approach to remote management. If you don't, in-band is the only other option.

After you make the decision about your remote management interface, you need to wire up your device and then configure the management interface.

Setting Up Out-of-Band Management

Out-of-band management is handled through special management interfaces on Juniper Networks devices. These interfaces are Fast Ethernet interfaces located on the front of all Juniper Networks devices. They're designed so that traffic that arrives on these interfaces does not get routed on other network interfaces on the router. This setup separates management traffic and network traffic.

In Chapter 6, we provide an example of management interface during initial device configuration. This section is more detailed. To connect your out-of-band interface to your management network, follow these steps:

1. **Connect an Ethernet cable from your device's out-of-band interface to your management network (typically a switch).**

2. **When your link lights are up, configure the IP address.**

   The out-of-band management interfaces on Juniper Networks routers are named fxp0 on M-, MX-, and T-series devices. On these product lines, the interface settings are configured under the interface name fxp0.

   On J-series devices, the management interfaces are named fe-0/0/0. Interface settings are configured under either fxp0 or fe-0/0/0. However, the router architecturally recognizes the J-series management interface as fe-0/0/0 and uses that name when reporting any interface information via operational commands. Therefore, using the fxp0 name when configuring J-series management interfaces is confusing; instead, use the fe-0/0/0 name.

3. **To configure the management interface, simply set the IP address on the interface:**

```
interfaces {
    fe-0/0/0 {
        unit 0 {
            family inet {
                address 192.168.71.246/32;
            }
        }
    }
}
```

Setting Up In-Band Management

For in-band management, you must first decide which interface you want as your management interface. Generally, management traffic is not excessive, or even substantial, so picking any of the slower interfaces on your router is likely to be enough. On most devices, a Fast Ethernet connection is more than sufficient to handle management traffic. On lower-end devices, you might choose a serial interface or T1/E1 interface, if there is one.

Connecting the interface is identical to connecting any other interface on the router. Here are the details for using `fe-0/1/1` (refer to Chapter 6 for more details on this interface):

1. **Connect the cable to the port and ensure that the remote connection is in place.**

   When the link lights come up, you're ready to configure the interface.

   Some interfaces, such as serial interfaces, require some minimal configuration before the link is active. For such interfaces, you must configure the interface as you do with any other interface *before* the link lights come up.

2. **After wiring up the management interface, configure the interface so that it has an IP address.**

   Typically, this configuration is enough to enable the interface:

   ```
   interfaces {
       fe-0/1/1 {
           unit 0 {
               family inet {
                   address 192.168.71.246/32;
               }
           }
       }
   }
   ```

When you configure an in-band management interface, if you are configuring a Layer 3 device such as a router, you need to be aware of how the routing protocols and routing policies will be affected. For more details on this concern, see Chapters 10 and 14.

Generally speaking, you don't want to enable routing protocols on the management interface because you want to prevent other routers from establishing adjacencies with your management interface. (In many cases, the management network is the shortest path between two routers! But that's not what it's for.) Make sure that none of the protocols configured on the router (especially those enabled using the `interface all` configuration statement) are active on the management interface. To disable a protocol on the management interface, use the `disable` statement:

```
[edit protocols]
user@Router# set ospf interface fe-0/1/0 disable
```

```
[edit protocols]
user@Router# show
```

```
ospf {
    interface all;
    interface fe-0/1/0.0 {
        disable;
    }
}
```

In this example, the OSPF protocol is enabled on all interfaces on the router. The `disable` statement ensures that OSPF doesn't run on the management interface (`fe-0/1/0`, in this case).

Similarly, you don't want route policies to advertise management interface addresses to peering networks. You can prevent advertising management interface addresses to peering networks by explicitly filtering management addresses using a route filter or by carefully constructing routing policies to ensure that routes are not leaked. For more information about routing policies and filtering routes, see Chapter 14.

Accessing the Device

Many places, you need a backstage pass to see what is going on behind the curtain, and different levels can get you access to the dressing rooms or tour bus. The following sections explore the kind of "backstage" passes Junos OS devices offer and how close you can get to what goes on behind the curtain.

Accessing your device with Telnet

The basic way of accessing a remote device is using Telnet. After you configure an IP address on the management interface (whether that interface is out-of-band or in-band), you can access the device by opening up a Telnet session to that address. For example, if you configure your device with a management interface address of 192.168.71.246, you should be able to access the device with the Telnet session:

```
> telnet 192.168.71.246
Trying 192.168.71.246...
telnet: connect to address 192.168.71.246: Connection refused
telnet: Unable to connect to remote host
```

Oops, something went wrong. Access to the device must be explicitly configured on the device (which is part of the initial setup in Chapter 6, but many people don't complete it!). More specifically, particular modes of access must be explicitly enabled. In this case, you're trying to access the device using Telnet, so you must tell the device to allow Telnet connections. To configure the Telnet service on the device, do the following:

```
[edit]
system {
    services {
        telnet;
    }
}
```

After Telnet services are enabled on the device, the Telnet request is successful:

```
> telnet 192.168.71.246
Trying 192.168.71.246...
Connected to device.domain.net.
Escape character is '^]'.
```

```
dummies (ttyp0)
```

```
login:
```

When your Telnet session is established, access is then based on user authentication. The exact authentication mechanism is based on your configuration. (See Chapter 6 for information on setting up user names and authentication.)

Root access to the device is restricted to only those connections that are made via the console (indicating physical access to the router) or via an encrypted session (such as SSH or HTTPS). If you try to log in with the root username, your login will fail regardless of the password you enter. If you must use Telnet to access the device and you must have root access, try setting up a user ID with super-user privileges. (See Chapter 6 for details.)

Accessing your device with SSH

Although Telnet is the old-school original remote access method and it may hold a fond place in your heart, when it comes to accessing devices, Telnet can be fairly insecure. Traffic exchanged via a Telnet session isn't encrypted, and no safeguards ensure that traffic being sent across a Telnet session is received by the end device and not intercepted somewhere between you and the machine you're accessing. Unfortunately, this setup makes it fairly simple to sniff the traffic and steal logins and passwords.

To be more protective with your login credentials, you want to use *Secure Shell* (SSH). SSH differs from Telnet in that it enables the exchange of data between you and your device over a secure channel. Just as with Telnet, you must explicitly enable the encrypted SSH service on the device:

```
[edit]
system {
    services {
        ssh;
        telnet;
    }
}
```

After you enable SSH on the device, you can access the device through an encrypted session. Because this session is encrypted, you can now log in to the device remotely using the root login:

```
> ssh -l root router
root@device's password:
```

```
--- JUNOS 11.1I (JUNIPER) #3: 2011-07-30 02:18:17 UTC
root@device%
```

When you log into the device as `root`, you log in directly to the FreeBSD shell. To start the CLI, issue the `cli` command at the prompt.

A fairly simple way to help strengthen your device against attack is to limit the number of access sessions that can be attempted per minute. If you imagine an automated script trying thousands, or even millions, of login/password combinations, you can see how a hacker might try to gain access to your device. Use the `rate-limit` statement to limit the number of tries to something reasonable:

```
[edit]
system {
    services {
        ssh {
            rate-limit 15;
        }
        telnet {
            rate-limit 15;
        }
    }
}
```

Managing Devices with Simple Network Management Protocol

Simple Network Management Protocol (SNMP) is an Internet standard protocol for managing all devices on an IP network. SNMP has centralized systems called clients (which SNMP calls *managers*) that actively monitor servers (which SNMP calls *agents*) by querying them and collecting status information and statistics from them. The managers generally run on dedicated computers called *Network Management Systems* (NMSs), and routers are one type of agent.

When you want the NMS on your network to be able to monitor the device, you need to configure the device to be an SNMP agent (Chapter 6 looks at some of this configuration):

```
[edit]
user@junos-device# set snmp community public authorization read-only
```

To transform the router into an agent, you place the router into an SNMP community using `set snmp community public authorization read-only`. This command uses one of the common SNMP communities, `public`. The second part of the command defines how the agent (your Junos OS) will respond to requests from the NMS system. An authorization of `read-only` means that the device will send its information to the NMS, but the NMS will not be able to modify any settings on the device (which it could do if you specified an authorization of `read-write`). You can configure the device to respond to multiple communities, each with its own authorization level.

You can configure basic information about the device for the NMS to collect when it queries the device, such as the device's location and description and who to contact about the device. This information corresponds to leaves in the `system` group in the standard MIB-II, and NMS on the network can collect this information when querying the device (in this case, a router):

```
[edit snmp]
user@junos-device# set description "Juniper Router"
```

```
[edit snmp]
user@junos-device# set location "Sunnyvale, California machine room"
```

```
[edit snmp]
user@junos-device# set contact "page-repair@juniper.net,
        cell phone +1-408-555-2000"
```

It's always a good idea to make the SNMP community permission string something other than `public`. If you don't, you can bet at some point someone will change the SNMP for every network device to contact you whenever anything goes wrong.

In normal SNMP operation, the NMS periodically queries the device. If any unexpected events occur on the device, the NMS finds out only after sending a query and examining the response. However, you can configure the device to send notifications to the NMS when unexpected events occur. This notification means that the NMS, and the people monitoring the NMS, can find out about device problems more quickly. These notifications of serious events are called *traps*, and you can configure the types of events that trigger the device to send traps. (Table 7-1 lists a variety of trap categories used in the Junos OS software.)

SNMP acronyms/definitions

SNMP uses a set of acronyms all its own:

- **SMI:** Structure of Management Information defines the way data is stored in a Management Information Base (MIB).

- **MIB:** Management Information Bases (not Men In Black!) are hierarchical databases, like a directory structure on a PC or Mac, in which SNMP agents (such as a router) store their status information and statistics. The information in each MIB is arranged as a hierarchical tree structure, with branches that move down from the root node. Each branch eventually ends at a leaf. Branches are just like directories on a computer, and leaves are just like the files in directories. One difference between MIBs and computer directories is that each branch and leaf in the MIB is identified not only by a name, but also by a number. SNMP defines standard MIBs, and individual network equipment vendors can also define proprietary MIBs. The standard MIB for use in TCP/IP networks is called MIB-II because it is the second version of this MIB. For your SNMP client to be able to retrieve information stored in these MIBs, it must know the structure of the MIB. You can download all Juniper Networks MIBs, both the standard and proprietary ones, from the Juniper website (www. juniper.net).

- **OID:** Object Identifier is the number that uniquely identifies a branch or leaf in the MIB. The OID is actually a string of numbers, with one number for each branch in the hierarchy and one number for the final leaf in the hierarchy. The OID generally begins with a period to indicate the top of the tree (the root node), and each subsequent number is separated by a period. An example of an OID from the standard MIB-II MIB is .1.3.6.1.2.1.1.1, which points to the device's description (sysDescr).

The following command configures the router to send traps when an NMS system uses the wrong community string when trying to access the device:

```
[edit snmp]
fred@junos-device# set trap-group authentication-traps targets 192.168.10.30
fred@junos-device# set trap-group authentication-traps categories authentication
```

Table 7-1	SNMP Trap Categories	
Configuration Option	**MIB**	**Description**
authentication	Standard MIB-II	Authentication failures on the agent (the device)
chassis	Juniper proprietary	Chassis and router environment notifications

(continued)

Table 7-1 *(continued)*

Configuration Option	MIB	Description
configuration	Juniper proprietary	Configuration mode notifications
Link	Juniper proprietary	Interface transitions, such as transitioning from up to down
rmon-alarm	Juniper proprietary	SNMP remote monitoring (RMON) events
routing	Juniper proprietary	Routing protocol notifications
startup	Standard MIB-II	Device reboots (soft/warm and full reboots)

Monitoring a Device with System Logging

You can use other techniques to remotely manage the Junos OS. Gaining access to the device is essential for remote management, and it allows you to issue diagnostic commands to monitor the health and state of the device. However, monitoring even a single box in real time using interactive commands is impossible. For example, to monitor a router — and by extension, your network — you must be able to generate router messages that you can either act on or use for historical data, without having to be actively on the router.

The Junos OS software supports extensive system logging capabilities, as well as tracing functionality, which makes watching over your network easier.

The Junos OS software generates system messages (known as *syslog messages*) when system events occur. A *system event* can be anything from a user logging on to the device, to a particular command being issued, to a process on the device failing and restarting. As we mention in Chapter 6, these syslog messages are constantly being generated and are either saved or processed by the device, providing you with the real-time and historical data you need to remotely monitor your network.

Now, take a look at these syslog messages in more detail.

Digging into syslog messages

The most important aspect of logging is understanding what and when something is logged. Events across the entire system, covering both hardware and software conditions, are included in the Junos OS software syslog repertoire:

- ✔ Every time the device is accessed, queried, or modified

- ✔ Every time a process starts, fails, or restarts

- ✔ Every physical threshold that is reached (temperature within the chassis, CPU utilization, fan speed, and so on)

- ✔ Various system conditions that affect or reflect the operation of the device

These events are divided into different categories, called *syslog facilities*. Each of these facilities is assigned a facility code, which ties a particular message to the syslog facility. Table 7-2 lists the Junos OS syslog facilities along with their corresponding facility code.

Table 7-2	JUNOS Syslog Facilities	
Syslog Facility	*Facility Code*	*Event Source*
Any	None	Any facility
Authorization	AUTH, AUTHPRIV	Authentication and authorization attempts
change-log	CHANGE	Configuration changes on the router
conflict-log	CONFLICT	Configuration changes that are in conflict with the router's hardware
	CONSOLE	Kernel messages to the console
	CRON	Scheduled processes
Daemon	DAEMON	Individual JUNOS software processes
Firewall	FIREWALL	Packet filtering performed by firewall filters
ftp	FTP	FTP activities
interactive-commands	INTERACT	Commands executed from the CLI or through the XML API
Kernel	KERNEL	JUNOS kernel
	NTP	Network Time Protocol process
Pfe	PFE	Packet forwarding engine
	SYSLOG	System logging
User	USER	User processes

Each of these syslog facilities contains many different syslog events. To help differentiate among these events, in addition to the facility, each event is assigned a severity level. Table 7-3 lists the syslog severities. (We in the industry tend to list the worst severity last, because we never want to see them!)

Table 7-3	JUNOS Syslog Facilities	
Severity Name	*Severity Number*	*Severity Description*
any	None	All severity levels
none	None	No severity levels
debug	7	Information to be used for debugging
info	6	Informational events about normal operations
notice	5	Conditions that aren't errors but are of more interest than normal operations
warning	4	General warnings for significant events
error	3	General errors
critical	2	Critical errors, including hardware failures
alert	1	Errors that require immediate intervention
emergency	0	Conditions that stop router function

All syslog messages contain both the facility and the severity. When searching through the hundreds, or even thousands, of log messages, you can match on these two values so that you can quickly identify the information you need when monitoring your network.

Here's what a syslog event looks like:

```
Nov  2 19:02:49  router mgd[8039]: UI_LOAD_EVENT: User 'michael' is performing
        a 'rollback 2'
```

In addition, this syslog event contains these key pieces of information:

✔ **Timestamp:** The system time at which the event occurred. In this example, the event took place at 7:02 p.m. on November 2.

✔ **Router name:** The configured name of the router. In this example, the router is creatively named `router`.

✔ **Process information:** The name of the process that generated the syslog event, including the process ID to uniquely identify the particular instance of the process. In this example, the Management daemon (MGD) process created the event. Specifically, it was the MGD instance with process ID `8039`.

✔ **Syslog message:** The syslog message, including the event name and relevant information to the event. In this example, the user `michael` has issued a `rollback 2` command on the router.

The timestamp associated with each `syslog` message doesn't indicate the time zone in which the device resides. If you have multiple devices across more than one time zone, you must remember the time zone each device is in. Imagine a situation where traffic between Los Angeles and Denver is interrupted at 1:00 p.m. PST. For you to effectively sift through the syslog messages, you must know the system time on each device when the events were logged. And in this case, the system times are different, so you have to know to look at 1:00 p.m. on the Los Angeles router and 2:00 p.m. on the Denver device. To simplify this kind of log perusal, configure the system time on each device using coordinated Universal Time Clock (UTC) — refer to Chapter 6 for more on using UTC. If all the devices are configured within the same time zone, all the timestamps will show the same time, making your life much simpler when it comes to wading through log files.

You can send syslog messages to a number of places. You can view them in real time by sending them to a console session. You can store them in files on the device so that you can look through them later. You can even store all the syslog messages from all your devices on a single syslog server so that you can go to a single place to monitor your network. How you configure your device determines which method you use.

Mood music: Turning on logging

To activate logging on the device, you must configure what you want logged and where you want to log it. You have to specify both the types of messages and where you want those messages to be sent.

The most common, and simplest, form of logging writes individual `syslog` messages to one or more log files stored locally on the device. Suppose that you want to log every interesting condition, regardless of the specific facility, as well as all user login activity on the box, and you want to store those messages in a file called `messages`. Turn on this logging by configuring system logs under the `[edit system]` configuration hierarchy:

```
[edit system]
syslog {
    file messages {
        any notice;
        authorization info;
    }
}
```

In this example, all message types of severity of notice or higher (that's what "any notice" does), for all facilities, will be logged. Also, all messages related to user authorizations (logins, authentications, and so on) of severity, info or higher, will be logged.

When you specify a severity for logging, all events with that specific severity or higher are included in the logging.

Viewing syslog messages

The previous syslog configuration is actually the default level of logging on the router — logs are saved to a file called messages, which resides in the default log file directory /var/log/ (on M-, MX-, and T-series routers), or /cf/var/log/ (on J-series routers).

You can view the file from the device with this command:

```
user@my-device> show log messages
Nov 7 15:24:36  my-device smartd[4239]: atastandbyarmset: ioctl: Inappropriate
                ioctl for device
Nov 7 15:24:36  my-device smartd[4239]: standby_request: Error:
                atastandbyarmset(TRUE): Inappropriate ioctl for device
Nov 7 15:31:01  my-device xntpd[4364]: kernel time sync enabled 2001
Nov 7 16:07:10  my-device mib2d[4365]: SNMP_TRAP_LINK_DOWN: ifIndex 195,
                ifAdminStatus up(1), ifOperStatus down(2), ifName at-1/0/0
```

In this kind of output, you can see a number of events, each timestamped and identified by its process and corresponding process ID. But the show log messages command basically concatenates the entire log file to the screen. If you're interested in only a subset of the entire log file or if you're searching for specific criteria, this kind of raw output is difficult to use — or to be honest, bordering on completely useless. To filter the output from the command, specify filter criteria. For example:

```
user@my-device> show log messages | match mib2d
Nov 7 16:07:10  my-device mib2d[4365]: SNMP_TRAP_LINK_DOWN: ifIndex 195,
                ifAdminStatus up(1), ifOperStatus down(2), ifName at-1/0/0
```

By specifying the match condition, only the syslog event containing the string mib2d is returned.

Filtering syslog to different files

Dumping all syslog events to a single log file makes parsing out significant events difficult, especially those events that may be of critical importance. For example, at a minimum, you need to know who accesses the box and when they do so in order to determine whether your device is the target of hacking attempts. You can configure logging so that these types of events are saved to a separate file called `security`:

```
[edit system]
syslog {
    file messages {
        any notice;
    }
    file security {
        authorization info;
    }
}
```

Here, you have a separate log file called `security` that has all the login attempts and authorization information. To view such a file:

```
user@my-device> show log security
Oct 28 12:41:44  my-device mgd[27893]: UI_AUTH_EVENT: Authenticated user
                'michael' at permission level 'j-superuser'
Oct 28 12:41:44  my-device mgd[27893]: UI_LOGIN_EVENT: User 'michael' login,
        class 'j-superuser' [27893]
```

This log file shows that the user `michael` was authenticated and then logged in. This user had super-user privileges.

Refining your access to events

You often have two separate files with logging information in them: a messages file with all `syslog` events with a severity of notice or higher, and a `security` file with all authorization events with a severity of `info` or higher.

Even with this separation, the syslog messages can still be cumbersome to sift through when viewing the files from the device. What if you want to view the messages file, but you want to see only events of severity warning or higher? The severity value doesn't appear in any of the syslog events.

To include both the syslog facility and the severity values in each message, configure the `explicit-priority` statement:

```
[edit system]
syslog {
    file messages {
        any notice;
        explicit-priority;
    }
    file security {
        authorization info;
    }
}
```

This syslog configuration includes the facility and severity values for all the syslog messages included in the messages file. Now you can view the log file and see only the messages of severity warning or higher:

```
user@my-device> show log messages | match -4-
Nov 30 16:07:10 my-device mib2d[4365]: %DAEMON-4-SNMP_TRAP_LINK_DOWN: ifIndex
     196, ifAdminStatus up(1), ifOperStatus down(2), ifName at-1/0/1
```

In this output, you filter the messages and retrieve only the message that has -4-. This filter returns the SNMP link category "link down" trap, which has a facility of DAEMON and a severity of 4. Using the explicit-priority configuration statement, you can make your log files substantially easier to parse.

Managing your log files

If you've created loads of log files, shuttling different types of events to different types of files for ease of use, you need to manage those files.

By default, Junos OS software limits the size of the log files to 128K. As events are logged, when the total size of the messages exceeds 128K, something has to give. You don't want to stop logging, but you also don't want to lose any historical information that may be necessary or useful.

When files reach the 128K limit, those files are compressed and archived on the device with a file extension that identifies the file's relative age. Looking at the /var/log/ directory shows this behavior:

```
% show /var/log/messages*
messages            Size: 62145, Last changed: October 27 17:15:45
messages.0.gz       Size : 9213, Last changed: October 25 09:23:01
messages.1.gz       Size : 7814, Last changed: October 24 23:14:53
messages.10.gz      Size : 8467, Last changed: October 17 03:11:28
messages.2.gz       Size : 8863, Last changed: October 24 06:31:09
messages.3.gz       Size : 8749, Last changed: October 23 19:51:00
messages.4.gz       Size : 9003, Last changed: October 22 22:05:37
messages.5.gz       Size : 7191, Last changed: October 20 14:10:22
messages.6.gz       Size : 9059, Last changed: October 19 14:21:59
messages.7.gz       Size : 7834, Last changed: October 19 02:46:01
messages.8.gz       Size : 8559, Last changed: October 18 09:29:52
messages.9.gz       Size : 8272, Last changed: October 17 21:45:38
```

Junos OS rotates the log files. Each time the current file reaches the size limit, that file is compressed and saved with the .0 file extension. Each file's extension is then incremented, and the tenth file is deleted.

If you're using log files to actively troubleshoot a current problem, you may find it useful to clean up the log files so that you can reduce the number of old messages you have to sort through while debugging the issue. To clear the messages for a particular log, use the `clear log` command:

```
user@my-device> clear log messages
```

When you issue this command, the messages log file is emptied, which makes sorting through incoming syslog messages considerably easier.

Monitoring a Device Using Trace Logging

In addition to logging system events, Junos OS software allows you to monitor events through trace logging. Trace logging is configured and behaves in almost the exact same way as system logging (see preceding section). That is, you specify what you want to trace and where you want the messages to be stored. The biggest difference in trace logging is where the logging is actually configured. That is, system logging (as the name implies) is system-wide, whereas tracing is a more localized function of specific protocol and processes.

Because trace logging is used to monitor and troubleshoot protocols, tracing isn't enabled at the `[edit system syslog]` level in the configuration hierarchy. Instead, the tracing options (or `traceoptions`) are configured at the various protocol levels in the configuration hierarchy. For example, if you want to enable `traceoptions` to monitor the routing protocol OSPF activities, you configure `traceoptions` under the `[edit protocols ospf]` hierarchy in the configuration. For example:

```
[edit protocols]
ospf {
    area 0.0.0.0 {
        interface fe-0/0/0.0;
        interface fe-0/0/1.0;
    }
    traceoptions {
        file ospf-log {
            flag hello error general;
}
```

In this example, `traceoptions` are configured for OSPF. Whenever a `hello`, `error`, or general OSPF event occurs, the message is written to the file `ospf-log`. The trace log file is very similar to the syslog files:

```
user@my-device> show log ospf-log
Nov 30 16:07:10  OSPF rcvd Hello 10.0.16.2 -> 224.0.0.5 (fe-0/0/0.0, IFL 0x42)
Nov 30 16:07:10  OSPF Version 2, length 48, ID 192.168.19.1, area 0.0.0.1
Nov 30 16:07:10  checksum 0x0, authtype 0
Nov 30 16:07:10  mask 255.255.255.0, hello_ivl 10, opts 0x2, prio 128
Nov 30 16:07:10  dead_ivl 40, DR 10.0.16.1, BDR 10.0.16.2
```

The trace file has the timestamped OSPF events specified by the traceoptions. Using `traceoptions` can be quite useful when debugging routing
issues within your network. Subsequent chapters discuss specific traceoptions for each protocol within the context of those protocols (for example,
see Chapter 13 for more on BGP and Chapter 16 for more on MPLS).

Chapter 8

Monitoring Junos

*I*n Chapter 7, you find out how to set up the Junos OS device to allow remote access for management purposes, and you take a look at SNMP basics, as well as a long look at syslog files and the information they provide. If you've read that chapter, you may be wondering what else could possibly be needed to keep the network humming along. Actually, quite a bit.

This chapter covers the basic diagnostic tools and commands that are essential to the maintenance of a healthy network. The chapter describes how to check connectivity, monitor activity, and make sure that traffic is flowing at the highest possible speeds.

Checking Host-to-Host

You'll probably begin monitoring your network immediately after setting up your protocols. The first thing most people do after configuring their device is check to see whether they can send traffic across links to other nodes within the network. This initial test is where the `ping` command comes into play. Examine the network topology shown in Figure 8-1.

If you were to run the OSPF routing protocol across all the links in the network, you'd expect to be able to reach any host from any other host. You still need to verify if things are working correctly, however.

From the Junos OS command prompt, you can issue the `ping` command. Log in to the device you want to start from and send a ping to an address on the remote host; that is, to the address you expect to have a path to through the network. For example, in the topology shown in Figure 8-1, you might log in to `router1`. From there, you want to ensure that you have connectivity to `router7`. So you pick any network address on `router7` (any of the interface addresses, or even the loopback address will work) and issue a `ping` command:

```
user@router1> ping 10.0.24.2
PING 10.0.24.2: 56 data bytes
64 bytes from 10.0.24.2: icmp_seq=0 ttl=62 time=0.520 ms
64 bytes from 10.0.24.2: icmp_seq=1 ttl=62 time=0.417 ms
64 bytes from 10.0.24.2: icmp_seq=2 ttl=62 time=0.497 ms
64 bytes from 10.0.24.2: icmp_seq=3 ttl=62 time=0.424 ms
64 bytes from 10.0.24.2: icmp_seq=4 ttl=62 time=0.501 ms
^C
--- 10.0.24.2 ping statistics ---
5 packets transmitted, 5 packets received, 0% packet loss
round-trip min/avg/max/stddev = 0.417/0.472/0.520/0.043 ms
```

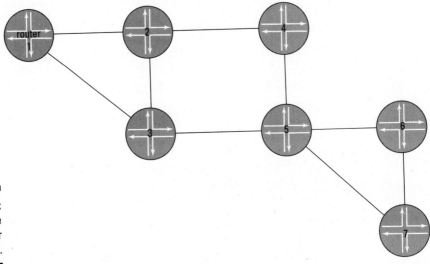

Figure 8-1:
A simple
7-router
network.

After you issue the command, the router sends packets to the remote address. When the remote node receives these packets, it generates a response packet and sends that packet back to the original sender. Upon receipt of this response packet, the router records a successful ping and measures the time between sending the original request and receiving the response. This process happens over and over until you stop the command by pressing Ctrl+C.

Associating an address with the hostname

If you try to send a ping to the name of the host, you have to make sure that the hostnames are being resolved on your device. In other words, you have to first configure a DNS server so that an address is associated with the hostname. (In Chapter 5, you do this as part of your initial device setup, but not everyone does so.)

Typically, even if DNS is configured, when you're using ping to diagnose a new network, you haven't yet added names to the DNS server, so you must use one of the configured addresses.

Now, if you're going with the address approach, which address should you use? You can pick any of the configured interface addresses, or you can pick the loopback address. If you want to ensure that the device itself is up, use the loopback address.

If you pick an interface address, and that interface happens to be down (because of a link error or because it hasn't been configured correctly, for example), your ping will fail. You may think the device is unreachable, but really only the interface is unreachable.

You may notice that in the ping output, each ping has an Internet Control Message Protocol (ICMP) sequence number associated with it. Each request and response is flagged with this sequence number so that the devices know which response goes with which request. If you know that you sent request 3 at a certain time, you can check the time that you receive response 3 and record the time it took for the entire roundtrip.

The ping command gives you a wealth of information. First, you know the remote address that you chose is up and responsive because the command yielded some output. Second, if you examine the summary data at the bottom of the output, you can see important statistics about the path. For example, notice that five packets were transmitted and five responses were received. This information tells you that all the ping requests were received by the remote device. If the network is having issues or the packets are lost, you will see that not all packets transmitted resulted in a received response packet. The packet loss is an indicator that something is wrong in the network.

Additionally, the summary output shows the minimum, maximum, average, and standard deviations for the response times. In this example, the round-trip transit time for the ping and response is on the order of .500 milliseconds, which is exceptionally fast. If the round-trip time exceeds 150 or 200 milliseconds, you probably want to take a look at the network to determine where the latency is originating.

TECHNICAL STUFF

The origin of ping

The concept of a ping is very similar to the way that SONAR works. Using SONAR, ships send out pulses of sound. The sound waves strike objects in the water and echo back. The transmitter can hear these echoes and use those to map out underwater obstacles. As you've probably seen in movies, these SONAR pulses make a pinging noise, and that noise is the namesake for the `ping` command.

After the concept was created by Mike Muuss, an acronym was associated with it. David L. Mills called the ping "Packet InterNet Groper," but don't let the presence of an acronym fool you as to the origin of the name.

Looking at Figure 8-1, you may wonder what happens if there is no path to `router7` from `router1`. The `ping` command reveals that information as well:

```
user@router1> ping router7
PING router7 (192.168.24.1): 56 data bytes
ping: sendto: No route to host
ping: sendto: No route to host
ping: sendto: No route to host
ping: sendto: No route to host
ping: sendto: No route to host
^C
--- router7 ping statistics ---
5 packets transmitted, 0 packets received, 100% packet loss
```

In this case, `router7` isn't reachable from `router1`. The ping fails, and one hundred percent of the packets sent are lost, meaning that there's no response. To find out whether the lack of response means the router is down or whether a problem occurred somewhere between `router1` and `router7`, you can issue a `traceroute` command, as discussed in the following section.

Tracerouting the Network

As shown in the preceding section, `ping` is useful for figuring out whether you can reach one host from another host; however, to find out the path that packets take through intermediate hops from source to destination, you can use the `traceroute` command.

For example, in Figure 8-2, the network is running the OSPF routing protocol. OSPF calculates a path from `router1` to `router7` (highlighted on the topology map). If you issue a `ping` command from `router1`, the ping fails. But to try to find out exactly where the failure is (the destination router or an immediate hop), you issue the `traceroute` command.

```
user@router1> traceroute router7
traceroute to router7 (192.168.24.1), 30 hops max, 40 byte packets
 1  router2 (192.168.26.1)  0.869 ms  0.638 ms  0.536 ms
 2  router3 (192.168.27.1)  24.968 ms  0.727 ms  0.363 ms
 3  *
 4  *
^C
```

The `traceroute` command works by sending an ICMP packet from the source to the destination node with an initial hop count of one. At each hop, the packet is processed, the hop count decremented, and if the hop count is now zero, the intermediate hop sends a response back to the source letting it know that it was received but the hop count expired. This information forms the first line of the output (from `router2` in this case). Then an ICMP packet with a hop count of 2 is sent out, and makes its way to the second device, and so on until either the destination is reached, a reply to a packet is not received (*), or the hop count (30, in this case) is exceeded.

So as a traceroute process makes its way hop by hop from `router1` to `router7`, you start to see responses showing how that packet is traversing the network. In the preceding output, the first hop along the way is `router2`. As part of the traceroute process, `router1` sends three separate ICMP packets. `router2` responds to each of these three as shown in the output.

The output shows the round-trip time for each of the three traceroute packets, which gives you an idea not only of which hops are being reached, but also how long it's taking to send traffic back and forth between those routers. As with the `ping` command, you want to keep an eye on the round-trip times to identify latency issues within your network.

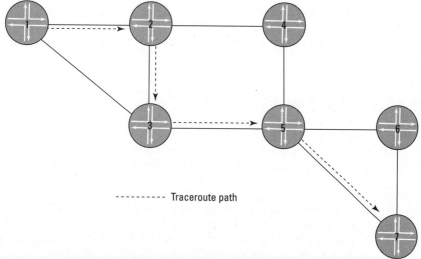

Figure 8-2:
Network
with path
from
`router1`
to
`router7`
highlighted.

In this example, the output shows that responses are being received from `router3`, but beyond that, nothing is received. Looking at the topology, the next hop in the path is `router5`. Because the traceroute isn't receiving a response from `router5`, you know that the problem is somewhere between `router3` and `router5`. You still don't know what the issue is, but at least now you know where to look.

It's tempting to look at the `traceroute` output shown and say, "Aha! The problem is at `router3`!" After all, that's when the good replies stop. But `traceroute` means that the packets are making their way just fine from `router1` to `router3` and back. The problem is with the link or router *beyond* that last good entry.

Using Diagnostic Commands

You'll find yourself using the same commands again and again to monitor, troubleshoot, and diagnose your network. These commands are the `show` commands that display important information about your interfaces and your routing (next-hop or forwarding) tables.

Almost every feature within the Junos OS software comes with corresponding *show* commands so that you can see what is happening on the device. Here are the show commands that you'll use most frequently:

✔ `show interfaces`

✔ `show route`

✔ `show <protocol>`

The following sections cover each of these commands in detail.

Monitoring your interfaces

You'll often want to look at how your interfaces are behaving to figure out what is happening to the traffic within your device. As such, you need to become an expert in the `show interfaces` command.

As with all `show` commands, this command has several variations:

✔ `show interfaces` (no modifier): The `show interfaces` command, issued with no modifier, gives you a summary of some of the most important fields and counters tracked for interfaces. This command is an excellent starting point for most interface activities.

✔ `show interfaces brief`: The brief version of the same command pares down the output even more. This command is useful when you're looking for big things such as whether an interface is up. If you need detailed statistics or counters, you must delve a little deeper than the `brief` command.

✔ `show interfaces detail`: The detailed output for `show interfaces` includes all the information from the previous commands, and it also includes detailed statistics about the interface, including the interface counters for packets and bytes, as well as queuing information, which is useful when you have class of service (CoS) configured (see Chapter 15 for more about CoS).

```
class-of-service      Show class-of-service (CoS) information
```

Which version of the command you use depends on your goal.

Taking a quick peek

If you just want to see whether an interface is operational, you can start with the `show interfaces brief` command (this section looks at a router):

```
user@router> show interfaces brief
Physical interface: fe-0/0/0, Enabled, Physical link is Down
  Link-level type: Ethernet, MTU: 1514, Speed: 10m, Loopback: Disabled,
  Source filtering: Disabled, Flow control: Enabled
  Device flags    : Present Running Down
  Interface flags: Hardware-Down SNMP-Traps Internal: 0x4000
  Link flags      : None
```

This command shows all the interfaces on the router, though the preceding snippet shows only a single interface. For each interface, you see the name of the interface, whether it's enabled, and the state of the physical link. For this Fast Ethernet interface, the physical link is down, which means that the interface isn't operational (the link light is down).

The device flags confirm that the interface is `present` (that is, it's on the box and the line card has been detected), `running` (meaning the line card is functioning), and `down` (the link light is down).

The output from the `show interfaces brief` command shows that the interface is `Enabled`. Remember that you can administratively disable an interface using the `disable` configuration statement within the interface configuration:

```
fe-0/0/0 {
    disable;
    unit 0 {
        family inet {
            address 10.0.24.2/32;
        }
```

```
      }
  }
```

If you disable an interface, the output from the `show interfaces` command
will indicate that the interface is administratively down:

```
user@router> show interfaces brief
Physical interface: fe-0/0/0, Administratively down, Physical link is Down
  Link-level type: Ethernet, MTU: 1514, Speed: 10m, Loopback: Disabled,
  Source filtering: Disabled, Flow control: Enabled
  Device flags   : Present Running Down
  Interface flags: Hardware-Down Down SNMP-Traps Internal: 0x4000
```

Viewing just the interface you want to see

Many times, you may not want to see every interface on the device. In fact,
more often than not, you're checking the status of a particular interface. To
see only the output for a specific interface, include that interface's name as
an argument in the command:

```
user@router> show interfaces brief fe-0/0/0
Physical interface: fe-0/0/0, Enabled, Physical link is Down
  Link-level type: Ethernet, MTU: 1514, Speed: 10m, Loopback: Disabled,
  Source filtering: Disabled, Flow control: Enabled
  Device flags   : Present Running Down
  Interface flags: Hardware-Down SNMP-Traps Internal: 0x4000
  Link flags     : None
```

This command limits the output to only the specific interface included in the
command. Sometimes, you may want to see all interfaces of a certain type.
Imagine, for example, that you want to monitor all your Fast Ethernet interfaces. You can use interface wildcards to view all your `fe` interfaces:

```
user@router> show interfaces fe* brief
Physical interface: fe-0/0/0, Enabled, Physical link is Down
  Link-level type: Ethernet, MTU: 1514, Speed: 10m, Loopback: Disabled,
  Source filtering: Disabled, Flow control: Enabled
  Device flags   : Present Running Down
  Interface flags: Hardware-Down SNMP-Traps Internal: 0x4000
  Link flags     : None

(output snipped)
```

Getting a closer look

If simply knowing whether your interface is up is not quite enough (see preceding section), you can use the base `show interfaces` command:

```
user@router> show interfaces
Physical interface: fe-0/0/0, Enabled, Physical link is Down
  Interface index: 128, SNMP ifIndex: 23
  Link-level type: Ethernet, MTU: 1514, Speed: 10m, Loopback: Disabled,
  Source filtering: Disabled, Flow control: Enabled
  Device flags   : Present Running Down
  Interface flags: Hardware-Down SNMP-Traps Internal: 0x4000
  Link flags     : None
  CoS queues     : 4 supported, 4 maximum usable queues
  Current address: 00:05:85:02:a4:00, Hardware address: 00:05:85:02:a4:00
  Last flapped   : 2008-03-05 14:30:58 PST (4w3d 23:00 ago)
  Input rate     : 0 bps (0 pps)
  Output rate    : 0 bps (0 pps)
  Active alarms  : LINK
  Active defects : LINK
```

The base `show interfaces` command includes a bit more information than its brief counterpart. In addition to the basic interface information, the `show interfaces` command includes these tasty informational nuggets:

✔ `CoS queues`: This is the total number of CoS queues configured for the particular interface card. If you've configured eight queues, it shows a value of eight. For this particular interface, only the default four queues are available.

✔ `Current address` and `Hardware address`: The `Current address` is the configured MAC address for the interface card. The `Hardware address` is the actual MAC address tied to the hardware.

✔ `Last flapped`: The `Last Flapped` field indicates the last time the interface went down and came back up. This information can be very helpful when you're trying to figure out why traffic is lost on your network. If you look at the last flapped date and time, you can try to correlate that data with changes in your network (maintenance calls, configuration changes, and so on), which can help you track down the source of the flap.

✔ `Input rate` and `Output rate`: The input and output rates identify the total input and output in packets per second. In this case, the interface is down, so the values are 0.

✔ `Active alarms` and `Active defects`: The active alarms and defects list the link alarms that are associated with the particular interface. In this case, the link is down, which has generated a `LINK` alarm. That alarm is listed as both an alarm and a defect.

Giving a full examination

If you find that the information provided by the `show interfaces` command (see preceding section) isn't enough information, you can try the `detail` version of the same command, as shown in Listing 8-1.

Listing 8-1: Monitoring Output with the show interfaces detail Command

```
user@router> show interfaces detail
Physical interface: fe-0/0/0, Enabled, Physical link is Down
  Interface index: 128, SNMP ifIndex: 23, Generation: 303
  Link-level type: Ethernet, MTU: 1514, Speed: 10m, Loopback: Disabled,
  Source filtering: Disabled, Flow control: Enabled
  Device flags   : Present Running Down
  Interface flags: Hardware-Down SNMP-Traps Internal: 0x4000
  Link flags     : None
  CoS queues     : 4 supported, 4 maximum usable queues
  Hold-times     : Up 0 ms, Down 0 ms
  Current address: 00:05:85:02:a4:00, Hardware address: 00:05:85:02:a4:00
  Last flapped   : 2008-03-05 14:30:58 PST (4w3d 23:03 ago)
  Statistics last cleared: Never
  Traffic statistics:
   Input  bytes  :                 0                0 bps
   Output bytes  :                 0                0 bps
   Input  packets:                 0                0 pps
   Output packets:                 0                0 pps
   IPv6 transit statistics:
    Input  bytes  :                      0
    Output bytes  :                      0
    Input  packets:                      0
    Output packets:                      0
  Egress queues: 4 supported, 4 in use
  Queue counters:     Queued packets  Transmitted packets  Dropped packets
    0 best-effort                  0                    0                0
    1 expedited-fo                 0                    0                0
    2 assured-forw                 0                    0                0
    3 network-cont                 0                    0                0
  Active alarms  : LINK
  Active defects : LINK
```

When you get to this level of detail, you're usually troubleshooting the interface. This view of the interface gives you even more information, including (but not limited to) the following:

✔ `Traffic statistics`: The counters displayed here indicate the total number of bytes and packets both received by and transmitted out of the interface. These numbers give you an indication of how much traffic your interface is handling. Note that these statistics are cumulative from the last time the statistics were cleared (displayed in the field `Statistics last cleared`, which is harder to find than it seems it should be).

✔ `Egress queues`: The egress queues correspond to the total number of outbound CoS queues you've configured on the box. In this case, the default CoS queues are all that are configured. Each queue is listed, along with the number of packets in each queue as well as the number of transmitted packets. The dropped packets should be 0 unless you're experiencing congestion. (For more details on CoS and outbound queues, see Chapter 15.)

If you find that you still lack the information you need to troubleshoot your network or even a particular interface, you can use another level of detail: the `show interfaces extensive` command. The output for that command is a superset of the detailed version of the same command. It includes all the same information presented here, along with a detailed listing of input and output errors, and a slew of MAC (Layer 2) statistics.

Monitoring your routing information

The foundation command for monitoring all the routing information on your router is the `show route` command. This command has a host of various knobs and parameters that you can use to fine-tune your quest for knowledge, and following are the most useful versions of that command:

- `show route` (no modifiers): The base `show route` command, issued with no modifiers, gives you a basic listing of the routes in your routing table. This information is helpful when you're trying to figure out whether an expected route is actually present, which is typically a first step toward finding out why devices in your network are unreachable.

- `show route detail`: This more detailed view of the routing information includes a significant amount of additional information for each route in the routing table, which is useful when troubleshooting routing issues. This command is typically the second step in diagnosing a routing problem (following the base `show route` command).

- `show route summary`: The `summary` command gives you some high-level statistics about the routes that are in your routing table. It tells you how many routes are in the routing table for each protocol.

- `show route exact`: The `exact` modifier allows you to see only a specific route or route prefix, which should be used in conjunction with the appropriate detail modifiers (`brief`, `terse`, `detail`, or `extensive`).

A quick peek at your routes

The most basic task when monitoring the routing information on your router is to look at the routes that are in the routing table. See the `show route` command in Listing 8-2.

Listing 8-2: Monitoring Output with the show route Command

```
user@router1> show route

inet.0: 10 destinations, 10 routes (9 active, 0 holddown, 1 hidden)
+ = Active Route, - = Last Active, * = Both
0.0.0.0/0          *[Static/5] 1w5d 20:30:29
```

(continued)

Listing 8-2: *(continued)*

```
                        Discard
10.255.245.51/32    *[Direct/0] 2w4d 13:11:14
                     > via lo0.0
172.16.0.0/12       *[Static/5] 2w4d 13:11:14
                     > to 192.168.167.254 via fxp0.0
192.168.0.0/18      *[Static/5] 1w5d 20:30:29
                     > to 192.168.167.254 via fxp0.0
192.168.40.0/22     *[Static/5] 2w4d 13:11:14
                     > to 192.168.167.254 via fxp0.0
192.168.64.0/18     *[Static/5] 2w4d 13:11:14
                     > to 192.168.167.254 via fxp0.0
192.168.164.0/22    *[OSPF/10] 2w4d 13:11:14
                     > via fxp0.0
192.168.164.51/32   *[OSPF/10] 2w4d 13:11:14
                       Local via fxp0.0
207.17.136.192/32   *[BGP/170] 2w4d 13:11:14
                     > to 192.168.167.254 via fxp0.0
```

This command lists the active entries in the routing table, along with some basic information for each route. For each route, you see route, route prefix, and the following:

- ✔ Route origin: The origin identifies how the route was learned. Listing 8-2 contains *direct routes* (indicating the route is directly accessible through one of the router's interfaces), static routes, OSPF routes, and BGP routes.

- ✔ Route preference: Listed alongside the route origin is the route preference. Remember that each protocol has a default route preference associated with it, or you can manually override the default. The higher preference values (lower numbers are higher preference) are selected as active routes.

- ✔ Next-hop **to the destination:** The address listed after the to keyword is the IP address of the next-hop address in the routing table. To get to route 172.16.0.0/12, the router uses the next hop 192.168.167.254.

- ✔ Outbound interface: The outbound interface tells you the interface that the router is going to use to send traffic to the next-hop address. For the route to 172.16.0.0/12, the router will send traffic out its fxp0 interface.

In the show output in Listing 8-2, the router sends traffic destined for next hop 192.168.167.254 out interface fxp0.0. Remember that the number that appears after the dot indicates the logical interface, which is defined as the unit number:

```
[edit interfaces]
fxp0 {
   unit 0 {
      family inet {
         address 10.255.245.51/32;
      }
   }
}
```

When you look at the routing table, you need to check that all expected routes are in the table. If you don't see a route you expect to see, you know something is wrong with the protocols on the router. In this case, you then must examine more closely how your device is configured and how your routing protocols are operating.

It's good to remember that the routing table contains *all* of the information gathered by the routing protocols. This information is used to derive the *forwarding table,* which is the table actually used to determine the correct next hop for a packet. Just because a route appears in the routing table doesn't guarantee that the forwarding table uses the route to forward packets. However, lots of network people use the term "routing table" loosely, but in networking, the requirement for breaking a rule is to know what the rule is.

Getting more information about your routes

If a quick glance at your routes doesn't satisfy your hunger for knowledge, you can get a bit more detailed in your examination. To see more routing information, use the detail modifier, as shown in Listing 8-3.

Listing 8-3:   Monitoring Output with the show route detail Command

```
user@router1> show route detail

inet.0: 22 destinations, 23 routes (21 active, 0 holddown, 1 hidden)
10.10.0.0/16 (1 entry, 1 announced)
        *Static Preference: 5
                Next-hop reference count: 29
                Next hop: 192.168.71.254 via fxp0.0, selected
                State: <Active NoReadvrt Int Ext>
                Local AS:     69
                Age: 1:31:43
                Task: RT
                Announcement bits (2): 0-KRT 3-Resolve tree 2
                AS path: I

10.31.1.0/30 (2 entries, 1 announced)
        *Direct Preference: 0
                Next hop type: Interface
                Next-hop reference count: 2
```

(continued)

Listing 8-3: *(continued)*

```
                Next hop: via so-0/3/0.0, selected
                State: <Active Int>
                Local AS:    69
                Age: 1:30:17
                Task: IF
                Announcement bits (1): 3-Resolve tree 2
                AS path: I
        OSPF    Preference: 10
                Next-hop reference count: 1
                Next hop: via so-0/3/0.0, selected
                State: <Int>
                Inactive reason: Route Preference
                Local AS:    69
                Age: 1:30:17    Metric: 1
                Area: 0.0.0.0
                Task: OSPF
                AS path: I
(output snipped)
```

The detailed listing for your routes lists a little more information for each route. Most of that information is a bit esoteric, but some of it can be downright helpful. Here are a couple of output fields that you may enjoy knowing more about:

- ✔ Age: This field tells you how long the route has been in the routing table. Imagine that traffic destined for a particular address experiences some problems. You may want to check the age to see whether there was a problem where the route was dropped from your routing table. So you look at the detailed routing information, and if the age is less than anticipated, you know that the route was newly added (or added again) to the routing table — a certain clue that something is amiss and you need to delve deeper.

- ✔ Inactive reason: You may have an inactive route that is being supplanted by some other route to the same host. For example, if you've set up label-switched paths (LSPs) in your network with multiprotocol label switching (MPLS), which are covered in detail in Chapter 16, you may be expecting traffic to flow a certain way. The inactive reason gives you an idea as to why a particular route has been preempted by another route. In Listing 8-3, you can see that you have multiple routes to the destination 10.31.1.0/30. In this case, the OSPF route is inactive because the route preference for an OSPF route is of lower priority than that of a direct route (*nothing* beats a direct route, which has a priority of 0 and means the router is directly connected to the destination sub-net).

Most of the other fields in the show route detail output are used very rarely.

Summarizing your routing information

Sometimes you may just want a quick summary of the routing information on your router. As an example, you have just configured OSPF in your network, and you're expecting to see a certain number of OSPF routes in your routing table. You can issue a `show route summary` command to see that all the routes are there (see Listing 8-4).

Listing 8-4: Monitoring Output with the show route summary Command

```
user@router1> show route summary

Autonomous system number: 69
Router ID: 10.255.71.52


inet.0: 24 destinations, 25 routes (23 active, 0 holddown, 1 hidden)
Restart Complete
            Direct:       6 routes,      5 active
             Local:       4 routes,      4 active
              OSPF:       5 routes,      4 active
            Static:       7 routes,      7 active
              IGMP:       1 routes,      1 active
               PIM:       2 routes,      2 active

inet.3: 2 destinations, 2 routes (2 active, 0 holddown, 0 hidden)
Restart Complete
              RSVP:       2 routes,      2 active

iso.0: 1 destinations, 1 routes (1 active, 0 holddown, 0 hidden)
Restart Complete
            Direct:       1 routes,      1 active

mpls.0: 7 destinations, 7 routes (5 active, 0 holddown, 2 hidden)
Restart Complete
              MPLS:       3 routes,      3 active
              VPLS:       4 routes,      2 active

inet6.0: 5 destinations, 5 routes (5 active, 0 holddown, 0 hidden)
Restart Complete
            Direct:       2 routes,      2 active
               PIM:       2 routes,      2 active
               MLD:       1 routes,      1 active
```

The route summary includes several key pieces of information:

✔ `Autonomous system number`: The AS number configured for your router (if any exists) is displayed here. This number really just reflects and validates your AS number configuration.

✔ `Router ID`: If you've configured a Router ID, it shows up here. If you haven't, the router uses the `lo0` address (the first non-127.0.0.1 address) as the router ID.

✔ `Routing table name`: Each stanza in the output corresponds to a different routing table within the router. You'll generally be looking in the base table, which is the `inet.0` table in this example. If you've configured MPLS, you'll see routes in the `inet.3` and `mpls.0` tables. The `inet.6` table is reserved for IPv6.

✔ `Routes`: Each routing table has a summary of the total number of routes in the table. In this case, they're categorized as follows:

- `active`: Routes that are `active`, meaning they are being used in the forwarding table.

- `holddown`: These routes are in holddown state, which basically means that they're in the process of becoming inactive. This state is rarely seen as it's a transitional state between active and inactive status.

- `hidden`: These routes exist on the router, but aren't being used for forwarding packets because of some routing policy in use. For example, you may be using a filter of some sort to select one route over another. The route that would have been selected is a hidden route. The route that is selected for forwarding must be an active route.

A major reason that otherwise functional routes are no longer being used in the forwarding table is that they have somehow become hidden!

Getting specific with your output

When you're looking for a particular route or a set of routes, it can be quite painful to have to go through 50 pages of routing information. You don't want your route to be the proverbial needle in a haystack. You need a way to search for a particular route. To find a specific route, use the `exact` modifier:

```
user@router1> show route exact 207.17.136.0/24

inet.0: 24 destinations, 25 routes (23 active, 0 holddown, 1 hidden)
Restart Complete
+ = Active Route, - = Last Active, * = Both
207.17.136.0/24    *[Static/5] 2d 03:30:22
                    > to 192.168.71.254 via fxp0.0
```

This command pretty much limits the output to only the requested route. You can use it with the various detail modifiers (`terse`, `brief`, `detail`, or `extensive`).

Keeping an Eye on Latency

One of the things you'll want to monitor in your network is latency. *Latency* is a measure of how long it takes for traffic to get from one device to another device. Latency is a combination of *propagation delay* (how long it takes the bits to flow from device to device over an interface) and *nodal processing delay* (how long it takes bits to flow from interface to interface through a device). Usually, you don't focus on one component of latency over the other. Examine the network topology shown in Figure 8-3.

In this simple network, traffic flows from `router1` through the network to `router5`. That path will take some amount of time on a normal day. If you know what that average time (or *network latency*) is, you can basically monitor your network and evaluate the current performance against the expected performance. So when you see a spike in network latency, you know that something has run amok in your network.

Real-time performance monitoring

The Junos OS supports a tool called *real-time performance monitoring* (RPM). RPM essentially is a set of tests, run periodically, that help you measure the latency between two devices on a network.

RPM works only if the two devices you're measuring both run the Junos OS.

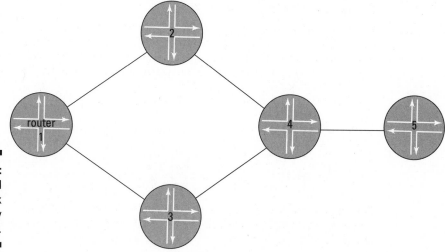

Figure 8-3:
A typical network connectivity diagram.

When RPM is enabled, your router generates a series of probes that are sent to the target device. These probes are timestamped when they're sent. When the target device receives the probes, it generates a response and sends that response back to the sender. By measuring the time between sending the probe and receiving the response, your router can tell you what the round-trip time is between the two devices.

This send/receive process is repeated for each probe within a test. By averaging the times over some sample, you can get a better idea of what the average time is across the network. Then these tests are run between fixed intervals to provide you with information about average latency over time.

For Layer 2 devices such as switches, the Junos OS supports standards for using a form of RPM over Ethernet links.

Configuring RPM

To configure RPM on your network, you need to decide on a few things. First, you have to figure out where you want to do the measurement. Looking at Figure 8-4, you see that you need to select two points in the network that will provide meaningful data.

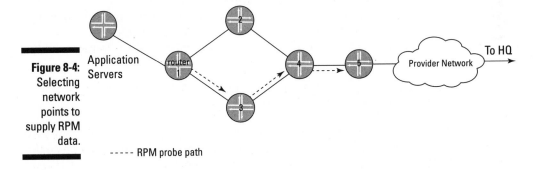

Figure 8-4: Selecting network points to supply RPM data.

In Figure 8-4, application servers are connected to router1. Ultimately, this traffic is transmitted via VPN through router5 to your service provider (and eventually back to some headquarters). In this case, you want to measure the latency between router1 and router5. Any increase in latency may potentially impact the application data (such as packetized voice or video) being routed between those nodes.

Here's how you configure this test:

```
[edit services]
rpm {
    probe app-server-network {
        test icmp-test {
            probe-type icmp-ping-timestamp;
            target address 192.168.24.1;
            probe-count 15;
            probe-interval 1;
            test-interval 600;
        }
    }
}
```

This configuration defines an RPM test for the `app-server-network`. The probe owner in this case is really just a name so that you can quickly see what the test is for. Typically, you name the probe owner after whatever network you're testing (in this case, the application server network).

Most of the RPM configuration is done within an RPM test configuration stanza. Name the test something intuitive (in this case, it's named `icmp-test`). Then you have to configure the test details.

ICMP ping probes are easy to configure and generally provide enough information to diagnose latency issues in your network. The more experienced user can use TCP or UDP probes, but they require the configuration of the remote end to act as a probe server. If you use ICMP packets, the device already knows how to respond (all IP devices must understand ICMP pings), and the configuration is simpler.

Configure the target address as the loopback address of the remote device (in this case, the loopback address on `router5`).

You must also configure the number of probes in each test, the length of time between probes, and the length of time between tests. We recommend configuring between 10 and 20 probes at one-second intervals. This particular test is going to run every ten minutes.

Monitoring RPM tests

Configuring a test is certainly a great step in the right direction, but you need to somehow see the results of those tests. To view the results of the RPM measurements, use the `show services rpm probe-results` command:

```
user@host> show services rpm probe-results

    Owner: app-server-network, Test: icmp-test
    Probe type: icmp-ping-timestamp
    Minimum Rtt: 312 usec, Maximum Rtt: 385 usec, Average Rtt: 331 usec,
    Jitter Rtt: 73 usec, Stddev Rtt: 27 usec
    Minimum egress time: 0 usec, Maximum egress time: 0 usec,
    Average egress time: 0 usec, Jitter egress time: 0 usec,
    Stddev egress time: 0 usec
    Minimum ingress time: 0 usec, Maximum ingress time: 0 usec,
    Average ingress time: 0 usec, Jitter ingress time: 0 usec,
    Stddev ingress time: 0 usec
    Probes sent: 15, Probes received: 15, Loss percentage: 0
```

The output can be a bit hard to parse, but focus on the following fields:

- Owner, Test: This field tells you which RPM test is summarized below.

- Probe type: Put simply, this field is what you configured as the probe type.

- RTT: The RTT fields are the round-trip time measurements. You can see the minimum measurement, the maximum measurement, and the average measurement for the probes over the entire test — in this case, 15 probes.

- Jitter: This is the variation in delay over time. The Jitter value lets you know how consistent the tests were. If one test took three seconds and the second test took 500 usecs, the jitter would be high, an indication that you might want to run the test again because some issues are affecting your network. Ideally, you want a small jitter and a small standard deviation, which means that all traffic more or less takes the same amount of time to traverse your network.

- Loss percentage: Although you shouldn't see it as non-zero very often, probes can be lost for many reasons. If you're seeing probe loss, you have an indication that your network is dropping packets somewhere; a firewall filter may be discarding them; or some device along the path is experiencing congestion. (Pings are generally treated as best effort, and this type of traffic is generally first to get dropped in times of congestion.) Check into the problem accordingly.

In terms of what kinds of times you should be seeing, as a general rule, you probably want to see round-trip times on the order of 200 to 500 microseconds (usecs). Because these RPM probes are using ICMP ping packets, the times should really be the same as when you issue several pings to the remote destination.

Chapter 9

Securing Your Junos OS Devices

. . . .

In This Chapter

▶ Ensuring the physical security of your network

▶ Getting the rundown on Junos OS default security settings

▶ Knowing who's logged on

▶ Logging out

▶ Creating a firewall filter to control SSH and Telnet access

▶ Limiting traffic on router interfaces by using policers

▶ Using the loopback (lo0) interface to protect the routing engine

▶ Enabling authentication to secure routing protocols

. . . .

*T*his chapter is about taking security measures using Junos on your switches, routers, and gateways. Security is critical today because you can move traffic, both wanted and unwanted, very quickly across a network. A hacker can take control of an unsecured or an improperly secured device and wreak havoc on your network, using the compromised device as a launching pad for denial-of-service and other types of attacks — faster than you can make a sandwich and eat it (maybe even before you can toast the bread).

In this chapter, we cover several security features and practices you can take advantage of that are built into the Junos OS. After you finish this chapter, you will be able to protect your device with basic security measures that can stop all sorts of attacks. (See Chapter 12 for information about implementing special security services on your network using the SRX Services Gateway.)

Note: In this chapter, we're assuming that you've installed and done the initial configuration (refer to Chapter 6) and have set up management and monitoring (refer to Chapters 7 and 8, respectively) on your device(s).

Stop! Physical Security

A basic way to secure your device is to limit physical access to it. This precaution prevents someone from accidentally or deliberately turning off the router or removing or replacing cables and power cords connected to the router.

Also, anyone who has physical access to a router can connect to the router's console port. If someone manages to log in as the root user, that person can take control of the router, issuing any and all commands and modifying the router configuration.

Keep your routers in an area with restricted access, such as a locked room or a room that requires badge access. then limit the number of people who have access to that area. this advice may seem like basic stuff, but you'd be surprised at the number of routers operating in the corner of some administrator's open cube.

Go! Junos Default Security Features

Junos OS has a number of default behaviors that contribute to router security, behaviors that immediately take effect once you perform the initial router configuration (see Chapter 6 for the initial configuration process).

- ✔ **Router access:** By default, the only way to access the router is by physically connecting to the router's console port. To configure the router initially, you must connect a laptop or other terminal directly to the console port. All other remote management access and management access protocols, such as Telnet, FTP, and SSH (secure shell), are disabled. (On the J-series routers, the Web interface is enabled by default to aid in initial system configuration.) Once the initial configuration is complete, you need to enable a way to remotely log in to the router so you don't have to be there physically to connect to the router's console port. SSH provides the best security, and you configure it as follows:

```
[edit]
fred@router# set system services ssh
```

- ✔ **Configuring the router with SNMP set commands:** Junos OS does not support the SNMP set capability for editing configuration data, which allows an NMS to modify the configurations on managed network devices. Junos OS does, by default, allow SNMP to query the status of the router, although no known security risks are associated with this.

- ✔ **Directed broadcast messages:** Junos OS doesn't forward these messages, which are datagrams with a destination address of an IP subnetwork broadcast address. Directed broadcasts are easy to spoof, which is a method used in DoS attacks.

✔ **Martian addresses:** Junos OS ignores routes for several reserved addresses (but not including the private addresses defined in RFC 1918). Martian addresses should never be seen on the Internet, but routes for these addresses are sometimes advertised by misconfigured routers. You can modify the list of Martian addresses, if you so desire.

Martian addresses are host or network addresses about which all routing information is ignored. They commonly are sent by improperly configured systems on the network and have destination addresses that are obviously invalid. For more on Martian addresses, beam yourself to Chapter 14, and turn on some retro sci-fi music.

✔ **Password encryption:** When configuring the router, you need to enter passwords for various features. All these passwords are secured — either by *encryption* (a one-to-one mapping, which is possible to decrypt), or by *hashing* (a many-to-many mapping, which is impossible to unhash), or by algorithms — to keep them from being discovered. Even in cases where the Junos OS prompts you for a plain-text password, the software encrypts it immediately after you type it. When you display the password in the configuration file, you see only the encrypted version, marked as SECRET-DATA. For example, if you configure a plain-text password for a user login account, you see that the Junos CLI encrypts it right away using SHA1:

```
[edit system]
fred@router# set login user mike authentication plain-text-password
New password:
Retype new password:
```

```
[edit system]
fred@router# show
user mike {
  authentication {
    encrypted-password "$1$bRzNS9Tm$yG6vt2U0aXHBR5f9U1twy/"; ## SECRET-DATA
  }
}
```

✔ **Partial enforcement of strong passwords:** Junos OS enforces the use of strong passwords to a certain extent, requiring that all passwords you configure be at least six characters long, have a change of case, and contain either digits or punctuation. The software rejects passwords that don't meet these criteria:

```
[edit system]
fred@router# set login user mike authentication plain-text-password
New password:
error: require change of case, digits or punctuation
```

You can enhance the enforcement of strong passwords by configuring a longer minimum password length and by increasing the minimum number of case, digit, and punctuation changes:

```
[edit system]
fred@router# set login password minimum-length number
```

```
[edit system]
fred@router# set login password minimum-changes number
```

Encryption and hashing algorithms

If security is your issue, it may be important for you to know that Junos OS uses the following encryption and hashing algorithms to protect data and packets:

- ✔ **DES:** An encryption algorithm that uses a 56-bit key.

- ✔ **MD5:** A message-hashing algorithm that produces a 128-bit hash function. Because of the longer hash, it's more secure than DES.

- ✔ **SHA1:** Produces a 160-bit message digest. It has the longest length and hence is the most secure of the algorithms.

- ✔ **SSH:** A security protocol that creates keys for authentication. You configure the public key on the router and only users with the corresponding private key can authenticate against that key. Determining a private key from a public key is generally considered to be impossible.

Tighten the root login account

During the initial configuration of a new router, you set the root password as a plain-text password. Because the root user is able to perform any and all operations on the router, tightening access to the root login account is a good idea. One way to do so is to configure the root password using SSH key authentication, which is more secure than the plain-text password (provided you protect the private key appropriately):

```
[edit system]
fred@router# set root-authentication ssh-dsa "ssh-dss
    AAAAB3NzaC1kc3MAAACBAMQrfP2bZyBXJ6PC7XXZ+MzErI8J16jah5L4/
    O8BsfP2hC7EvRfNoX7MqbrtCX/9gUH9gChVuBCB+ERULMdgRvM5uGhC/
    gs4UX+4dBbfBgKYYwgmisM8EoT25m7qI8ybpl2YZvHNznvO8h7kr4kpYuQEpKvgsTdH/
    Jle4Uqnjv7DAAAAFQDZaqA6QAgbW3O/zveaLCIDj6p0dwAAAIB1iL+krWrXiD8NPpY+
    w4dWXEqaV3bnobzPC4eyxQKBUCOr80Q5YBlWXVBHx9elwBWZwj0SF4hLKHznExnLer
    VsMuTMA846RbQmSz62vM6kGM13HFonWeQvWia0TDr78+
    rOEgWF2KHBSIxL5l1mIDW8Gql9hJfD/Dr/NKP97w3L0wAAAIEAr3FkWU8XbYy
    tQYEKxsIN9P1UQ1ERXB3G40YwqFO484SlyKyYCfaz+yNsaAJu2C8UebDIR
    3GieyNcOAKf3inCG8jQwjLvZskuZwrvlsz/xtcxSoAh9axJcdUfSJYMW/
    g+mD26JK1Cliw5rwp2nH9kUrJxeI7IReDp4egNkM4i15o=
    mike@server"; ## SECRET-DATA
```

As you can see, this is a lot to type! If you don't feel like entering so much text, you can also load an SSH key file from a network server:

```
[edit system]
fred@router# set root-authentication load-key-file server-name:/dir/filename
```

When SSH is enabled, anyone with the root password or SSH private key can log in as the root user from anywhere on the network. This capability is useful in large networks or when you can't get physical access to the router.

Generally, however, no one on the network should have any reason to log in to the router using the root account, so you can ratchet up the router security one level by forcing anyone logging in as root to log in directly from the router's console port. To do so, you disable root login through SSH:

```
[edit system]
fred@router# set services ssh root-login deny
```

Although unlikely, if you lose network access to the router, you may find that you can't connect to a router over the network as usual. If this issue occurs, the only way to access the router is to connect a laptop or terminal to the router's console port. This port is enabled by default on all Junos routers. Although you can disable console access to the router, we really don't recommend it. Also, the only way you can remain logged in to a router while its rebooting is by connecting to the console port. You may want to do so when trying to troubleshoot and debug problems with the router or the Junos OS.

Choosing passwords

Password selection is one of the most important ways to protect a router from hackers and other types of unwanted attacks. Be sure that the root and user accounts you create on the router all have passwords and that the passwords are strong:

✔ Choose a password that is a combination of uppercase and lowercase letters, digits, and punctuation characters.

✔ Choose a password that is a phrase or a shortened version of a phrase that you can easily remember without writing it down.

✔ Don't choose the router vendor name (such as juniper), the string admin, or the string password.

✔ Don't choose an easily guessable password, such as your birthday or spouse's name.

✔ Don't use a word that's in a dictionary in any language. Brute-force, automated programs can rapidly try all words in all online dictionaries when attempting to break into a router.

Checking Who's on the Router

More than one person can log in to a Juniper router at any given time, logging in either with an individual user account name or with a group name that is shared by many users. (An example of a group account is *root.*) Each person who is on the router can perform whatever operations they're allowed, depending on their privileges (see Chapter 7 for more on logging in and log in status), and it's possible that another person's work may interfere with what you're doing.

Knowing who's logged in

When you log in to the router, the CLI doesn't tell you whether anyone else is already logged in. You need to check manually:

```
fred@router> show system users
```

If you discover that an unwanted user is logged into the router or if you need to perform an operation, such as rebooting the router or installing new software, that would be easier if no one else were logged in to the router, you can forcibly log people out. The show system users command shows you the names of users who are logged in. Use the name to forcibly log the person out, in this case Mike:

```
fred@router> request system logout mike
```

Now, Mike sees the following on his terminal window:

```
mike@router> Connection closed by foreign host.
[server.mycompany.com] mike@server%
```

You can also ask people to log out. You can ask an individual with a command like this one, with any message you want:

```
fred@router> request message user mike message "End router session now!"
```

You can also have the message go to everyone currently logged in to the router:

```
fred@router> request message all message "End router session now!"
```

Figuring out who's configuring

Junos OS also allows multiple people to be in configuration mode at the same time. When you enter configuration mode, the CLI displays a message letting you know whether anyone else is also editing the configuration. However, if someone enters configuration mode after you, you won't receive any kind of message. You can check periodically using the status configuration mode command:

```
[edit]
fred@router# status
Users currently editing the configuration:
  fred terminal p0 (pid 13329) on since 2008-03-23 15:15:12 UTC
     [edit]
```

If more than one person is changing the configuration, when one of them issues a commit command to activate the configuration, all changes made by all users are activated. To check the changes before committing the configuration, move to the top of the configuration hierarchy and use the following version of the show configuration mode command to look at the differences:

```
[edit]
fred@router# show | compare
[edit protocols]
+   mstp;
[edit interfaces]
-   ge-0/0/1 {
-     unit 0 {
-        family inet {
-          address 192.168.1.4;
-        }
-     }
-   }
- }
```

The plus sign (+) indicates lines that have been added to the configuration since it was last activated, and the minus sign (–) shows what has been deleted. In the preceding example, the MSTP protocol has been enabled, and one of the Gigabit Ethernet interfaces has been removed from the configuration.

If you need to ensure that no one else can modify the router configuration while you're editing, lock it when you enter configuration mode with this command:

```
fred@router> configure exclusive
```

If someone else has an exclusive lock on the configuration, the CLI displays a message when you enter configuration mode:

```
fred@router> configure
Users currently editing the configuration:
  mike terminal p0 (pid 13329) on since 2008-03-23 15:15:12 UTC
  exclusive [edit]
```

Logging Out

Most people remember to log out when they're no longer working on the router to monitor it or modify the configuration, but even when you walk away from your desk or office, be sure to log out to prevent unauthorized people from walking up to your keyboard and accessing the router.

Log out with this simple operational mode command:

```
fred@router> exit
```

If you're in configuration mode, use the exit or quit command to return to operational mode first. If you're not at the top level of the configuration, use one of the following command sequences to get there:

```
[edit protocols bgp group isp-group]
fred@router# top
```

```
[edit]
fred@router# exit
Exiting configuration mode
```

```
fred@router>
```

or

```
[edit protocols bgp group isp-group]
fred@router# exit configuration-mode
Exiting configuration mode
```

```
fred@router>
```

Controlling SSH and Telnet Access to the Router

SSH and Telnet are the two common ways for users to access the router. Both require password authentication, either through an account configured on the router or an account set on a centralized authentication server, such as a RADIUS server. Even with a password, Telnet sessions are inherently insecure, and SSH can be attacked by brute-force attempts to guess passwords.

One way to limit the number of people who can log in to the router is to restrict which network systems people can use to connect to the router.

You restrict SSH and Telnet access by creating a firewall filter, which regulates the traffic on a specific interface, deciding what to allow and what to discard. (Firewall filters are discussed in more detail in Chapter 14.) Creating a filter is a two-part process:

1. You define the filtering details.
2. You apply the filter to a router interface.

Now, when you want to control access to the router, you'd normally need to apply those restrictions to every interface as the router can be contacted through any interface. However, to make things easier, Junos OS allows you to apply firewall filters to the lo0 interface. Firewall filters applied to the lo0 interface affect all traffic destined to the router's control plane, regardless of the interface on which the packet arrived. So to limit SSH and Telnet access to the router, you apply the filter to the lo0 interface.

To create a filter, you name it and define the filtering conditions. A firewall filter looks at the contents of packets on an interface and compares them to conditions you define. If the packet matches all conditions, the filter takes the actions you configure.

The filter shown in the following process is called limit-ssh-telnet, and it has two parts, or terms. The Junos OS evaluates the two terms sequentially. Traffic that matches the first term is processed immediately, and traffic that fails is evaluated by the second term. Here's how the process works:

1. The first term, limit-ssh-telnet, looks for SSH and Telnet access attempts only from devices on the 192.168.0.1/24 subnetwork.

   Packets will match this term only if the IP header includes a destination address from the 192.168.0.1/24 prefix, the IP header shows the packet is a TCP packet, and the TCP packet header shows that traffic is headed for the SSH or Telnet destination ports.

   If all these criteria are met, the filter's action is to accept the access attempt and traffic:

   ```
   [edit firewall]
   fred@router# set filter limit-ssh-telnet term access-term from
        source-address 192.168.0.1/24
   ```

   ```
   [edit firewall]
   fred@router# set filter limit-ssh-telnet term access-term from
        protocol tcp
   ```

```
[edit firewall]
fred@router# set filter limit-ssh-telnet term access-term from
       destination-port [ssh telnet]
```

```
[edit firewall]
fred@router# set filter limit-ssh-telnet term access-term then accept
```

2. The second term, called `block-all-else`, blocks all traffic that does not meet the criteria in Step 1.

   You can do this step with a basic `reject` command. This term contains no criteria to match, so, by default, it's applied to all traffic that fails the first term:

```
[edit firewall]
fred@router# set filter limit-ssh-telnet term block-all-else term reject
```

From a vigilance point of view, you need to track failed attempts to access the router so that you can determine whether a concerted attack might be underway. The `block-all-else` term counts the number of failed access attempts (the first command in the next example keeps track of these attempts in a counter named `bad-access`), logging the packet, and sending information to the syslog process about the packet. (These actions are taken in addition to the `reject` command you already configured.)

```
[edit firewall]
fred@router# set filter limit-ssh-telnet term block-all-else term count
       bad-access
```

```
[edit firewall]
fred@router# set filter limit-ssh-telnet term block-all-else term count log
```

```
[edit firewall]
fred@router# set filter limit-ssh-telnet term block-all-else term count syslog
```

Creating a filter is half the process. The second half is to apply it to a router interface, in this case to the router's loopback interface, lo0:

```
[edit interfaces]
fred@router# set lo0 unit 0 family inet filter input limit-ssh-telnet
```

You apply the filter as an input filter, which means that the Junos OS applies it to all incoming traffic destined to the control plane.

Firewall filters have two basic characteristics to consider in order to design them properly:

✔ On most devices, you can apply multiple firewall filters in an ordered chain. If you apply the `limit-ssh-telnet` filter to the router's loopback interface, this interface accepts SSH and Telnet traffic but nothing else. So if you've configured other protocols, such as SNMP, BGP, OSPF, and IS-IS, to use the loopback address as the router address, packets from those protocols are blocked and don't reach the router.

However, you can write a number of smaller firewall filters and apply them in a chain, which allows you to reuse smaller pieces of firewall filters multiple times instead of writing custom firewall filters for each interface. When you configure a chain of firewall filters, the Junos OS acts as though you had just created one large firewall filter, composed of the terms of each filter in order. (This means if you put this `limit-ssh-telnet` filter first in a chain, all other traffic is rejected regardless of the remaining firewall filters, because the second term of the chain rejects all traffic.)

✔ Junos OS evaluates the terms in a firewall filter (or chain of firewall filters) in order, starting with the first one. The router processes each packet through the terms in a firewall filter in order until it finds a match. When the router finds a match, it takes the actions indicated by that term's `then` clause, which means that you must ensure traffic will be accepted or rejected at the right place, but not sooner.

So, for example, if you want to allow all Telnet traffic, but deny all other TCP traffic, you need to put the term allowing Telnet traffic before the term denying TCP traffic. If you put them in the reverse order, the router will deny the Telnet traffic (because Telnet uses TCP) and never reach the term to allow Telnet traffic. You do not, however, need to worry about optimizing your firewall filters, because the Junos OS does that for you. Having the software take care of your filtering makes your job easy. You just worry about making sure that the filter logic is in the correct order, and the router takes care of optimizing it for you.

Limiting Traffic on Router Interfaces

Some DoS attacks on routers work by inundating the router with traffic, sending so much traffic to router interfaces so quickly that the interfaces are overwhelmed and can't handle the regular traffic that should be passing through the interface. One method to combat this attack is to use Junos policers, which you can specify when you define the action a firewall filter should take. *Policers* allow you to place limits on the amount of traffic (or even just a type of traffic) that an interface can receive, which can limit the impact of DoS attacks. Policers control the maximum allowed bandwidth (the average number of bits per second) and the maximum allowed size of a single burst of traffic when the bandwidth limit is exceeded. Any traffic received beyond the set limits is dropped.

Policers are used in the action (then) portion of a firewall filter. To use them in a firewall filter, you first define the policer. The following example creates a policer called `police-ssh-telnet` that sets a maximum traffic rate (bandwidth) of 1 Mbps and the maximum size of a traffic burst exceeding this limit (burst size) of 25K. Traffic exceeding these limits is discarded.

```
[edit firewall]
fred@router# set policer police-ssh-telnet if-exceeding bandwidth-limit 1m
```

```
[edit firewall]
fred@router# set policer police-ssh-telnet if-exceeding burst-size-limit 25k
```

```
[edit firewall]
fred@router# set policer police-ssh-telnet then discard
```

Then include the policer in a firewall filter action. For example, add it to the SSH-Telnet firewall filter from the previous section that you applied to the router's loopback interface:

```
[edit firewall]
fred@router# set filter limit-ssh-telnet term access-term then policer
     police-ssh-telnet
```

```
[edit firewall]
fred@router# set filter limit-ssh-telnet term access-term then accept
```

Traffic that conforms to the limits in the policer will take the action you specify in the firewall term — in this case, it is accepted — whereas traffic that exceeds the limits in the policer will take the action specified there — in this case, it is discarded. (We didn't need to re-specify the accept action configured earlier, but we did so for clarity, just in case you skipped over that part.)

Rate-limiting traffic flow to the Routing Engine by defining policers is a good security practice to prevent the Routing Engine from being overwhelmed by unwanted traffic or by possible attacks on the router. All the routing protocol processes run on the Routing Engine, which is critical to the core operation of the router itself. When these processes can't run normally, the result can be a destabilization of the network.

Protecting the Routing Engine: A More Complete Strategy

Although all interfaces are important, the loopback (lo0) interface is perhaps the most important because it is the link to the Routing Engine, which runs and monitors all the routing protocols.

This section shows the skeleton of a firewall filter that protects the Routing Engine by allowing only desired traffic and rejecting all other traffic. You can use this example as a blueprint to design the appropriate filter for your router. The filter is applied to the router's `lo0` interface.

This filter is for a router configured for a common IPv4 setup:

- ✔ IPv4
- ✔ BGP and IS-IS routing protocols
- ✔ RADIUS, SSH, and Telnet access
- ✔ SNMP NMS access
- ✔ NTP

Because firewall filters are evaluated in order, place the most time-critical items — the routing protocols — first. Accept traffic from your known BGP peers and from the known IS-IS neighbors with the AS using the following `set` commands:

```
[edit firewall filter routing-engine]
set term bgp-filter from source-address peer-address1
set term bgp-filter from source-address peer-address2
set term bgp-filter from protocol tcp
set term bgp-filter from port bgp
set term bgp-filter then accept
```

Then accept DNS traffic (for hostname resolution):

```
[edit firewall-filter routing-engine]
set term dns-filter from source-address network-address
set term dns-filter from protocol [ tcp udp ]
set term dns-filter from port domain
set term dns-filter then accept
```

Next, accept RADIUS, SSH, Telnet, and SNMP NMS traffic:

```
[edit firewall-filter routing-engine]
set term radius-filter from source-address radius-server-address1
set term radius-filter from source-address radius-server-address2
set term radius-filter from source-port radius
set term radius-filter then accept
set term ssh-telnet-filter from source-address network-address1
set term ssh-telnet-filter from source-address network-address2
set term ssh-telnet-filter from protocol tcp
set term ssh-telnet-filter from destination-port [ ssh telnet ]
set term ssh-telnet-filter then accept
set term snmp-filter from source-address network-address1
set term snmp-filter from source-address network-address2
set term snmp-filter from protocol udp
set term snmp-filter from destination-port snmp
set term snmp-filter then accept
```

The last traffic to accept is from the NTP time servers and the ICMP protocol (which sends IPv4 error messages):

```
[edit firewall-filter routing-engine]
set term ntp-filter from source-address server-address1
set term ntp-filter from source-address server-address2
set term ntp-filter from source-address 127.0.0.1
set term ntp-filter from protocol udp
set term ntp-filter from port ntp
set term ntp-filter then accept
set term icmp-filter from protocol icmp
set term icmp-filter from icmp-type [ echo-request echo-reply unreachable time-
            exceeded source-quench ]
set term icmp-filter then accept
```

The final part of the filter explicitly discards all other traffic:

```
[edit firewall-filter routing-engine]
set term discard-the-rest then count counter-filename
set term discard-the-rest then log
set term discard-the-rest then syslog
set term discard-the-rest then reject
```

You need to create the file in which to place the syslog messages:

```
[edit system]
fred@router# set syslog file filename firewall any
```

And lastly, apply the firewall filter to the router's loopback interface:

```
[edit interfaces]
fred@router# set lo0 unit 0 family inet filter input routing-engine
```

Securing Routing Protocols

Another way to protect the routing protocols is to enable authentication so that the protocols accept traffic only from routers known to you. This approach ensures that only trusted routers contribute routes to the routing table and, hence, participate in determining how traffic is routed through your network.

You enable authentication for each routing protocol separately.

Securing RIP

The most secure authentication RIP supports is MD5:

```
[edit protocols]
fred@router# set rip authentication-type md5
```

```
[edit protocols]
fred@router# set rip authentication-key key-string
```

MD5 creates an encoded checksum, which is verified by the receiving router before it accepts packets. You must configure the same password on all RIP routers on the network and the same authentication type. (RIP also lets you use a simple, unencrypted password for authentication.)

Securing IS-IS and OSPF

IS-IS supports MD5 and a simple password authentication, which uses a clear-text, unencrypted password. When authentication is enabled, IS-IS validates that all LSPs are received from trusted routers.

Each IS-IS area can have its own encryption method and password. The following commands set encryption in the IS-IS Level 2 area:

```
[edit protocols]
fred@router# set isis level 2 authentication-type md5
```

```
[edit protocols]
fred@router# set isis level 2 authentication-key key-string
```

All routers within the same area must have the same authentication key.

Securing OSPF

OSPF also supports MD5 and a simple password authentication. When authentication is enabled, OSPF validates its Hello and LSA protocol packets.

The following command sets the OSPF encryption for an interface in an area, here the backbone area. For OSPF, you must set the encryption on each interface separately:

```
[edit protocols]
fred@router# set ospf area 0.0.0.0 interface interface-name authentication md5
    1 key key-string
```

Routers will be able to form adjacencies only over interfaces with other routers that are configured to use the same authentication key for that network.

Authenticating BGP peers

BGP sessions are often the subject of external attacks on the network because the sessions are visible on the Internet. Enabling the authentication of the BGP packets exchanged by EBGP peers prevents the router from accepting unauthorized packets. For BGP, you also use MD5. Each BGP group can have its own authentication password:

```
[edit protocols]
fred@router# set bgp group group-name authentication-key key-string
```

You can also set individual authentication passwords between each BGP peer in an EBGP session:

```
[edit protocols]
fred@router# set bgp group group-name neighbor address authentication-key
        key-string
```

The neighbor in an EBGP session is often in another AS, so you be sure to coordinate authentication methods and keys with the administrator of the external AS.

You can also enable authentication between IBGP peer routers. Even if the IBGP peers are all within your administrative domain and you know them to be trusted routers, it may be worth enabling authentication in order to prevent attempts to maliciously spoof these sessions.

Enabling authentication on MPLS signaling protocols

You use a signaling protocol with MPLS — either LDP or RSVP — to allocate and distribute labels throughout an MPLS network. Enabling authentication for these two protocols ensures the security of the MPLS LSPs in the network.

Enabling authentication for LDP protects the TCP connection used for the LDP session against spoofing. Junos OS uses an MD5 signature for LDP authentication. You configure the same key (password) on both sides of the LDP session:

```
[edit protocols]
fred@router# set ldp session address authentication-key key-string
```

RSVP authentication ensures that RSVP traffic accepted by the router comes from trusted sources. RSVP uses MD5 authentication, and all peers on a common network segment must use the same authentication key (password) in order to communicate with each other:

```
[edit protocols]
fred@router# set rsvp interface interface authentication-key key-string
```

Part III
Deploying a Device

The 5th Wave   By Rich Tennant

NETWORK ADMIN

"We found where the security breach was originating. It was coming in through another rogue robot-vac. This is the third one this month. Must have gotten away from its owner like all the rest."

In this part . . .

In this part, you graduate from the academy and receive your first assignment. This is where software meets hardware, and the union creates a unique opportunity. That's because with a single operating system like Junos, all devices are capable of doing unique and sometimes similar things. An SRX firewall can route traffic, a MX router has firewall filters protecting its routing engine, and an EX switch . . . well, switches back and forth.

Chapter 10

Deploying a Router

- -

In This Chapter

▶ Understanding how routers work

▶ The differences among routing, bridging, and switching

▶ Finding the Next Hop for a packet

▶ Running the RIPv2 routing protocol

▶ Running the standard OSPF routing protocol

▶ Running the standard IS-IS routing protocol

- -

The previous five chapters show how to install a device, set it up with the CLI or J-Web, and manage, monitor, and secure it. In the next three chapters, we show you how to turn your Junos OS device loose and see what it can do.

This chapter helps you understand routers. We discuss how packets make their way through a network hop-by-hop, and why this should guarantee the "best" route to a destination. Then we consider how a router chooses the correct next hop. We also look at the configuration basics of three routing protocols: RIPv2, OSPF, and IS-IS.

Note: This chapter explores the definitions for network devices like *routers*, *bridges*, and *switches*. We don't talk about *hubs* or *repeaters* to any extent. That's a little like talking about steam engines when considering modern railroads — nice to know about, but you won't see many.

Understanding Network Routing

The basic routing concept is that of a *route*. Routes on a network, whether the global Internet or the network within your company, are the path that messages take to reach their destination.

The way routes are determined is similar to how you might choose to drive from your home to work. Most people know several different ways to get to work and each day choose the one that will be best because it's less congested, or avoids a construction project, or whatever. Network routes work the same way. The router's job is to keep track of available routes and to send network traffic along the route that it decides is best at that moment.

Most of the time, however, we tend to take the same route to work. This route is unchanging, or static. On a network, as the administrator, you may want packets from a specific router to always follow the same path to reach another router. You, again as the administrator, explicitly configure these *static routes* on the router.

Static routes are the simplest way to direct traffic along a path in the network and to always know what that path will be. A static route provides straightforward directions to the router. When the router sees a packet destined for a particular address in the network, the static route instructs the router to send the message to a specific IP address or out a specific interface. The IP address that the message goes to isn't necessarily the destination network, but it's generally just the next router in the right direction. This next router then has to determine how it will continue forwarding the message toward its destination.

Unlike your drive to work, where you decide the route to take, each router along the path decides the route in IP networks. So even if a static route on Router A always moves packets to Router B, Router A has no control over the path that Router B will choose to move that packet along.

Most of the time, you want to let a router determine the best path for a packet to take as it travels through the network. But sometimes a router should always use the same path — for example, when an enterprise router connects directly to your upstream service provider. In this case, you need to hard-code a static route on the router such as a static route from your router to the SP's router.

To reach a system on the network that doesn't or can't run a dynamic routing protocol for some reason, you can use a static route, as shown here:

```
[edit routing-options]
user@junos-router# set static route 192.168.1.1 next-hop 10.1.0.1
```

This command says that any packets that are destined for the system at 192.168.1.1 should be sent through the router at 10.1.0.1.

Why use routes that are subject to change?

Just as traffic conditions tend to be stable when you drive to work (apologies to those with a killer commute), the routes through the network tend to be, though not always, stable. So if a neighboring router goes down or a physical cable connecting two cities on the Internet is severed, dynamic routing protocols become aware of these network topology changes and automatically perform calculations to choose different routes. Best of all, the protocols perform the route calculations by themselves, without any intervention from a network administrator!

Dynamic routing protocols

When you drive to work along your normal route, you might listen to the radio for reports on traffic conditions ahead. If you hear about an accident, you can use your knowledge of the city (and perhaps the advice from the traffic report) to decide on a different route. Routers use dynamic routing protocols to do essentially the same thing. *Dynamic* routing protocols keep track of which routers are present in the network as they change and which paths are being used to send traffic. Dynamic routing protocols use this network traffic information to decide which path is the best one to reach a certain destination and to dynamically decide on alternate routes.

Dynamic IP routing protocols choose the best route toward a destination, the best route being the shortest one. The protocols define what *short* means in two ways:

- ✔ Some protocols count how many routers it takes to get to the destination. Each router is a *hop* along the way, and the next router in the path is called the *next-hop router*. Each destination has a hop count associated with it, which is the number of hops, or routers, to reach that destination. This routing algorithm is called a *distance-vector algorithm*. On Junos routers, the only protocol that uses this algorithm is RIP (Routing Information Protocol), which is one of the original Internet routing protocols.

- ✔ *Link-state protocols* use a different mechanism to determine the best route. Two of the routing protocols, Open Shortest Path First (OSPF) and Intermediate System to Intermediate System (IS-IS), use this mechanism. These protocols send out special packets — OSPF calls them link-state advertisements (LSAs), and IS-IS calls them link-state protocol data units or link-state PDUs (LSPs) — to find out who their neighboring routers are and the speed of the connections between routers. From this information, the routing protocols create a database that defines the network topology. They then run the Dijkstra shortest-path first (SPF) algorithm on the information in the database to determine the shortest path to each destination in the network.

Routing tables

When you select your route on the way to work, you may consult a map or ask your coworkers or friends for suggestions. You probably store all this information in your head and then use it to make choices based on the commute conditions each day.

Routers have a mechanism called a *routing table,* which is similar to a map, that they use to store information about destinations on the network that they know how to reach. A routing table entry contains two basic types of information: a network destination and the address of a next-hop router that can accept traffic for that destination. The destination is a network address or prefix that has been learned from either static and dynamic routing protocols or directly from the router's network interfaces.

The destination can be reached through an interface on another router somewhere on the network, or it may be right on the router itself. When the network is reached through another router, the next-hop router is one of the router's directly connected neighbors. When the router receives a packet destined to a network address, the router determines which destination in the routing table best matches the destination address in the IP packet. The router then forwards the packets to the next-hop router (or neighbor) associated with that destination in the routing table. This process moves the packet one step closer to its destination.

Routers actually maintain several routing tables to separate the information they learn from different types of routing protocols, for example IPv4, IPv6, ISO, and multicast routes (see Table 10-1).

Table 10-1	Junos OS Routing Tables
Routing Table Name	*Description*
inet.0	Default table for IPv4 unicast routes, including configured static routes. RIP, OSPF, IS-IS, and BGP stored their routes in this table.
inet.1	Multicast forwarding cache, used by DVMRP and PIM.
inet.3	Stores paths and label information for traffic engineering (MPLS).
inet6.0	Default table for IPv6 unicast routes.
iso.0	ISO routes for IS-IS.
mpls.0	Next hops for MPLS label-switched paths (LSPs).

The show route command lists all the entries in the routing table, as detailed in Listing 10-1.

Listing 10-1:   Using show route to List a Router's Routing Table

```
user@junos-router> show route

inet.0: 6 destinations, 6 routes (6 active, 0 holddown, 0 hidden)
+ = Active Route, - = Last Active, * = Both

2.0.0.0/24          *[Direct/0] 06:01:36
                     > via fe-0/0/2.0
2.0.0.120/32        *[Local/0] 06:01:36
                      Local via fe-0/0/2.0
10.5.0.0/16         *[Static/5] 5d 00:25:00
                     > to 10.93.15.254 via fxp0.0
10.10.0.0/16        *[Static/5] 5d 00:25:00
                     > to 10.93.15.254 via fxp0.0
10.93.4.52/32       *[Direct/0] 5d 00:25:00
                     > via lo0.0
10.93.8.0/21        *[Direct/0] 5d 00:25:00
                     > via fxp0.0
                      [Static/5] 5d 00:25:00


__juniper_private1__.inet.0: 14 destinations, 14 routes (8 active, 0 holddown,
      6 hidden)
+ = Active Route, - = Last Active, * = Both

10.0.0.0/8          *[Direct/0] 5d 00:25:00
                     > via fxp1.0
10.0.0.1/32         *[Local/0] 5d 00:23:09
                      Local


__juniper_private1__.inet6.0: 2 destinations, 2 routes (2 active, 0 holddown,
      0 hidden)
+ = Active Route, - = Last Active, * = Both

fe80::/64           *[Direct/0] 5d 00:25:00
                     > via fxp1.0
fe80::200:ff:fe00:4/128
                    *[Local/0] 5d 00:25:00
                      Local via fxp1.0
```

The command lists the contents of all the routing tables that the Junos OS routing process (RPD) is using. Scan the output of the show route command in Listing 10-1 and notice that the routing table has both IPv4 and IPv6 routes. Notice, too, the first part of the output shows the contents of the inet.0 routing table, which is the default IPv4 routing table. The prefixes starting with 2.0.0.0 and ending with 10.93.8.0 are IPv4 unicast routes that are used to route traffic. The prefixes listed under __juniper_private1__.inet.0 and __juniper_private1__.inet.6 are the routes in internal routing tables that only Junos OS software uses.

If you closely examine the entries in the routing table in Listing 10-1 (look just at the IPv4 routes because the detail is the same for both IPv4 and IPv6 routes), the first line summarizes the contents of the `inet.0` routing table. The router has learned six destinations and has six routes, all of which are active. No routes are in hold-down state, which occurs just before a route is removed from the routing table, and no routes are hidden as a result of a policy that you've configured on the router or a problem with the route.

The second line of output in Listing 10-1 is just a key to symbols used in the output. An active route is one that the router is currently using as the best route to reach a destination. All the routes shown in the output are active, so they're marked with an asterisk (*) in the right column.

The first column in the routing table lists all the prefixes that the router knows how to reach.

The text in the brackets lists how the router learned about the route. This router has learned routes directly, from local interfaces, and from configured static routes. If any routing protocols, such as OSPF or BGP, were running on the router, the routing table would also show the routes learned from these protocols. The final text on the first line of each routing table entry shows how long the route has been in the routing table.

Inside the brackets, the number after the slash is a value the router uses to choose between multiple routes to the same destination. This value is called the route's preference, and we talk about it more in the next section.

The second line of each routing table entry shows which interface the router will use to forward traffic toward the prefix and, in some cases, the IP address of the next-hop router. Some of the prefixes in this routing table are reached through the Fast Ethernet interface `fe-0/0/2`.

You can practice this kind of close examination on your own routing tables, which are chock full of network and routing information.

Choosing the best route

The router chooses the best routes from all the routes it learns about (see the preceding section). It makes the decision about which route is the best by looking at a route's *preference*. The route preference is a number from 0 through 4,294,967,295 ($2^{32} - 1$) that is assigned based on the protocol from which the route was learned (see Table 10-2). If the router learns several routes to the same destination, it chooses the one with the lowest preference value, marks it as the active route, and uses that route to forward packets. The other routes remain in the routing table, but are inactive and are not marked with an asterisk.

Table 10-2   **Default Route Preferences in Junos OS**

How Route Is Learned	Default Route Preference
Directly connected router or network	0
Configured static routes	5
MPLS	7
LDP	9
OSPF internal routes	10
IS-IS Level 1 internal routes	15
IS-IS Level 2 internal routes	18
SNMP	50
RIP	100
PIM	105
DVMRP	110
Aggregate	130
OSPF external routes	150
IS-IS Level 1 external routes	160
IS-IS Level 2 external routes	165
BGP	170
MSDP	175

Sometimes two routes will have the same preference, and the router still has to pick one of them to be the active route. The Junos OS software goes through a fairly complex decision tree for choosing the best route. Because you generally don't need to know how this decision-making process works unless you're analyzing the overall flow of traffic through your network, we're punting to the Juniper product documentation, which has dozens and dozens of pages devoted to the actual decision tree.

Choosing the Next Hop

The router sends a packet hop-by-hop (router-by-router) through a network from source to destination. Generally, a router does not send a packet inside a frame directly to a destination. The exception is when the router is the "last hop" and is directly connected to the LAN (subnet) containing the destination host. Usually, the router looks at a certain number of bits in the network portion of the destination IP address and consults a forwarding table, which contains a list of prefixes for subnets that the router knows about — that is, prefixes derived from the routing table. Each prefix points to the interface to the router on the next hop closer to the destination. The router always chooses the longest match if there are multiple forwarding table entries with closely matching prefixes (such as 192.168.27/24 and 192.168.27.1/25).

That's a lot to digest! And because it is, we will back up a bit and consider the preceding information in more detail.

Routing, Bridging, and Switching

A network node, which is just a device that forwards packets toward a destination, can be a router, bridge, or switch. They operate on different layers of a networking protocol (layered protocols make it easier to modify and implement the networking task). Routers operate at Layer 3, the packet layer. The basic routing concept is that of a *route*. Routes on a network, whether the global Internet or the network within your company, are the path that messages take to reach their destination. But Layer 3 packets are placed inside Layer 2 frames (like Ethernet frames), and a network node that only looks at frames is called a bridge. A switch, as defined in this book, is a bridge that uses frames with special tags called *virtual LANs* (VLANs), to forward traffic.

Layer 1, the *Physical Layer*, "spits bits" across a medium directly connecting two devices, called *adjacent systems*. At each adjacent device, or even mid-span on long links, bits are cleaned up and regenerated by a device called a *repeater*. Repeaters used to be a big deal, but their operation is pretty much a given today, so we won't dwell on them any further. That's all there is to Layer 1.

However, for the purposes of this chapter about routing, bridging, and switching (and for Chapter 11 on EX switches), Layer 2 and Layer 3 are important, and you need to know the differences between networking at Layer 2 and networking at Layer 3. We explain these differences in the following sections.

Layer 2: Bridging

Bits at Layer 1 are organized into *frames* at Layer 2. Ethernet frames, which are the only frame *data units* a lot of networking people care about, have a source and destination address and a type field in the header, followed by the "data" (as you might imagine, by definition, *all* data units at any level carry data). At the end of the Ethernet frame comes a trailer that contains some error-detecting information.

Now, here's the key: *Bridges* are the network devices that look at the frame (Layer 2) header to figure out which *adjacent system* should get the frame next. Bridges adjust the frame source and destination addresses (called Media Access Control addresses, or *MAC addresses*) so that the frame addresses show each network device that a frame came from and where it is going on each hop from source to destination.

Layer 3: Routing

Wait a minute! A bridge changes the source and destination addresses each hop along the way, which makes it hard for the end systems to figure out where the frame came from and whom to reply to.

That's where the layers come in. Although a different frame (at least as far as MAC addresses are concerned) is sent hop-by-hop through the network, the *data content of the frame*, called the Layer 3 *packet*, remains intact from source host to destination host. The Layer 3 packet can't use Layer 2 MAC addresses (it is not obvious why, but there are sound reasons beyond the scope of this book), so we'll invent an address scheme just for Layer 3. The result is, of course, the IPv4 or IPv6 address. We'll use IPv4 in this book for the most part, but the more you know about IPv6, the better.

Although end systems (hosts) will continue to use IPv4 addresses for a long time (possibly until the next Ice Age), service provider networks are all busily transitioning to IPv6, especially for mobile networks.

Okay, drum roll, please: Network devices that look at the packet (Layer 3) header to figure out which adjacent system should get the frame next are called *routers*. Routers *cannot* adjust the packet source and destination addresses (the IP addresses) so that the receiver knows that the packet is for them and where to reply. However, routers *do* adjust the MAC addresses in the Layer 2 frame hop-by-hop, just like bridges.

All routers are also in some sense bridges. When networking was new (1990s-web new, not modem-on-a-voice-link new), it was common to read things like "A router is a feature-rich Layer 2 bridge" or "A bridge is a router with some Layer 3 stuff turned off." You don't read things like that anymore because a lot of modern network nodes do some repeating, bridging, and routing, depending on circumstance and configuration. And also because they were silly things to say to begin with.

Figure 10-1 illustrates the relationship between repeaters, bridges, and routers in the context of the 5-layer TCP/IP model, not the OSI-RM.

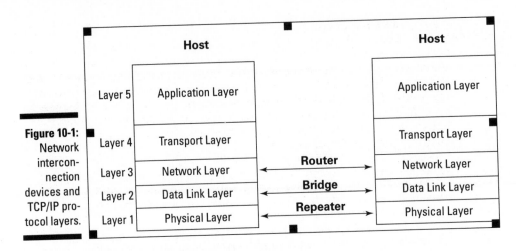

(Layer 2) Switching

However, if you define a bridge as a MAC-frame-address-examining-device and a router as an IP-packet-address-examining-device, then there does not seem to be anything left for a switch to do.

Today, when people say "switch," they usually mean a LAN switch. When applied to LANs, a *switch* is a device with a number of characteristics that can be compared to bridges and routers.

The *LAN switch* is really a complex bridge with many interfaces. LAN switching is a form of *multiport bridging*, where a bridge device connects not just two, but many LANs on different ports. (For more about multiport bridging, turn to Chapter 11). Essentially, though, a LAN switch has every device on its own LAN segment (piece of a LAN), giving each system the entire LAN bandwidth.

Much more can be said about switching, of course, enough to fill a book or two. For now, just remember that switching normally involves *virtual LANs*, or VLANs, which we cover in Chapter 11.

Note that on a WAN (wide area network), the term *switch* means a class of network nodes that behave very differently than routers. Before Ethernet more or less conquered all, fast packet network devices such as Frame Relay and ATM switches were network nodes that were not routers. WAN switches are beyond the scope of this book.

Running RIPv2

RIPv2 is a distance-vector routing protocol and uses the distance, measured in hops, to determine the best route to a destination. (A distance-vector routing protocol uses only the number of routers on a path to determine the next hop.) In RIPv2, each hop corresponds to a single router, and the number of hops to a destination is the sum of the number of routers a packet has to pass through, starting at its origin.

There is also a RIP version 1 (RIPv1). It works well for networks that have not changed since 1985, but not so well for today's networks. We recommend dealing only with RIPv2.

RIPv2 is generally used in smaller or less complex networks, partly because it's something of a simple protocol, and partly because of a design limitation. The maximum hop count that a route can have is 15. If a destination is more than 15 routers away, RIPv2 can't forward packets to that destination and simply discards (drops) the packets. The two other IGPs discussed later in this chapter, OSPF and IS-IS, don't have this limitation. For this reason, and also because OSPF and IS-IS provide more features than RIPv2, they're used more often for a network's IGP (which is why this discussion of RIPv2 is fairly short!).

You want to use RIPv2 on the Juniper router when you're connecting the router to a network that is already running RIPv2. The router configuration is very straightforward. You activate RIPv2 on each interface that is directly connected to a neighboring router running RIPv2. In the following configuration, the Junos OS router connects to the neighbor using the Fast Ethernet interface `fe-0/0/1`'s unit 0 logical interface, and sets the router to send and receive RIPv2:

```
[edit protocols]
user@junos-router# set rip group user-group neighbor fe-0/0/1.0
user@junos-router# set rip receive version-2
user@junos-router# set rip send version-2
```

Let 'er RIP!

The Routing Information Protocol (RIP) is one of the first routing protocols, developed as part of the ARPANET project in 1969. It was included in the UNIX BSD operating system in the early 1980s, before specialized devices called routers had even been developed, and as a result, became the de facto routing protocol and was widely used. RIP is an IGP, meaning that it routes traffic within a single administrative domain, such as a company or a university. RIP was standardized by the IETF in 1988 and became known as RIP version 1. The protocol was updated to version 2 in 1994 to add support for Classless Interdomain Routing (CIDR) and MD5 authentication.

The Junos OS configuration requires that all RIPv2 neighbors be part of a group, which you define with the `group` keyword. Here, the group has a name of `user-group`, but you can name it almost anything you like. For a simple network, you can configure all the RIPv2 interfaces and routers to be in a single group. If you want to enable RIPv2 packet authentication and want routers to have different passwords, you need to configure the routers to be in different groups.

The RIPv2 configuration on the neighboring router is similar. You can use the same group name and the appropriate interface. Use the `show rip neighbor` command to check that the interface is configured:

```
user@junos-router> show rip neighbor
                        Source          Destination     Send    Receive   In
Neighbor      State    Address         Address         Mode    Mode      Met
--------      -----    -------         -----------     ----    -------   ---
fe-0/0/1.0             Up 10.0.29.2    224.0.0.9       mcast   both      1
```

The first column of the output shows that you're running RIPv2 on the configured interface, `fe-0/0/1.0`, and the `State` column shows that the connection is `Up`. The two `Address` columns show the address of the local interface and the interface to which the router is sending updates (in this case, a well-known multicast address used by RIPv2 routers). The last column reports the inbound metric, which is how many hops will be added to received routes. Here, the metric is the expected value of 1.

Running OSPF

OSPF is a more advanced interior gateway routing protocol. Unlike RIP, which is a distance-vector protocol, OSPF is a link-state protocol. Instead of determining the best route by looking at the distance (number of hops), link-state protocols run a shortest-path first (SPF) algorithm to create a database of the network's topology and, from that database, to determine the best (that is, shortest) path to a destination.

The nice thing about OSPF is that not only can hops be used as metrics, as in RIP, but you can set OSPF to determine the best path. The best path might use the fewest number of hops or the highest bandwidth links, while using one route for multicast and another for regular unicast packets. Setting up all this multi-topology OSPF routing is a lot of work, but doing so is often worth the effort.

As an IGP, OSPF operates within a single network administrative boundary or domain, which is sometimes called an *autonomous system (AS)*.

Each router running OSPF goes through the following process to discover the network topology and determine the best path to each destination:

1. OSPF creates link-state advertisements (LSAs), which describe the network topology that the router has in its link-state database.

2. The router floods the LSAs to all routers in the domain.

3. When the router receives LSAs from other routers, it adds the information to its link-state database.

4. The router runs the Dijkstra SPF calculation to determine the shortest path to each destination in the domain.

   The result of the calculation is a pair of values for each destination, consisting of the destination address and the next hop toward that destination. OSPF places this information in its OSPF routing database. Although each router performs the SPF calculation independently, all routers end up with identical link-state databases (though the routers may have different next hops for the destinations). Another way to look at it is that OSPF routers all have essentially the same routing table information, but derive distinct forwarding tables.

   All OSPF routers within a domain must have the same link-state databases for OSPF to work.

5. When changes occur in the administrative domain, this information is transmitted in LSAs, and all the OSPF routers rerun the SPF calculation and update their link-state databases.

Dividing an OSPF network into areas

As an OSPF network gets larger, one of the challenges is keeping all the link-state statements on all the routers in sync. One way to control the size of the OSPF network is to divide it into smaller pieces, which OSPF calls *areas*. Each area has the same properties: All the routers within the area exchange their network topology information in LSAs, and this smaller group of routers runs the SPF calculation to keep its link-state databases identical. An OSPF network must have at least one area, the backbone area, called *Area 0*.

Routers that connect only to other routers within an area are called *internal routers*.

Some of the routers within an OSPF area sit on the boundary of two areas. These *area border routers* (ABRs) connect the areas within the larger OSPF network. They run two SPF calculations, one for each area to which they're connected, and they maintain two link-state databases, one for each area. The ABRs pass route information between the two areas, but condense (summarize) it before sending it into the neighboring area. The summarization improves the overall stability of the OSPF network.

Areas and area border routers sit in a single OSPF administrative domain. Another type of router sits at the boundary between one OSPF administrative domain and another administrative domain or routing protocol. This router is the AS boundary router (ASBR). These routers are responsible for advertising externally learned routes into the OSPF administrative domains.

Areas come in several different flavors. The main one is the *backbone area* because it forms the backbone of the OSPF network. The backbone area has the area ID 0, which is normally written as the 32-bit value 0.0.0.0. All areas in the OSPF network connect to the backbone, and as a result, all area border routers are part of the backbone area. Also, any networks that have an area ID of 0.0.0.0 must also connect to the backbone area.

All routers in the OSPF backbone must be physically connected to each other. If any routers aren't physically contiguous, they must be connected by an OSPF virtual link so that they appear to be contiguous.

In a simple (if you can conceive of that right now) OSPF network, all nonbackbone areas (areas numbered other than 0) connect directly to the backbone area (area 0). By default, these non-0-numbered areas are referred to as *regular areas*. To minimize the amount of LSA traffic on segments of the OSPF network, OSPF has two other types of areas that don't advertise route information into other areas. *Stub areas* receive only summarized routing information about other areas within the OSPF domain, and they don't receive any information about external OSPF routes. As a result, stub areas can't connect to external networks. Not-so-stubby areas (NSSAs) are a slight variant of a stub network. These areas can connect to external networks.

Configuring and monitoring OSPF

Although OSPF in theory may seem overly complicated, configuring OSPF on a Junos OS router is straightforward and easy. First, you must define the OSPF areas to which the router will connect, and then you must enable OSPF on the interfaces on which you want OSPF to run. You can configure these two properties as follows:

```
[edit protocols]
user@junos-router# set ospf area 0.0.0.0
user@junos-router# set ospf area 0.0.0.0 interface interface-name
```

Once OSPF is configured, you can use the commands listed in Table 10-3 to monitor OSPF routing on your network.

You can use the `interface all` statement to run OSPF on all interfaces. But be careful — be sure to disable OSPF (or *any* routing protocol) on the management interface or you might find customer traffic on your network management devices!

Table 10-3	Commands to Monitor OSPF
Command	**Purpose**
`show ospf database`	Displays entries in the OSPF link-state database.
`show ospf interface`	Displays the interfaces on which OSPF is configured.
`show ospf neighbor`	Displays the router's OSPF neighbors.
`show ospf route`	Displays the contents of the OSPF routing table.
`show route protocol ospf`	Displays the routes learned by OSPF.

Running IS-IS

IS-IS is a link-state interior gateway routing protocol. Like OSPF, IS-IS runs the Dijkstra shortest-path first (SPF) algorithm to create a database of the network's topology and, from that database, to determine the best (that is, shortest) path to a destination.

Unlike OSPF, which was developed and standardized by the Internet Engineering Task Force (IETF), IS-IS is an ANSI ISO protocol and was originally based on the Digital Equipment Corporation DECNET Phase V Network Technology.

IS-IS uses a slightly different terminology than OSPF for naming its protocol packets. The packets that IS-IS routers send to each other describing the network topology are called *link-state protocol data units* (link-state PDUs, or LSPs). In addition to describing the network topology that the router knows about, the link-state PDUs include IP routes, checksums, and other information.

Similar to OSPF, all IS-IS routers place the information in the received link-stated PDUs into their link-state database, and all routers have the same view of the network's topology. IS-IS runs the SPF algorithm on the information in the link-state database to determine the shortest path to each destination on the network, placing the destination/next-hop pairs that result from the SPF calculation into the IS-IS routing database.

Using IS-IS addresses only when needed

Unlike other IP routing protocols, which typically run on TCP, UDP, or IP, which are OSI Layer 3 or Layer 4 protocols, IS-IS runs directly on the data link layer (Layer 2). As a result, an interface that runs IS-IS doesn't need an IP address to exchange IS-IS information, and you don't need to configure an `inet` family on interfaces running IS-IS. Instead, only the router needs an IP address, which makes the router configuration simpler (but not necessarily better).

Because it was developed as part of the OSI network protocols and not part of TCP/IP, IS-IS doesn't use IP addresses. IS-IS addresses are called NETs, or network entity titles. While IP addresses are 32 bits long and are normally written in dotted quad notation (such as 192.168.1.2), NETs can be 8 to 20 bytes long, but are generally 10 bytes long and are written as shown in this example:

```
49.0001.1921.6800.1002.00
```

The IS-IS address consists of three parts:

✔ **Area identifier:** The first three bytes are the area ID. IS-IS areas are similar to OSPF areas (see the next section), but for this example, the area ID is `49.0001`. The first byte of this — `49` — is the address family identifier (AFI) of the authority, which is equivalent to the IP address space that is assigned to an autonomous system. The AFI value 49 is what IS-IS uses for private addressing, which is the equivalent of RFC 1918 address space for IP protocols. The second two bytes of the area ID — `0001` — represent the IS-IS area number. In this example, the area number is 1.

✔ **System identifier:** The next six bytes identify the node (that is, the router) on the network. The system identifier is equivalent to the host or address portion on an IP address. Although you can choose any value for the system identifier, a commonly used method is to use binary-coded decimal (BCD) which involves taking the router's IP address (the address you assigned to the `lo0 loopback` interface), filling in all leading zeros, and then repositioning the decimal points to form three two-byte numbers. In this example, if you pad the IP address `192.168.1.2` with zeros, the result is `192.168.001.002`. Rearranging the decimal points gives you `1921.6800.1002`.

Another common way to assign the system identifier is to start with the router's media access control (MAC) address, which is a six-byte address and rearrange the decimal points to create three two-byte numbers. So, for example, for a router MAC address of `00:1B:63:31:86:BE`, the IS-IS system identifier is `001b.6331.86be`.

✔ **NET selector:** The final two bytes are the NET selector (NSEL). For IS-IS, they must always be `00`, to indicate "this system."

Minding your IS-IS areas

To control the amount of IS-IS protocol traffic sent within the local network, IS-IS networks are divided into areas, just as OSPF networks have areas. Each IS-IS area consists of a set of networks and routers that are administratively grouped together. All the routers within an area exchange their network topology information in IS-IS LSPs, and this smaller group of routers run the SPF calculation to keep their link-state databases identical. Routers within an area share the information in their link-state databases with each other by exchanging LSPs. This process ensures that all the link-state databases in the area are identical, hence all routers within an area have the same view of the area's network topology. Routers within an area can send summaries of their routes to other areas in the IS-IS network.

IS-IS areas contain two types of routers:

- ✔ **Level 1 systems:** These routers route traffic within an IS-IS area. When they receive traffic destined for somewhere outside the area, they send the packet toward a Level 2 system.

- ✔ **Level 2 systems:** These routers route traffic between two IS-IS areas. They also route traffic to other ASs.

A single IS-IS router can be both a Level 1 and a Level 2 system, which is similar to the OSPF area border router. These routers maintain two link-state databases, one for the Level 1 area and a second one for the Level 2 area.

Configuring and monitoring IS-IS

To configure IS-IS on a Junos router, you enable family `iso` processing on the interfaces on which you want IS-IS, and then you tell the router to form IS-IS adjacencies over that interface. Here's how you do so for the `ge-1/2/0.0` interface:

```
[edit]
user@junos-router# set interfaces ge-1/2/0 unit 0 family iso
```

```
[edit]
user@junos-router# set protocols isis interface ge-1/2/0.0
```

When IS-IS is configured, you can use the commands listed in Table 10-4 to monitor IS-IS routing on your network.

Table 10-4	Commands to Monitor IS-IS
Command	*Purpose*
`show isis adjacency`	Displays the router's IS-IS neighbors.
`show isis database`	Displays entries in the IS-IS link-state database.
`show isis interface`	Displays the interfaces on which IS-IS is configured.
`show isis route`	Displays the contents of the IS-IS routing table.
`show route protocol isis`	Displays the routes learned by IS-IS.

Chapter 11

Deploying an EX Switch

● ●

In This Chapter

▶ Using VLANs with Juniper EX Series switches

▶ Setting up the switch to connect LANs

▶ Creating LAN segments with Virtual LANs

▶ Interconnecting EX switches with Virtual Chassis

▶ Using the Layer 2 switch as a Layer 3 router

● ●

*Y*ou may think that routers and switches are the same because you use them to connect to the Internet or to a network in your office or campus. But from a technological point of view, as shown in Chapter 10, they're different.

Remember, routers, routing protocols, and the Internet Protocol (IP) operate at Layer 3, the network layer, of the OSI protocol stack. They use IP addresses to route traffic, and — for Ethernet networks — to map these addresses to each network device's media access control (MAC) address, which is the Layer 2 hardware address of the device. Switches operate at Layer 2, the data-link layer, of the OSI protocol stack, so they use only the MAC address to forward traffic through the network.

This chapter concentrates on two key components in modern networks: VLANs and switches. We'll see how VLANs help make large arrays of networked devices more manageable, and how switches make everything look like a unified whole.

Ethernet, VLANs, and Juniper EX-Series Switches

Ethernet is the most common LAN technology today, so to understand virtual LANs (VLANs) switches, you need to understand Ethernet. VLANs, made up of pieces of what would ordinarily be massive, unwieldy collections of networked devices, make Ethernets more tractable for the modern world.

Finally, because the collection of VLANs and Ethernets must all still work and feel as one to users and managers, we'll look at how switches tie it all back together.

Understanding Ethernet

Over the years, Ethernet, which is technically *IEEE 802.3 CSMA/CD LANs* (although no one uses that terminology), has become the most commonly used standard for enterprise networks. These networks carry voice, graphics, and video traffic over interfaces that run considerably faster than the original Ethernet. The most common top speed, for example, is a full thousand times faster than the original Ethernet — 10 gigabits per second (Gbps) versus 10 megabits per second (Mbps).

With so much data being carried, the potential increases for more and more packet collisions in the *collision domain*. When a collision occurs, both data frames must be resent and this cuts down drastically on the throughput of the LAN. The collision domain is established by the number of hosts that can be transmitting at the same time and cause a collision. If you can have two hosts blasting away at the same time, you have at least two collision domains on the LAN.

The IEEE addressed this issue by defining *transparent bridging*, which is generally just called *bridging*, in the IEEE 802.1D-2004 standard. You can bridge two collision domains, each a LAN in itself, together to make one big LAN, just by plugging them into the same transparent bridge device.

However, extending a LAN by transparently bridging frames still creates one collision and broadcast domain. (A *broadcast domain* is established by all systems that receive a broadcast "send this to everyone" message. Many protocols use broadcasts in IPv4.) Table 11-1 shows the collision and broadcast domains created by repeaters, bridges, routers, and switches.

Table 11-1	Collision and Broadcast Domains	
Internetwork Device	*Collision Domains*	*Broadcast Domains*
Repeater	One	One
Bridge	Many	One
Router	Many	Many
Switch	Many	Depends on VLAN configuration

The use of the Internetwork devices listed in Table 11-1 is not mutually exclusive. In other words, a router can be used to segment a LAN into two (or more) segments, and each resulting segment can be divided further with bridges. In an extreme case, each individual system has its own port and the full media bandwidth available. Think of a *LAN switch* as a device that bridges many collision domains together but that keeps them apart as far as broadcast domains are concerned.

Understanding VLANs

As LANs grew bigger and bigger and faster and faster, the need to segment to cut down on collisions became more and more urgent. For flexibility, physical segmenting gave way to logical (virtual) segmenting with VLANs. However, this practice creates isolated pieces of LANs (even if virtual) that are tied together with a special type of bridge called a switch.

Bridges, discussed in the preceding section, reduce the chances for collisions by segmenting the network. Unlike the original Ethernet, where all stations on the Ethernet network received all traffic, bridges (the EX series switches, covered in this chapter, are a kind of bridge) receive traffic on a port, examine the traffic to determine the appropriate destination, and send the traffic on appropriate ports when able to do so. By using bridging, Junos OS reduces the collision domain to just the single switch port and the devices attached to it. In fact, when just a single host is attached to a single switch port, you no longer need to worry about collisions. In these cases, you can enable *full-duplex* operation, where both sides can transmit simultaneously and ignore collisions.

LANs have another concern besides collisions. In some cases, switches can't determine the appropriate ports on which to transmit packets. In these cases, they *flood* packets, sending them on every switch port, to make sure that the traffic reaches its destination.

Also, in the case of broadcast traffic (traffic intended to reach every host on the network, as described in the preceding section, "Understanding Ethernet"), the switches must send the traffic on every port to ensure that it reaches every host. In this case, the entire LAN is a single broadcast domain. On a normally functioning network, hosts send broadcast traffic for many reasons. Because this broadcast traffic must reach every host in the network, it can produce increasingly large amounts of traffic when the broadcast domain grows.

One way to reduce the size of a broadcast domain is to split LANs into smaller LANs, but this approach typically requires separate equipment for each LAN. Thankfully, there is a better way: VLANs.

Instead of thinking of each network as a single LAN, a switch can divide a LAN into subsets called *virtual LANs*, or VLANs. Switches treat VLANs as if each VLAN were a separate LAN. So, when a switch receives broadcast traffic from a device within a VLAN, it sends the traffic only to those devices in the same VLAN. In addition, when the switch needs to flood traffic, it sends the traffic only to other ports in the same VLAN on which the traffic was received. In this way, VLANs significantly reduce the amount of broadcast or flooded traffic that devices on the VLAN see, thus decreasing the amount of bandwidth used for this traffic.

Understanding LAN Switches

Now, using bridges to "separate" the network may make you think that devices on different VLANs can't communicate with each other. In a sense, that is true, because the devices aren't on the same Layer 2 network, and they can't communicate with each other directly at Layer 2. Do not fear! Traffic destined for a device outside one VLAN can be forwarded to a different VLAN by a Layer 3 router attached to both VLANs, or by the internal inter-VLAN routing feature of an EX series switch. (See the section "Trunking together VLANs," later in this chapter.)

Okay, so all of the ports on the switch establish their own broadcast domain. However, when broadcast frames containing ARPs or multicast traffic arrive, the switch floods the frames to all other ports. Unfortunately, this makes LAN switching not much better than a repeater (a device that duplicates bits) or a bridge when it comes to dealing with broadcast and multicast traffic (traffic sent to multiple destinations) (but there is an improvement because broadcast traffic cannot cause collisions that would force retransmissions).

To overcome this problem, a LAN switch can allow multiple ports to be assigned to a broadcast domain. The broadcast domains on a LAN switch are configurable, and each floods broadcast and multicast traffic only within its own domain. In fact, it is not possible for *any* frame to cross the boundary of a broadcast domain. When LAN switches define multiple broadcast domains, they create virtual LANs (VLANs). A VLAN defines membership to a LAN logically, through configuration, not physically by sharing media or devices.

Setting Up the Switch

Before you can configure the EX switch for VLANs and other features, you have to physically set it up. This process can be simple or involved, depending on the size of the switch.

Juniper switches ship in individual shipping crates. All EX switches except the EX 8200 devices come in cardboard boxes. The EX 8200 device comes on a wooden pallet. The series includes the EX 2200, EX 2500, EX 3200, EX 4200, EX 4500, and the super-sized EX 8200.

Unlike some of the larger Juniper routers, you can unpack and install these switches (except the EX 8200) without forklifts or other mechanical aids.

The EX 8200 models are much larger — the smaller one is about 24 inches high and about 250 pounds, and the larger model is about 38 inches high and about 400 pounds — so to install these switches, you'll need mechanical moving and lifting equipment and a team of three people.

Racking the switch

You can install EX series switches in a rack or cabinet, or even on a desk or table if you have the smaller models. If you're mounting the switches in a rack or cabinet, screw the mounting brackets onto the sides of the switch and then install the switch in the rack or cabinet. If you plan to set the switch on a desk or table, insert the rubber feet into the holes in the bottom of the switch to keep the chassis from sliding on the desk and aid airflow around the device.

You can install the larger EX 8200 only in a rack or cabinet. Attach the mounting brackets and use a mechanical lift to move the switch into the proper position.

The smaller EX series switches don't have on/off switches. When you plug them in, they start booting. If you need to power down the switch, you have to halt the software and then unplug it. The larger EX 8200 switch has an on/off switch.

Configuring the switch initially

One easy way to initially configure the switch is to use the J-Web GUI interface, as shown in Chapter 5. After the switch powers up, press the Menu button next to the LCD panel on the front of the box and navigate to the Maintenance Menu. Press Enter and then press the Menu button again until you see Enter EZ Setup. At this point, use an Ethernet cable to connect a PC to port 0 (which is called `ge-0/0/0`, the first Gigabit Ethernet interface) on the front panel of the switch:

1. **From the laptop browser, go to the address 192.168.1.1.**

2. **Log in as the user** `root` **with no password.**

3. **On the Basic Settings page, set the name of the switch (the hostname), the root password, and the date and time.**

4. **On the Management Options page, use either the default VLAN (called `default`) or create a new VLAN.**

   We talk about VLANs in the section "Segmenting a LAN with VLANs," later in this chapter.

5. **On the Manage Access page, you can enable Telnet, SSH, and SNMP services on the switch.**

6. **Click Finish to activate the initial configuration on the switch.**

Plugging devices into the switch

The ports for plugging network devices into the switch are on the front of the switch. On the models with copper ports, all the ports are 10/100/1000BASE-T ports, so you use the appropriate Ethernet cables to connect laptops, VoIP phones, wireless access points (WAPs), security cameras, and other network devices to the switch.

If you used the `default` VLAN when you initially configured the switch, all the devices you connect to the switch are placed into this VLAN and can begin transmitting traffic on the network without further configuration of the switch. If you configured a different VLAN, you'll have to configure the switch to add the appropriate ports to that VLAN. We cover this topic in the section "Configuring more VLANs," later in this chapter.

Connecting switches

When you want to create a Virtual Chassis unit from two or more (up to ten) EX series switches (not all models support this feature), you nor-mally interconnect them using the dedicated 64-Gbps Virtual Chassis ports (VCPs) on the back of the switch chassis, which are designed exclusively for interconnecting switches (and which require no extra configuration on the switch). You can also interconnect them using the 10-Gbps ports on the uplink module, but then you must configure these ports to be Virtual Chassis Extender Ports (VCEPs).

In the shipping box of each EX model that supports Virtual Chassis, you will find one Virtual Chassis cable for the dedicated 64-Gbps VCPs.

The Virtual Chassis unit you create can be in a single rack or wiring closet, or it can be spread out across different racks or different wiring closets. The only restriction on where you can place the switches is the maximum length of the VCP cable, which is about ten feet (three meters).

TIP

If you need a longer distance, you must connect the switches by configuring ports on the 10-Gbps uplink module to be VCEPs. You can use both VCPs and VCEPs in a single Virtual Chassis unit, if necessary.

Design the connections between the individual chassis to form a ring topology that ensures that the distance between any two switches in the Virtual Chassis unit is as short as possible. A ring topology configuration provides up to 128 Gbps of bandwidth between member switches, which they use to pass data packets and out-of-band traffic. Figure 11-1 shows a simple ring topology for an EX 4200 Virtual Chassis unit in a single location.

When you're connecting member switches that are in adjacent racks or in wiring closets scattered across a floor in your building or between floors, using a *chain* topology that joins each member switch to the previous and next switch in a line is often easier than trying to loop back to form a ring topology. The maximum bandwidth between member switches in a chain is slower than that in a ring, only 64 Gbps. Additionally, this topology provides no redundancy in case of a switch or link failure in the middle of the chain. For that reason, you should try to form a loop wherever possible. Figure 11-2 illustrates the sample cabling for a chain topology.

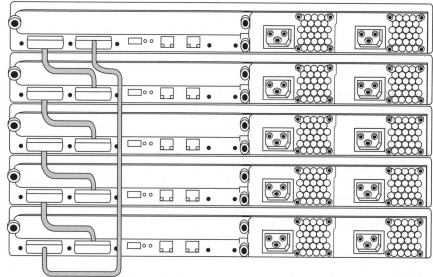

Figure 11-1: EX 4200 switches connected in a ring topology.

Figure 11-2:
EX 4200
switches
connected
in a chain
topology.

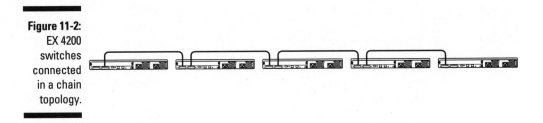

Segmenting a LAN with VLANs

To account for packet collisions that occur with broadcasting, Ethernet uses the carrier-sense multiple access with collection detection (CSMA/CD) protocol to detect frame collisions and to signal each device on the network to retransmit frames that aren't successfully sent the first time because of collisions.

Configuring the default VLAN

When you power on smaller EX models (or an individual EX 4200 that isn't part of a Virtual Chassis unit), bridging is enabled on all the interfaces (ports) on the switch, and all the ports are part of a preconfigured VLAN named `default`. So, for a small office or research lab, all you need to do to get the Juniper switch up and running is to power on the device, perform the initial configuration to give the switch a name and time, set the root password, and then connect your laptops, PCs, WAPs, printers, file servers, and other devices to the ports on the front of the switch.

The great thing about this setup is that you don't need to open the switch's configuration file to set up anything. The JUNOS software handles everything automatically. You can at some point look in the configuration file to see the results of the automatic configuration. The automatic switching portion of the configuration will look as follows:

```
[edit]
user@junos-switch# show
[...]
interfaces {
  ge-0/0/0 {
    unit 0 {
      family ethernet-switching;
    }
  }
  ge-0/0/1 {
    unit 0 {
      family ethernet-switching;
    }
```

```
    }
    [...]
  }
  protocols {
    lldp {
      interface all;
    }
    rstp;
  }
  poe {
    interface all;
  }
```

Look at the configuration to see that the `ge-0/0/1` interface supports bridging. First, the interface is configured with the `ethernet-switching` keyword, which enables the JUNOS Ethernet switch protocol family. Second, the `protocols` section of the configuration shows that two bridging protocols are enabled, `rstp` and `lldp`. The switch uses the Link Layer Discovery Protocol (LLDP) to learn which network devices are attached to each port on the switch.

A switch may find multiple paths to another device, or the path that it finds may go in circles, creating a loop. The second protocol, RSTP, is a rapid version of the original Spanning Tree Protocol (STP) that prevents loops in a bridged LAN or within a VLAN. Spanning tree protocols also determine new paths to devices on the VLAN after the topology in the VLAN changes — for example, when you add or move a laptop or a printer. The convergence times for RSTP are faster than those for STP.

The last protocol in the configuration is Power over Ethernet (PoE), which is enabled on all switch interfaces. This protocol ensures that PoE is enabled on all the ports that support PoE.

Another way to check that the `default` VLAN is configured on the switch is to use the `show vlans` command to list all the VLANs. We have configured only one interface, so the output of this command is short:

```
user@junos-switch> show vlans
Name            Tag      Interfaces
default

                         ge-0/0/0.0, ge-0/0/1.0, [...]
mgmt

                         me0.0
```

The output shows two VLANs: `default`, which contains the `ge-0/0/1` interface that you have plugged into the laptop, and `mgmt`, which is a switch management interface. The default VLAN has no VLAN ID, or tag, to identify which VLAN arriving packets originated from, so no tag name is listed in the `Tag` column. (The VLAN IDs, or tags, are used for VLAN trunking using the

802.1q specification, which we discuss in the next section, "Configuring more VLANs.") All packets sent on this VLAN are untagged, which is fine because the network has only one VLAN.

Configuring more VLANs

The basic VLAN configuration that switches set up automatically creates a single VLAN. This setup is fine for a small network, but for anything larger than that, you will want to subdivide your LAN into a number of VLANs.

In addition, when you have more than one VLAN, the switch needs a way to distinguish which packets originate where. To do so, each VLAN must have a unique name and a numeric tag, called a VLAN ID. Also, because each VLAN is a separate broadcast domain, any given IP subnet should usually not span VLANs.

As a simple example, look at two printers connected to the same switch, one in the physics department and the other in chemistry. To configure these VLANs, you follow these steps:

1. **Configure the ports that the printers are plugged into, namely** ge-0/0/1 and ge-0/0/2 **(the second and third ports on the front of the switch) and associate the interfaces with the VLANs you're about to create:**

```
[edit interfaces]
user@junos-switch# set ge-0/0/1 unit 0 family ethernet-switching
    vlan members physics
```

```
[edit interfaces]
user@junos-switch# set ge-0/0/2 unit 0 family ethernet-switching
    vlan members chemistry
```

Some people prefer an interface-centric approach to VLAN configuration, where you configure all the VLAN membership information in the interface configuration. Others prefer a VLAN-centric approach to VLAN configuration, where you configure all the VLAN membership information in the VLAN configuration. Fortunately, the Junos OS offers a CLI syntax that supports both approaches.

The following example illustrates the interface-centric approach, which is the approach we will continue to demonstrate. If you instead want to use the VLAN-centric approach, you need to configure the ge-0/0/1.0 and ge-0/0/2.0 interfaces for family ethernet-switching (which is included in the factory default configuration):

```
[edit interfaces]
user@junos-switch# set ge-0/0/1 unit 0 family ethernet-switching
```

```
[edit interfaces]
user@junos-switch# set ge-0/0/2 unit 0 family ethernet-switching
```

2. **Configure the VLAN membership under the VLAN configuration:**

```
[edit vlans]
user@junos-switch# set physics interface ge-0/0/1.0
```

```
[edit vlans]
user@junos-switch# set chemistry interface ge-0/0/2.
```

3. **Say that you want the EX series switch to route traffic between these two VLANs. To do so, you must configure two VLAN Layer 3 interfaces and assign IP addresses for each VLAN interface:**

```
[edit interfaces vlan]
user@junos-switch# set unit 100 family inet address 192.0.2.1/25
```

```
[edit interfaces vlan]
user@junos-switch# set unit 200 family inet address 192.0.2.129/25
```

4. **Define the VLAN ID so that all packets transmitted from the physics department are marked with the VLAN ID (or tag)** 100 **when the switch is performing VLAN trunking, while the chemistry packets are tagged with VLAN ID** 200**:**

```
[edit vlans]
user@junos-switch# set physics vlan-id 100
```

```
[edit vlans]
user@junos-switch# set chemistry vlan-id 200
```

5. **Associate the Layer 3 interface that you created with the two VLANs:**

```
[edit vlans]
user@junos-switch# set physics l3-interface vlan.100
```

```
[edit vlans]
user@junos-switch# set chemistry l3-interface vlan.200
```

In these two statements, the last keyword (vlan.100 and vlan.200) establishes the connection between Layer 3 routing and a VLAN, which performs Layer 2 switching. In assigning the IP addresses, we use two different logical units, or logical interfaces, for the VLAN. For physics, we use the command set unit 100... to create vlan.100, so unit 100 is the logical interface we specify as the physics department Layer 3 interface. For chemistry, we use set unit 200... to create vlan.200, so we specify vlan.200 as the logical interface. In this case, we have chosen to use the same numbers for the units and the VLAN IDs; however, you aren't required to do so.

In the Junos OS software, you can use <interface>.<unit> to refer to a particular unit on a physical interface. So, ge-0/0/1 unit 0 is ge-0/0/1.0, and vlan unit 10 is vlan.10. When you reference an interface elsewhere in the configuration, you almost always need to specify unit numbers. If you forget, the CLI usually will assume that you meant to specify unit 0, which can save you time — if it's the right choice!

Trunking together VLANs

Access ports are simply ports that connect to network devices. By default, all switch ports are in access mode, so you don't need to specify this mode in the configuration. When you connect one switch to another, or to a router, they are usually connected with *trunk ports*. On trunk ports, the devices add a short header to each Ethernet frame, which includes the VLAN ID. The receiving device reads the VLAN ID and puts the traffic into the correct VLAN. This information in the header lets the two devices exchange traffic for multiple VLANs, while keeping all the data straight.

You convert a port into a trunk port simply by configuring it to be a trunk port. Although you can make any port a trunk port, you generally connect switches together using the uplink ports, which are numbered starting at ge-0/1/0 or xe-0/1/0. (Depending on the uplink module, it will have either two or four ports.)

Suppose that the physics and chemistry departments have two separate switches and you've connected them by plugging in a cable to ge-0/1/0 on the physics side and to ge-0/1/1 on the chemistry side. Here's how you configure the trunk port on the physics switch:

```
[edit interfaces]
user@physics# set ge-0/1/0 unit 0 family ethernet-switching port-mode trunk
```

```
[edit interfaces]
user@physics# set ge-0/1/0 unit 0 family ethernet-switching vlan members
        [ physics chemistry ]
```

The configuration on the chemistry switch is similar:

```
[edit interfaces]
user@chemistry# set ge-0/1/1 unit 0 family ethernet-switching port-mode trunk
user@chemistry# set ge-0/1/1 unit 0 family ethernet-switching vlan members
        [ physics chemistry ]
```

The remaining switch configuration is similar to what we describe in the previous section.

Two strategies for architecting VLANs

The following are two common ways to design VLANs:

✔ **Group devices by type:** In this architecture, each VLAN contains only one type of network device, meaning you have one (or more) VLAN for printers, another one for office PCs and laptops, a third one for WAPs, a fourth one for VoIP telephones, another for IP security cameras, and so on. The advantage of this design is that the VLAN carries the same type of traffic, so less contention for bandwidth occurs among applications that use a lot of

bandwidth, such as security cameras and computers simply sending e-mail to each other.

✔ **Group devices by organizational structure:** This architecture segments network devices according to the organizational boundaries of your company or enterprise. For example, at a university, you can create separate VLANs for the physics, chemistry, and computer science departments when each department is responsible for procuring and maintaining their own network equipment.

Controlling access to VLANs

The VLAN configuration described in the preceding sections of this chapter set up the network so that anyone who can plug their computer into the switch or who can get on the wireless network through your WAPs can use your network. To limit network use only to valid users, whether employees, department or group members, or anyone else, you need to set up network admission control (NAC) policies on the switches. Admission control allows you to strictly control who can access the network, preventing unauthorized users from logging in and enforcing policies for network access (such as ensuring that authorized users have the latest antivirus software and operating system patches installed on their PCs and laptops).

The Junos OS software on EX series switches can use the IEEE 802.1X protocol (often just called *dot-one-ex*) to provide authentication of all devices when they initially connect to your LAN. The actual authentication is done by separate software or a separate server, generally a RADIUS authentication server that is connected to one of the switches on your LAN. When you configure the EX series switch to use 802.1X and a network device of any type attempts to connect to the LAN, this connect attempt kicks off the following authentication process on the switch:

When you configure the EX series switch to use 802.1X and a network device of any type attempts to connect to the LAN, the network device of any type attempting to connect to the LAN kicks off the following authentication process on the switch:

1. When the switch detects that a device has connected to the LAN, the switch puts on its authenticator hat and blocks all traffic to and from the network device, which at this point is an unauthenticated device.

2. When the client indicates it wants to start 802.1X authentication, the switch asks for the client's identity and then sends an access request message to the RADIUS server, asking the server to verify whether the network device is allowed to access the LAN.

3. If the RADIUS server sends an access challenge to the switch, the switch sends an access challenge to the network device, asking for a password to connect to the network.

4. When the network device responds, the switch forwards this password to the RADIUS server.

5. If the RADIUS server accepts the response, it sends a message to the switch telling it to allow the user and, optionally, assigning certain parameters (such as VLAN assignment or firewall filters) that the switch should use for this client.

   The device is then allowed to send and receive traffic on the LAN.

   If the RADIUS server rejects the access request or the user enters an invalid password, the network device remains unauthenticated and is denied access to the LAN.

6. When the network device disconnects from the LAN, the switch moves the port into an unauthorized state in which all traffic to and from that port is again blocked.

To set up admission control on the switch, follow these steps:

1. **Configure the address of the RADIUS servers, along with a password that the RADIUS server uses to validate requests from the switch.**

   This example uses the address `192.168.1.2`:

   ```
   [edit access]
   user@junos-switch# set radius-server 192.168.1.2 secret my-password
   ```

   The `secret` keyword in this command configures the password that the switch uses to access the RADIUS server.

   In case the switch has several interfaces that can reach the RADIUS server, you can assign an IP address that the switch can use for all its communication with the RADIUS server. In this example, you choose the address 192.168.0.1:

   ```
   [edit access]
   user@junos-switch# set radius-server 192.168.1.2 source-address
           192.168.0.1
   ```

2. Set up an authentication profile to be used by 802.1X:

```
[edit access]
user@junos-switch# set profile my-profile authentication-order radius
```

```
[edit access]
user@junos-switch# set profile my-profile radius authentication-server
        192.168.1.2
```

The first command requires the switch to contact a RADIUS server when sending authentication messages. (The other available options are LDAP servers or local password authentication.) The second command shows the address of the authentication server (which you just configured in the previous step).

3. Configure the 802.1X protocol itself, specifying the access permissions on the switch interfaces:

You can do so interface by interface, as follows:

```
[edit protocols]
user@junos-switch# set dot1x authenticator authentication-profile-name my-
        profile interface ge-0/0/1.0
```

```
[edit protocols]
user@junos-switch# set dot1x authenticator authentication-profile-name my-
        profile interface ge-0/0/2.0 supplicant single-secure
```

The `authentication-profile-name` statement associates the authentication profile established in the previous step with this interface.

Note that you specify the logical interface name (`ge-0/0/1.0`), not the physical interface name (`ge-0/0/1`).

In Step 3, the keyword `supplicant` (which is the 802.1X term for a network device seeking authentication on a network port — in other words, the 802.1x client) defines the administrative mode for authentication on the LAN:

✔ **Single mode:** Authenticates only the first device that connects to the switch port and allows access to any devices that later connect to the same port without further authentication. When the first authenticated device logs out, all other devices are locked out of the LAN. This mode is the default, so you don't need to include it in the configuration.

✔ **Single-secure mode:** Authenticates only one network device per port. In this mode, additional devices that later connect to the same port are not allowed to send or receive traffic, nor are they allowed to authenticate.

✔ **Multiple:** Authenticates each device that connects to the switch port individually. In this mode, additional devices that later connect to the same port are allowed to authenticate and, if successful, to send and receive traffic.

When using single mode, only the first device is authenticated, and this configuration can be considered to be a security hole. If you foresee problems, use the single-secure or multiple mode.

If the authentication mode is the same on all switch ports, you can configure 802.1X parameters to apply to all interfaces by using the keyword `all` instead of an interface name:

```
[edit protocols]
user@junos-switch# set dot1x authenticator interface all
```

Interconnecting Switches with Virtual Chassis

Creation of a Virtual Chassis unit with interconnected EX series switches establishes a single unit that you can manage as though it were a single chassis. One switch member in the Virtual Chassis is the primary or master switch, and a second member is a backup that provides redundancy if the master member fails for some reason. The forwarding (and routing) tables remain synchronized with those of the master member. If a failover to the backup occurs, this member switch can immediately step in to continue the forwarding of traffic on the LAN.

Going virtual

As a basic example to illustrate interconnecting switches, consider a Virtual Chassis configuration where two EX series switches are interconnected.

If you use the default configuration, you connect the two switches with the dedicated 64-Gbps VCPs on the rear panel of the switch and power on the switches, and the Virtual Chassis is operational. Connect each of the two VCPs on the chassis member to a VCP on the other member. You don't have to configure these ports.

After you power on the two switches in the Virtual Chassis unit, the JUNOS software picks one of them to be the master (the other one becomes the backup) and assigns member IDs to each one. You can see this information on the switch's LCD display, which is on the front panel. The master will show `Member ID: 0, Role: Master`, and the backup will show `Member ID:1, Role Backup`.

TIP

If you want a particular switch to be the master, power it on first.

Another way to check the master-backup assignment is to view the status of the Virtual Chassis unit:

```
user@junos-switch> show virtual-chassis status

Virtual Chassis ID: 0019.e250.47a0
                                           Mastership          Neighbor List
Member ID  Status  Serial No     Model     priority  Role     ID  Interface
0 (FPC 0)  Prsnt   AK0207360276  ex4200-48p     128  Master*   1   vcp-0
                                                               1   vcp-1
1 (FPC 1)  Prsnt   AK0207360281  ex4200-24t     128  Backup    0   vcp-0
                                                               0   vcp-1


Member ID for next new member: 4 (FPC 4)
```

The `Mastership priority` column shows that both members have an equal chance of being elected as the master. In this case, member 0 is the master because it was powered on first. Also check that the dedicated VCPs are up and running:

```
user@junos-switch> show virtual-chassis vc-port all-members
fpc0:
--------------------------------------------------------------------------
Interface        Type              Status
or
PIC / Port
vcp-0            Dedicated         Up
vcp-1            Dedicated         Up


fpc1:
--------------------------------------------------------------------------
Interface        Type              Status
or
PIC / Port
vcp-0            Dedicated         Up
vcp-1            Dedicated         Up
```

Junos OS treats each switch in a Virtual Chassis unit as though it were a FPC in the slot of an M-series router chassis. So, the software calls the first member switch `fpc0`, and it calls the second switch `fpc1`.

As your network expands, you add another member to the Virtual Chassis unit. Start by cabling the VCPs on the rear of the third chassis, as shown in Figure 11-3. But do not power on this switch yet.

To ensure that the first switch remains the master when you add the new member, you need to configure the mastership priority. This makes sure that the flow of traffic through the Virtual Chassis unit is not disrupted, and still has the second switch remain the backup You configure the mastership priorities on the existing Virtual Chassis unit. To configure the first switch to be the master, use this command:

```
[edit]
user@junos-switch0# set virtual-chassis member 0 mastership-priority 255
```

You use the highest possible value for mastership priority to ensure that this switch continues to function as the master. Configure the second switch with the same priority so that it remains first in line to become the master:

```
[edit]
user@junos-switch0# set virtual-chassis member 1 mastership-priority 255
```

Rear view

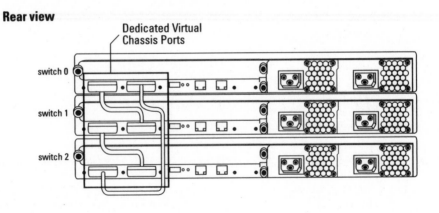

Front view

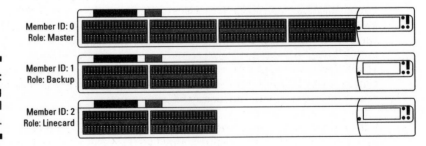

Figure 11-3:
Expanding
the Virtual
Chassis.

Note that this configuration will produce nondeterministic results on boot-up. It is possible that the second switch will become master if it boots first when the Virtual Chassis unit reboots. If you want switch 0 to always be master when it is available, you can set switch 0 to have a slightly higher priority than switch 1, but for both to have a higher priority than the default (128). In this case, switch 0 will assume the master role anytime it's available, even if switch 1 is already functioning as master and hasn't failed. (This behavior is commonly called *preemption.*) The one downside to this behavior is in a failure scenario: If switch 0 is continually rebooting, it will continue to become master, only to reboot a minute later. That's not so good! We recommend that you use the same mastership priority for master and backup.

When you commit any configuration changes to the Virtual Chassis unit (whether interface configuration, protocol configuration, or even Virtual Chassis configuration), use the `commit synchronize` command rather than the plain `commit` command. This command ensures that configuration changes are saved on both the master and backup switches.

Now you can power on the new third switch. You don't need to perform any configuration on this switch, and the expanded Virtual Chassis unit is ready to use.

Providing redundancy with Virtual Chassis

Because each switch member in an EX series Virtual Chassis unit has its own Routing Engine (RE), the Virtual Chassis unit has inherent redundancy. The configuration discussed throughout this chapter provides redundant failover. In addition, you can configure Graceful Routing Engine Switchover (GRES). Before explaining the difference between these two types of redundancy, you need to look at how the switch's REs work.

In a Virtual Chassis unit, the master member acts as the master RE, running the routing protocols, providing the forwarding table that the Packet Forwarding Engines (PFEs, the lower layer processors) on all the member switches of the Virtual Chassis unit use to forward traffic on the LAN, and running management and control processes for the entire Virtual Chassis unit. When you issue a `commit synchronize` command, the master RE sends the new configuration to the backup RE to ensure the configuration is synchronized; however, the backup RE does not actively run routing protocols or keep state with the master RE.

With redundant failover, when the master member fails, the backup RE assumes mastership and begins acting like the master RE (running routing protocols, building forwarding tables, and so on). Because the two REs haven't been synchronized, this change is rather traumatic for the PFEs.

Imagine being in the middle of intensely reviewing a spreadsheet and suddenly having all the numbers change on you! For this reason, the PFEs on all the member switches in the Virtual Chassis reinitialize their state to the boot-up state before connecting to the new RE. After they reboot, everything is better, and they begin talking to the new RE.

GRES allows the transition to the new master RE to occur with minimal interruption in network traffic. When you configure GRES, the master and backup REs synchronize certain information. This synchronization allows the PFEs to seamlessly switch from one RE to another. The PFEs never reinitialize their state to the boot-up state, preventing a forwarding outage.

Configuring GRES requires a single command:

```
[edit]
user@junos-switch# set chassis redundancy graceful-switchover
```

Even though the switchover may be fairly seamless for the PFEs, the new master RE still needs to restart the sessions with all its routing protocol peers. By default, the switchover will cause a forwarding outage while the old sessions are torn down and the new sessions are established. For this reason, on switches that perform Layer 3 routing, you'll likely want to combine GRES with graceful restart, which allows Layer 3 forwarding to continue with the existing routing information while the new master RE starts sessions with routing protocol peers and builds routing and forwarding tables. Once the new master RE has completed building new routing and forwarding tables, it sends updates to the PFEs. These updates prevent an outage while the new master RE gets up to speed. You configure graceful restart with this command:

```
[edit]
user@junos-switch# set routing-options graceful-restart
```

For graceful restart to work correctly, the routing protocol peers of the switch must support graceful restart in *helper mode*. Just like it sounds, devices that support graceful restart in helper mode will help peers that have failed and want to perform a graceful switchover. These devices will maintain routes for a failed switch while the backup RE is taking over, resend all routing information to the new RE, and receive new routing information from the new RE. Once the restart is complete, the helper device will compare the routes it has received from the new RE with the routes it had received from the former master RE. If it finds differences, only then will it update its routing table. Helper mode allows the network to keep forwarding traffic with the routing and forwarding tables that existed at the time of the switchover until the new RE has had a chance to build all its routing protocol adjacencies and exchange routes with them.

Thankfully, by default, all routers running the Junos OS software support graceful restart helper mode for all protocols except BGP. So, if you use only Juniper Networks routers and don't run BGP, you don't need to do anything else. You can configure the Junos OS software to support graceful restart for BGP simply by configuring graceful restart on the device. If you use another vendor's routers, you will need to check their documentation to determine how to enable their devices to run graceful restart for particular protocols.

Using the Switch as a Router

EX series switches support many of the standard Junos OS routing protocols, including static routing, RIP, OSPF, IS-IS, and BGP, as well as features such as VRRP. To enable inter-VLAN communication, you configure a Layer 3 (routing) logical interface on the switch for each VLAN, as discussed in the section "Configuring more VLANs." The switch treats these just like any other interface, so you can route traffic to and from VLANs through these interfaces.

The switch maintains routing tables to compile information learned from the routing protocols and from other routing information sources. The switch creates the same routing tables (and forwarding tables) and uses them in the same way as JUNOS routers do (see Chapter 10).

Connecting to the Internet

If you have a small LAN with a single connection to the Internet, you can easily connect to your service provider's edge router by configuring a static route from the switch to the router. The static route configuration is straightforward, and the route remains in the switch's routing table until you remove it, or until it becomes inactive for some reason.

You need just a few commands to configure the static route. First, set the IP address on the switch interface that connects to the service provider:

```
[edit interfaces]
user@junos-switch# set ge-0/0/10 unit 0 family inet address 192.168.0.2/30
```

As you can see in this example, you can configure any interface on an EX series switch to be a Layer 3 routed interface instead of a switch interface. You configure the interface to be a Layer 3 interface by configuring a Layer 3 `family` statement on the interface. Of course, if you do so, you can't also configure the `family ethernet-switching` statement on the same interface. That configuration would be very confusing — like telling your convertible car to have its top down and up at the same time — so the Junos OS software won't let you do that.

Then create a default route (a route with the address 0.0.0.0) to that switch interface:

```
[edit routing-options]
user@junos-switch# set static route 0.0.0.0/0 next-hop 192.168.0.1
```

Connecting to a router in your LAN

In larger networks, switches can perform different functions. Everything we describe in this chapter is for access switches, which are the switches that connect end-user network devices, such as computers and printers, to the LAN. But large LANs can have dozens of switches that need to connect to the LAN core or to WAN edge layer switches. The switches at the LAN core or WAN edge are called *aggregation,* or *distribution, switches.* (In some cases, the network is large enough that the distribution switches need to be connected together at another layer of aggregation. In those cases, you might use *core switches* to aggregate the distribution switches together.)

You may need to configure a distribution switch if, for example, you move traffic between a number of different switches within your organization. The switches can be in the same building, or they may be geographically dispersed across a campus, city, country, or even around the world. The switches can communicate using the bridging, spanning tree, and other mechanisms.

Or you may need to move traffic between your network and the Internet. In this case, your distribution switches link to routers that in turn connect to the Internet. The switch interfaces that connect to the routers usually communicate either with a single Layer 3 interface or with a single Layer 2 interface with VLAN trunking enabled. If you choose to use a Layer 3 interface, you need to get routing information on the switches by either configuring static routes or using a dynamic routing protocol (such as OSPF or IS-IS). If you choose to configure routing protocols on the switch, you do so in the same way as you do on any Junos OS software router. For more information, see Chapter 10 and the chapters in Part IV that are applicable to your network.

Chapter 12

Deploying Security with the SRX

. . . .

In This Chapter

▶ Setting up the SRX

▶ Getting the basics on flow processing

▶ Managing system security

▶ Writing security policies

▶ Configuring NAT Source Address Translation

. . . .

*N*ot too long ago, network administrators were not entirely convinced that a network required tight security measures. But when people began buying and selling everything from books to cars to stock portfolios over the Internet, the need to protect privacy, credit card information, and bank account details became obvious. The issue today is not whether a network requires security, but how much and how best to provide a secure environment for users.

This chapter looks at securing networks with a type of specialized equipment called the SRX. We look at how the system is set up and the key concept of flow processing. We then show you how to manage the system and write some security policies to prevent really bad things from happening on the protected network. Finally, we cover setting up NAT source address translation.

Setting Up the SRX

A popular way to provide network security is with a *services gateway*. The term *gateway* (an older term for what we now call a *router*) is used today for a device that connects two dissimilar types of networks: LAN and WAN, public and private, and so on. A modern gateway usually doesn't route because it has enough to do translating between one type of network and another. The *services* part of the term just means that the gateway supplies more than simple connectivity. Services are different than applications that a client might access and run on a server. Services are applied as traffic passes back and forth between client and server through the gateway. Security is one type of service; network address translation (NAT) is another. We cover both services in this chapter.

The SRX Series Services Gateway runs the Junos OS and is the device considered in this chapter. Because *SRX Series Services Gateway* is a handful to write and a mouthful to pronounce, we just call it the *SRX*.

Accessing the services gateway

After you install the SRX hardware, as covered in Chapter 5 (in general terms), you can access the services gateway for configuration in the following four ways:

- ✔ Connect via the console.
- ✔ Connect via the CLI interface.
- ✔ Connect via the J-Web interface.
- ✔ Connect via the Network and Security Manager (NSM).

Most users make sure they are familiar with both the CLI and J-Web interfaces. Other vendors make heavy use of graphical management interfaces, but many support staffs work with the CLI. Avoid frustration. Learn them both.

Any SRX running Junos 10.4 or higher makes use of wizards in J-Web to make the whole thing even simpler. If you're a newbie, start with the wizards to get it running; then take the time to experiment with other J-Web tools and the CLI.

Using the Network and Security Manager

The Network and Security Manager (NSM) is a Juniper Networks management platform for SRX platforms. NSM is not limited to SRX firewalls, but can potentially be used with any Juniper Networks device, including routers, switches, secure access (SA) devices, intrusion, detection, and prevention (IDP) appliances, and so on. NSM makes it easy to push changes to multiple devices with a few keystrokes. The SRX configuration must align with the NSM server, but once the configuration is set up, it is a good solution for logging network events. However, NSM is not intended for heavy-duty debugging.

Initial SRX console access

The most common way to configure a newly installed SRX is by using the RJ-45 serial console port. After all, someone has to actually be at the device to install it (remote hardware installation might be possible someday, but that's a long way off). Another reason is that access via any of the other methods (management port, J-Web, NSM) on high-end SRX platforms requires initial configuration of modular components, whereas the console port on low-end SRX devices uses the default factory configuration because of their fixed hardware configuration.

Note: As of this writing, the high-end, non-default configuration SRXs are the SRX3400/3600 and the SRX5600/5800. The low-end SRXs using the factory default configurations are the SRX100, 210, 240, and 650.

When you connect to the console port, you need the SRX console cable that shipped with the device, a computer (usually a laptop) with a serial port (or provide a USB-to-serial adapter), and a terminal emulation application on the computer, such as the Windows Hyper Terminal.

To access the SRX through the console port, do the following:

1. **Connect the cable between the computer port and the SRX console port.**

2. **Open the terminal emulation program by clicking on it or running it.**

3. **In the terminal emulation program, set the COM port options to 9600 bits per second, 8 data bits, no parity, 1 stop bit, and no flow control.**

4. **Click Open or Connect (the term varies in different applications).**

Apple computers are a little more complex. You'll need a USB-to-serial adapter to connect the cable to the console port, and you also need to know the name of the device using the $ ls /dev/ command. After you determine this name, open a terminal window and type $ **screen /dev/***device-name* **9600**, where *device-name* is the name determined for the SRX.

If you connect during the boot process, you will see a mass of scrolling messages on the screen. After the new SRX boots and is stable, you will see a login prompt for SRX Amnesiac (meaning the system has amnesia and does not remember who it is):

```
Amnesiac (ttyu0)
Login:
```

If the SRX is not new, the prompt may be very different. It may include a banner, and the system will recall its name. The key is that the word Amnesiac will not appear.

At this point, you can log in with "root" as the username and no password (especially in Amnesiac mode). Then you see something like this:

```
--- JUNOS 10.1R1.8 built 2010-07-12 18:31:54 UTC
root@%
```

If the "root" username does not work, the SRX is not using the default factory configuration. There may be legitimate reasons for not deleting all configuration information, and there is a way to reset the root or super-user account password. To reset the password, go to http://kb.juniper.net/ KB12167 and follow the directions.

Understanding Flow Processing

In TCP/IP, a *flow* is defined as a set of packets that shares the same values in a number of header fields. The fields required to establish a flow can vary, but usually at least source and destination addresses and ports, along with the protocol and a few other fields, are more than enough. TCP sessions are good candidates for packet flows, and often are the only flows defined on a device. The SRX enforces security policy by processing the flow of packets through the device. Therefore, flow processing is an important concept in SRX configuration and management.

Let's look at how flow processing works in the SRX.

The SRX actually does many complex things before it looks at the established security policies (rules), and a lot depends on whether the SRX has already seen the flow (session). If so, a great deal of information about the flow already exists and is installed on the SRX. When there is no match for the session, the SRX subjects the packet to *first path* processing. If the packet header fields match an installed session, the SRX subjects the packet to *fast path* processing (about half the steps of first path processing).

The use of the term *fast path* is unfortunate, but at least the first path is no longer called the slow path. These were very relative terms and the term "slow path" did not imply that the SRX would grind to a halt if a lot of new sessions occurred. Better terms might have been "full path" and "established path," but "first path" and "fast path" are the terms we must use when talking about flows.

Also, rules called policers are applied to the packets as they enter the SRX. These policers determine if the packet should be processed further or not. (On the output side, rules called shapers are applied to determine if and when the SRX should send the packet.)

Figure 12-1 shows the major steps in flow processing.

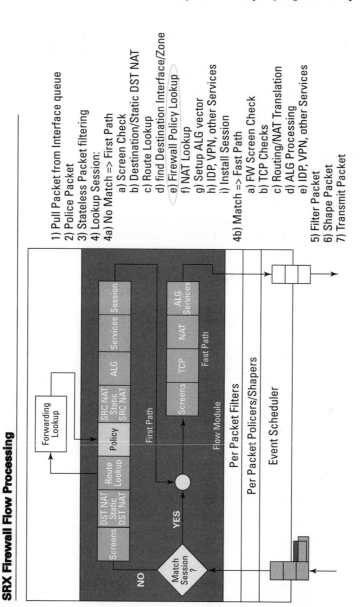

Figure 12-1:
SRX flow
processing
steps.

The major SRX flow processing steps are as follows:

1. **Pull the packet from the input interface queue.**

2. **Apply policers to the packet.**

3. **Perform stateless (that is, non-flow) packet filtering.**

4. **Decide on first path or fast path.**

5. **Filter the packet for output.**

6. **Apply shapers to packet.**

7. **Transmit the packet.**

Policing and shaping and stateless filtering are things that almost any router can do. The real value of the SRX is in the first path and subsequent fast path flow processing.

Here are the steps for first path flow processing:

1. **Perform a screen check, which we will describe in more detail below.**

2. **Perform destination or static destination NAT to substitute one set of packet header address information with another.**

3. **Perform route lookup to determine the next hop.**

4. **Find destination interface and zone.**

5. **Look up firewall policy.**

6. **Perform NAT lookup to substitute address information.**

7. **Set the application layer gateway (ALG) services vector (fields).**

8. **Apply intrusion detection and prevention (IDP), VPN, or other services.**

9. **Install the new session in the SRX.**

We cover zones and the actual security policies later in this chapter in sections Security Zones and Writing Basic Security Policies. For now, here are the steps for fast path flow processing:

1. **Perform screen check.**

2. **Perform TCP header and flag checks.**

3. **Perform route lookup and NAT translation.**

4. **Apply ALG services.**

5. **Apply IDP, VPN, and other services.**

Sure, fast path is faster than first path, but some jet aircraft are faster than others, too. From the perspective of a person walking by, all the jets overhead move pretty fast, whether they are "first path" or "fast path."

Just as a screen check at an airport precedes boarding a plane, all security flow processing begins with a screen check. In the SRX, a screen is a built-in (but tunable) protection mechanism that performs a variety of security functions. The tuning can adjust the screen protections for small enterprise or large carrier networks, for the network edge to the internal core. Screens are for detecting and preventing many kinds of malicious traffic, such as denial-of-service (DoS) attacks.

Screen checks take place before other security flow processing in an attempt to eliminate issues before attacks can make a mess of the other steps. Screen checks dig deeper into the packet and flow than firewall filters, and although screen checks take a lot of processing power, they also allow the SRX to block large and complicated attacks. On high-end SRX models, many of the screen checks take place in hardware, close to the ingress interface.

Notice that even if the flow session is established and the fast path is used instead of the first path, the screen check still takes place. Malicious traffic can still try and piggyback on an established flow, and the SRX can still block and drop mid-session packet attacks.

Screens are evaluated on inbound traffic and are grouped into screen profiles. Great care is required when changing or creating new screens, because they can have serious and unintended side effects.

You can use the `alarm-without-drop` keyword to detect traffic that would be caught by a screen profile without actually dropping it. This allows you to test the screen profile without affecting live traffic.

Managing the System

The SRX uses the concept of *nested security zones.* Zones are a critical concept in SRX configuration. The SRX is not the same as a router, and that point is immediately obvious after initial configuration of users and interfaces. Unlike routers, the SRX is a locked-down device. You can't even ping an interface on the SRX initially, even if it has a valid IP address. No traffic goes in or out unless the security zones are configured properly on the SRX interfaces.

Security zones

To configure a security zone, you need to associate the interface with a security zone, and then the security zones need to be bound with a routing instance (if there are multiple routing instances). Figure 12-2 shows the relationship between interfaces and zones on the SRX.

It sounds complicated, but it's not. First, you configure the zones and then you associate the interfaces with the zones. Here, we're assuming that you're using only one routing instance. You can configure a zone with more than one interface. However, each interface can belong to only one zone.

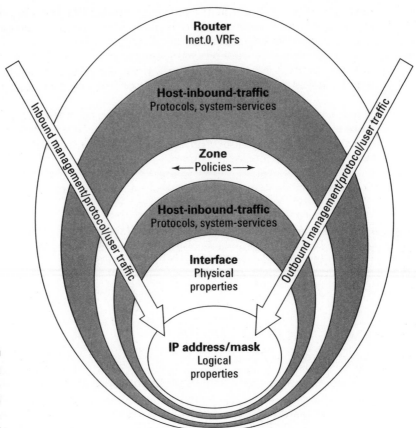

Figure 12-2:
SRX inter-
faces and
zones.

Security zones and interfaces

Now, establish two security zones for a simple SRX configuration. One zone
is for a local LAN called admins (administration) on interface ge-0/0/0.0,
and the other zone is for two links to the Internet called untrust with interfaces ge-0/0/1.0 and ge-0/0/2.0:

```
root# edit security zones
[edit security zones]
root# set security zone admins
root# set security zone untrust
root# set security zone admins interfaces ge-0/0/0.0
root# set security zone untrust interfaces ge-0/0/1.0
root# set security zone untrust interfaces ge-0/0/2.0
```

Always configure zones from the perspective of the SRX you are configuring. Many other zones may be on the LAN (`trust`, `accounting`, and so on). But this SRX only links to `admins` and `untrust`.

Now you can add services to the zones you just configured. Assume that inbound ssh, ftp, and ping traffic is permitted from the untrusted zone.

This is just an example. Before you enable any services at all on your SRX, make sure you truly need them. FTP in particular is often considered risky because FTP has no real security, and you just punched a big hole for it in your security zone.

```
[edit security zones]
root# set security zone untrust host-inbound-traffic ssh
root# set security zone untrust host-inbound-traffic ftp
root# set security zone untrust host-inbound-traffic ping
```

Your configuration now looks like this:

```
[edit security]
zones {
    security-zone untrust {
        host-inbound-traffic {
            system-services {
                ssh;
                ftp;
                ping;
            }
        }
        interfaces {
            ge-0/0/1.0;
            ge-0/0/2.0;
        }
    }
    security-zone admins {
        interfaces {
            ge-0/0/0.0;
            }
        }
```

If you haven't yet configured routing and applied licensing to your SRX, you will get a fetch error message when you try and commit the security configuration. This error will go away when configuration is complete.

Writing Basic Security Policies

If the SRX could only assign interfaces to zones and allow certain services in and out, there wouldn't be much to it. But the SRX is much more powerful.

After you have zones and interfaces set up, you can tap into the real power of the SRX: the security policies themselves.

Without security policies, all the SRX could do is create interface zones and screen out certain services. Security policies allow you to configure the details of what is and is not allowed through the SRX.

Multiple security policies

Large SRXs can have hundreds or even thousands of policies, because policies become more and more complex as they try and do too much. So, you can have multiple policies that are applied to traffic, all based on source and destination zone. The policies are applied one after another until an action is determined. The final default, of course, is to deny the traffic and discard the packet.

The exception to the default deny rule is traffic on the fxp0 management interface, which makes management of the SRX possible at all times (even when configurations go haywire), and allowing this traffic is a small risk because outside user traffic never appears on this interface.

Figure 12-3 shows this policy ordering on the SRX by zones.

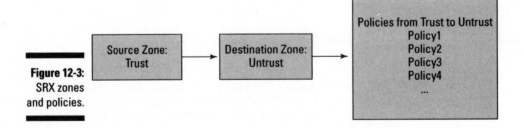

Figure 12-3:
SRX zones
and policies.

Source Zone: Trust → Destination Zone: Untrust →

Policies from Trust to Untrust
Policy1
Policy2
Policy3
Policy4
...

All SRX security policies follow an IF-THEN-ELSE algorithm. IF traffic X matches some rule, THEN action Y is performed, ELSE the default deny (drop) is applied.

The IF part of the policy examines five aspects of packets to test for a match:

✔ The predefined or configured source zone of the traffic inspected

✔ The predefined or configured destination zone where the traffic is headed

✔ The source IP address, or address book contents, of the traffic

✔ The destination address, or address book contents, where the traffic is headed

✔ The predefined or configured application or service to be allowed or denied

When an incoming packet matches all five default or configured parameters in the IF portion of the policy, one of these actions is applied:

- ✔ **Deny:** The packet is silently dropped.
- ✔ **Reject:** The packet is dropped, and a TCP-Rest is sent to the originator.
- ✔ **Permit:** The packet is allowed to pass.
- ✔ **Log:** The SRX creates a log entry for the packet.
- ✔ **Count:** The packet is counted as part of the SRX accounting process.

When an action is applied to a packet, the policy chain is terminated. So policy order counts! Generally, you configure the most specific rules at the top of the chain and more generic policies at the bottom. Otherwise, one policy might mask the intended effect of another.

Now, add an example policy to the security zones you've already configured. Here's what you want the policy to do:

- ✔ Permit any traffic from any hosts in the admins zone to any destination in the untrust zone.
- ✔ Permit certain traffic from any hosts in the admins zone to any other host in the same zone.
- ✔ Deny any traffic from the untrust zone to the admins zone.

Configuring address books

The first step is to configure an address book to hold a group of IP addresses or prefixes. The address book is referenced by *both* the source and the destinations in an SRX security policy, which makes the Junos operating system different than a lot of other vendors. Make sure you create the address book for the correct zone!

You create an address book called PC1 for a device on the admins LAN as follows:

```
[edit security zones security-zone admins]
root# set address-book address PC1 192.168.2.2
```

If you use this as a destination address book, only this single device will be reachable. If you want to allow access to all devices on the subnet, you can use the following prefix:

```
[edit security zones security-zone admins]
root# set address-book address PC-all 192.168.2.0/24
```

To create multiple address books for a zone and gather them together, use an `address-set`.

For this simple example, you won't establish address books at all. You just specify the addresses as `any` when the time comes.

Configuring services

You dealt with services like ssh and ping on the SRX earlier in this chapter when we dealt with zones. Generally, the security policy will match on the protocol and port in the packet header fields, along with a timeout. The timeout establishes how long the packet is held in the SRX memory before it is purged, if no other packets arrive to match the same security policy. SRX gateways are *stateful* firewalls, which means a session table records the history of host interactions. The stateful aspect helps increase processing speed.

You don't have to configure service parameters. The Junos OS supplies a list of predefined services on the SRX (which is why you configure only ssh or ping, and not everything about the protocol and port). You can see the groups like this:

```
[edit]
root# show groups junos-defaults applications
```

Of course, you can always configure your own service or application parameters. For example, you can match

✔ Source ports in the range from 2000 through 4000

✔ Destination port 1111

✔ Protocol TCP

✔ Timeout 1800 seconds (30 minutes)

You can even configure all these parameters at once as part of an application list called `SERVICE1`:

```
[edit]
root# set applications application SERVICE1 source-port 2000-4000 destination-
      port 1111 protocol tcp inactivity-timeout 1800
```

The configuration looks like this:

```
[edit applications]
application SERVICE1 {
    protocol tcp;
    source-port 2000-4000;
    destination-port 1111;
    inactivity-timeout 1800;
}
```

You can configure as many custom applications as you like. As with address books, you can group the services together with `service-sets`, making it easier to configure security policies. Here's an example for service set `MYSERVICES`, which adds `http` to the preceding custom service:

```
[edit]
root# set applications application-set MYSERVICES application SERVICE1
root# set application application-set http
```

Configuring the security policies

So far, you've configured addresses and applications (services). Now you're ready to configure the security policy itself. (This might seem a roundabout way to configure a security policy, with addresses and service first, but remember that this method allows defined addresses and services to be used in many policies so that if one address or service changes, it must be changed in only one place in order to change it in all policies.)

From the SRX perspective, traffic is always arriving from one zone and making its way to another zone. Technically, these zone crossings are called *contexts*. The context is where the security policies are applied. You have only two zones (`admins` and `untrust`), so there are two intra-zone policy contexts (`admins` to `admins` and `untrust` to `untrust`) and two inter-zone policy contexts (`admins` to `untrust` and `untrust` to `admins`). Not all of them will be configured here.

First, you want to give traffic originating on the `admins` zone permission to pass to the `untrust` zone:

```
[edit]
root# edit security policies from-zone admins to-zone untrust
[edit security policies from-zone amdins to-zone untrust]
root# set policy admins-to-untrust match source-address any destination-address
            any application any
root# set policy admins-to-untrust then permit
root# show
policy admins-to-untrust {
    match {
```

```
        source-address any;
        destination-address any;
        application any;
    }
    then {
        permit;
        }
}
```

Realistically, the policy will probably count the packets and log the session initiations and closes between the zones.

The second goal, which is to build a security policy to permit certain traffic between hosts in the admins zone is easy enough to do, using your service set:

```
[edit security policies from-zone admins to-zone admins]
root# set policy intra-zone-traffic match source-address any destination-address
      any application MYSERVICES
root# set policy intra-zone-traffic then permit
```

The second requirement is now satisfied. No configuration is required for the third point, denying traffic from untrust access to admins. Because "deny" is the default action, the SRX has already taken care of that.

Verifying the policies

The easiest way to verify that the policies are working as expected is to test data traffic. You can also inspect the SRX session table:

```
root# show security flow session
Session ID: 100001782, Policy name: admins-to-untrust/4, Timeout: 1796
  In: 192.168.2.2/4777 --> 216.52.233.201/443;tcp, If: ge-0/0/0.0
  Out: 216.52.233.201/443 --> 192.168.2.2/4777;tcp, If: ge-0/0/2.0
Session ID: 100001790, Policy name: admins-to-untrust/4, Timeout: 1800
  In: 192.168.2.2/4781 --> 216.239.112.126/80;tcp, If: ge-0/0/0.0
  Out: 216.239.112.126/80 --> 192.168.2.2/4781;tcp, If: ge-0/0/2.0
```

In the real world, these policies will perform logging and counting, but remember, these are just examples.

Configuring NAT Source Address Translation

Security services are not the only services supplied by the SRX (although security services are the most vital). You can configure other services, such as NAT source address translation, as well. In essence, NAT should solely be configured to extend the usefulness of IP addresses. NAT does so by substituting one set of packet header address information for another, according to a configured rule.

Some books also consider NAT as a kind of security service. However, NAT is not intended as a security service. Nevertheless, it is also true that disguising the host's real source address (and port!) provides a measure of security not readily available through other means.

By default, the SRX routes packets that pass the security policy tests, but it does not translate the source and destination IP addresses. The packets flowing through the session you established in the previous section demonstrate this point. Note that the In and Out addresses are unchanged as the packets flow to the destination and back.

```
root# show security flow session
Session ID: 100001790, Policy name: admins_to_untrust/4, Timeout: 1800
  In: 192.168.2.2/4781 --> 209.239.112.126/80;tcp, If: ge-0/0/0.0
  Out: 209.239.112.126/80 --> 192.168.2.2/4781;tcp, If: ge-0/0/2.0
...
<output truncated>
```

You can configure NAT to provide this address translation service on the SRX quite easily.

Major NAT options

Three major NAT options are available on the SRX: *source, destination,* and *static.* The first two translate the source or destination addresses based on a pool of addresses, whereas the last option statically maps addresses from one to another (so the servers and network printers have stable, but concealed, addresses).

Once you decide on the NAT option you want, you can adjust other options. In this section, you execute source address translation. Specifically, the available option is a choice between using source-to-egress interface translation or translating the port and IP address (technically, this is NATP — NAT with ports — but NAT people frustratingly tend to just call everything *NAT*).

Figure 12-4 shows the source NAT you configure in this section.

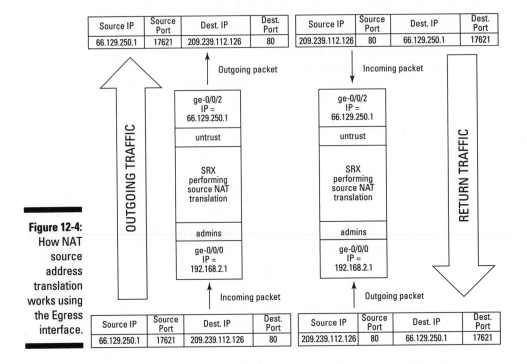

Source IP	Source Port	Dest. IP	Dest. Port
66.129.250.1	17621	209.239.112.126	80

Source IP	Source Port	Dest. IP	Dest. Port
209.239.112.126	80	66.129.250.1	17621

Outgoing packet   Incoming packet

ge-0/0/2
IP =
66.129.250.1

untrust

SRX
performing
source NAT
translation

admins

ge-0/0/0
IP =
192.168.2.1

ge-0/0/2
IP =
66.129.250.1

untrust

SRX
performing
source NAT
translation

admins

ge-0/0/0
IP =
192.168.2.1

OUTGOING TRAFFIC   RETURN TRAFFIC

Incoming packet   Outgoing packet

Source IP	Source Port	Dest. IP	Dest. Port
66.129.250.1	17621	209.239.112.126	80

Source IP	Source Port	Dest. IP	Dest. Port
209.239.112.126	80	66.129.250.1	17621

Figure 12-4: How NAT source address translation works using the Egress interface.

In Figure 12-4, note that in addition to translating the source IP address to the IP address on egress interface ge-0/0/2, the SRX also translates the source port. This is a very common form of NAT that conceals private local IP addresses and ports from the global public Internet.

However, you need to remember that the SRX is not designed to differentiate between a "private" LAN and the "public" Internet. The SRX knows only zones, and these must be configured correctly to supply the NAT service expected. Also, although the NAT rules may look very much like a security policy, the SRX treats the NAT service independently of the security service (the NAT rules are under a separate [edit security nat] hierarchy). This characteristic allows NAT rules to be adjusted without affecting the security policies, but it also requires careful consideration. NAT has nothing to do with whether a packet is accepted; only the security policies can do that.

NAT configuration

NAT can translate addresses in different ways. You can configure rules to apply to traffic to see what kind of NAT should be used in a particular case. You can configure the SRX to perform the following NAT services:

> ✔ Use the IP address of the egress interface.
>
> ✔ Use a pool of addresses for translation.
>
> ✔ Create a rule to exclude certain traffic from the NAT process.

Usually, you will not include the first two services on the same SRX, because they are two different things entirely. So if you do one, you can't do the other at the same time. But you may find reasons to use egress translation on one interface and a pool on another interface.

Configuring source NAT using the Egress interface address

First, you need to create a rule set called `internet-nat` with a distinctive name and establish the context of the traffic you're applying NAT to. In this case, the rule applies to traffic from the `admins` LAN zone to any untrusted zone (`untrust`). You can also specify interfaces or virtual routers, but it's best to think of everything on the SRX in terms of zones.

```
root# edit security nat source rule-set internet-nat
[edit security nat source rule-set internet-nat]
root# set from zone admins
root# set to zone untrust
```

Now, you configure the actual rule (`admins-access`) that matches all the LAN traffic going to any location and applies NAT to the packets:

```
[edit security nat source rule-set internet-nat]
root# edit rule admins-access
[edit security nat source rule-set internet-nat rule admins-access]
root# set match source-address 192.168.2.0/24
root# set match destination-address all
root# set then source-nat interface
```

The last line sets the NAT source translation to the egress interface. Here's what it looks like:

```
[edit security nat]
source {
    rule-set internet-nat {
        from {
            zone admins;
        }
        to {
            zone untrust;
        }
        rule admins-access {
            match {
                source-address 192.168.2.0/24;
                destination-address 0.0.0.0/0;
            }
            then {
```

```
            source-nat interface;
        }
    }
}
```

Configuring a source NAT translation pool

In many cases, the address space allocated to an interface is not sufficient to cover all the addresses in the LAN. If this is the case, it is better to establish a pool of addresses that devices on the LAN can use when they send traffic outside the trusted zone.

To reconfigure the previous example to use a pool of IP addresses, first, you must configure the pool, `public_NAT_range`. Here, you use a small pool of six addresses:

```
[edit security nat source]
root# set pool public_NAT_range address 66.129.250.10 to 66.129.250.15
```

This statement structure lets you change the pools in one place, rather than all over the rule sets. You apply the pool at the `then` level of the NAT hierarchy:

```
[edit security nat source]
root# edit rule-set internet-nat rule admins-access
[edit security nat source rule-set internet-nat rule admins-access]
root# set then source-nat pool public_NAT_range
```

Only one statement really changes, but that makes all the difference:

```
[edit security nat]
source {
    rule-set internet-nat {
        from {
            zone admins;
        }
        to {
            zone untrust;
        }
        rule admins-access {
            match {
                source-address 192.168.2.0/24;
                destination-address 0.0.0.0/0;
            }
            then {
                source-nat pool public_NAT_range;
            }
        }
    }
}
```

Configuring a rule to exclude traffic from NAT

Now, it's time to configure a rule that *excludes* certain traffic from NAT translation. This configuration can be done to allow certain servers (such as a public Web or FTP site) to have public IP addresses on otherwise private LAN address space, but the choice is really up to the network administrator.

Naturally, you need a new rule. This one applies to 192.168.2.2 and is called NO_translate:

```
[edit security nat source rule-set internet-nat]
root# set rule NO_translate
```

Now, you need a match rule and action for the new rule so you can turn NAT off for 192.168.2.2, as shown here:

```
[edit security nat source rule-set internet-nat rule NO_translate]
root# set match source-address 192.168.2.2/32
root# set then source-nat off
```

It might look like you're done, but you're not (and that's one reason we presented things in this particular order).

If you commit this configuration, the SRX continues to translate 192.168.2.2, even though the rule is fine and the SRX should not translate it.

Here's what happened: The order of the rules is established by the order in which they're configured in the CLI. The NO_translate rule was added after you configured the basic admins-access rule, so the NO_translate rule was simply added after the existing admins-access rule. Unfortunately, because admins-access matches the entire LAN address space (192.168.2.0/24), no traffic is left for the NO-translate rule to match!

This is a common policy issue with Junos and is easy enough to fix. One statement puts the rule in the correct order:

```
[edit security nat source rule-set internet-nat]
root# insert rule NO_translate before rule admins-access
```

Always make sure your configured rules are in the proper order to achieve the results you want. As the number of rules grows, the possibility of error grows even faster.

Part IV
Running a Junos Network

The 5th Wave   By Rich Tennant

In this part . . .

You don't get to sit in an airplane cockpit with your scarf in the wind if you don't maintain the plane. You don't get to ride in the Indy 500 without fine-tuning your Formula 1 car. And you don't get to sit at your computer with an outstanding connection to the world and all who work and collaborate with you without enabling policies, services, and protocols par excellence. Take it the extra mile. You've got a Junos network!

Chapter 13

Working with Border Gateway Control

*W*hile interconnecting the routers and other devices in your network is certainly an accomplishment, having your own network without any conduit to the rest of the world is kind of like living on a deserted island. If you want any kind of contact with the rest of the networking world, you need to have some way to talk to people on the mainland. That connectivity between your network island and the mainland Internet is typically provided via the Border Gateway Protocol (BGP).

In this chapter, we introduce you to BGP, describe why and how it is used, and how you can configure and tailor it to suit the specific needs of your network.

An Island of Their Own: Autonomous Systems

Interior Gateway Protocols like OSPF and IS-IS enable you to set up networks and exchange routing information within your network. These IGPs let you create your own network island, which you can interconnect so that they can exchange information. (For more on IGPs, refer to Chapter 10.)

Because these island networks are fully functioning networks, they are completely *autonomous*. Given their autonomy, such networks have been aptly labeled *autonomous systems* (AS). An AS is a set of routers and devices, or even a set of networks, controlled by a single entity.

Because they're all operated by a single entity, these ASs can freely exchange information among all the routers within their boundaries. They can allocate addresses with full knowledge of the rest of the network. Security is important, but less than usual because all the information and traffic is self-contained.

If you wonder why an EGP like BGP is needed along with an IGP, keep in mind that an IGP cares only about routes and destinations within a given AS. BGP basically takes all the routes (prefixes) inside an AS and makes sure that *other* ASs know about them. BGP lets a router in an AS say, "If you get any packets for destination 10.0/16, send them to me! I'll get them to the other AS."

Making AS Connections

An AS cut off from the rest of the Internet is only marginally useful. If you have any need to access the Internet, either to grab information or to use it as a transport to other networks, you must be able to connect outside the AS. These connections are established using peering relationships, where one AS connects to another (a peer) using Border Gateway Protocol (BGP).

To connect ASs to each other and establish a peering relationship, you must configure BGP on both peering routers.

Whereas an IGP like OSPF is easy to configure and works on its own once you enable it, you must explicitly configure BGP. BGP can be rather unwieldy at times, primarily because when you're using BGP, you're connecting to a router outside your control. Therefore, you're likely to want stricter security in terms of the information you make available to your peers as well as what they send to you.

Imagine that you have a simple network with two ASs, each of which has a gateway router, as shown in Figure 13-1. In this figure, notice that you want to connect the two networks using BGP. To establish a connection, BGP requires a little bit of information:

- ✔ **You must identify the AS to which each of the peering routers belongs.** Every AS in the world is uniquely identified by an AS number. These numbers are handed out by the Internet Assigned Numbers Authority (IANA) and are used to specify not only the peering router but also the peering AS for each BGP session.

- ✔ **You must decide on a group for the peering session.** BGP groups everything so that you can have logical sets of connections that all behave more or less the same way.

Imagine, for example, that you have multiple connections between your network and a neighbor network. You may have all the same configuration on these links except that they are between different routers (to provide a redundant link). To simplify the configuration, you group them and call them collectively "Those guys." All configuration for "Those guys" is employed on each individual session within the group.

✔ **You must know the specific IP address of the interface to which you're connecting.** This address is the neighbor address because it's the neighboring interface with which you are peering.

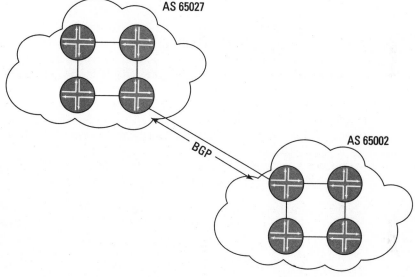

The need for the specific IP address is the reason why BGP is an EGP and not an IGP. While you can use BGP to interconnect all of the routers within your network, the fact that you have to explicitly configure each connection can be a pain. It is far simpler to use a lighter-weight protocol like OSPF and save the heavy-duty protocols for the connections outside your network. When we get to internal BGP (IBGP), you will understand even more why BGP is not well-suited for easily managing connections within your network. (For more on IBGP, see the section, "Configuring BGP," later in this chapter.)

As a general rule and best practice, you want your IGP to carry local and interface routes. You want to leave the heavy lifting for BGP. BGP was built to handle large numbers of routes. IGPs, on the other hand, were designed to reconverge as fast as possible in the event of a failure (link, router, or other type of failure). For more on IGPs, see Chapter 10.

Keep in mind that the other guy must have all the same information as well. For this session to work, both of you have to explicitly configure BGP to each other.

Configuring BGP

The configuration required for BGP to work can be broken into two parts:

- ✔ **A configuration that specifies who you are:** Who you are is really as simple as identifying your AS and specifying the address by which you want to be known. You configure "who you are" by setting your AS under `routing options`:

```
[edit]
routing options {
    autonomous-system 65001;
}
```

A lot of protocols include an address for the router in their exchange of information with other routers. Explicitly configuring the address to be used for this type of communication is generally a good idea so that messages between routers are always clear, making it far easier to troubleshoot things down the road. You should always explicitly configure the router ID:

```
[edit]
routing-options {
    router-id 192.168.14.3
}
```

A common best practice is to have the `router-id` correspond to your loopback interface IP address.

- ✔ **A configuration that establishes a session with your neighbors:** After configuring your own information, you need to set up the BGP session to your external neighbor, as shown in Figure 13-2.

Using the topology in Figure 13-2, configure a BGP session between router 3 to router 5, and vice versa, by working in the `protocols` section of the configuration hierarchy, such as shown here:

```
[edit protocols]
bgp {
    group those-guys {
        type external;
        peer-as 65002;
        neighbor 10.0.26.2;
    }
}
```

All you're doing here is explicitly defining the BGP session that will connect your AS to your peer AS. The neighbor address specified here is the interface address on the peer you're connecting to. The AS number you configure for this peer must match the AS number that the peer configured for itself. Also note that you configured this neighbor as `type external`. This configuration means that the neighbor will be connected via the external flavor of BGP called *E*BGP.

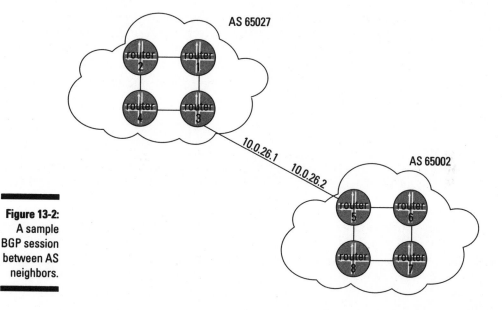

AS 65027

AS 65002

Figure 13-2:
A sample
BGP session
between AS
neighbors.

If you have an external BGP, you also have an internal version of BGP (known as IBGP). Whereas EBGP is configured between routers in different ASs, IBGP is configured between all routers within your internal network. Figure 13-3 shows the network topology.

IBGP allows the routers in the AS that are not the EBGP router to reach external routers. For example, with IBGP running, routers 6, 7, and 8 in AS 65002 know which routes are in AS 65027.

The external BGP (EBGP) session that you created established the connection between your AS and the peering AS. It did not, however, connect all your routers via BGP. You must configure IBGP between your routers. Configuring IBGP is very similar to configuring EBGP. To configure router 3:

```
[edit protocols]
bgp {
group my-guys {
   type internal;
   neighbor 192.168.14.1;
   neighbor 192.168.14.2;
   neighbor 192.168.14.4;
   }
}
```

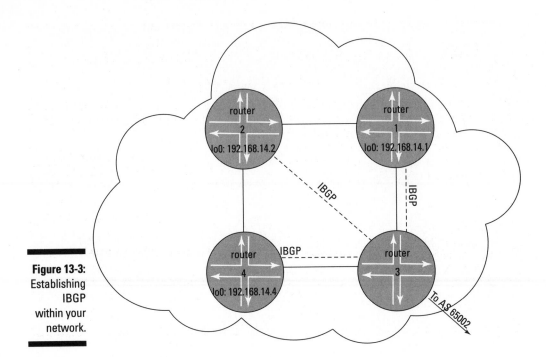

Figure 13-3:
Establishing
IBGP
within your
network.

Notice the type of connection being configured here: type internal. Because these are internal neighbors, JUNOS is intelligent enough to know that the AS number is the same as the AS number configured under the routing-options. Also, notice that you configured three neighbors, but the topology shows that you have only two immediate neighbors. Router 2 is accessible only via the other routers.

This is because IBGP has some restrictions. By default, IBGP can't advertise routes learned via IBGP to other IBGP neighbors (this is a routing loop prevention mechanism). So in Figure 13-2, shown earlier in this chapter, router 4 learns routes via EBGP from router 5. These routes have to be propagated to the rest of your network so that router 2 can send traffic to router 7. Router 4 sends those routes to routers 1 and 3 via the IBGP session between them. Because IBGP cannot re-advertise those routes, it can't share them with router 2.

This kind of information is used to prevent routing loops, which it must do with IBGP and the AS-Path attribute (or lack thereof). The AS-Path attribute is carried inside BGP to advertise the AS numbers that the route has traversed to get to your router. Every time the prefix goes through a new AS, that AS is added to the AS-Path. The AS-Path attribute is modified only when the route traverses EBGP peers.

Noting implementation differences between IOS and Junos OS software

You may have extensive experience implementing BGP in another network operating system. If you're familiar with the Cisco IOS software, for example, you may want to note some differences in implementation between that software and the Junos OS software. It's helpful to know that in BGP configurations, Junos OS software does the following:

✔ By default, disables synchronization and auto-summarization.

✔ By default, enables the sending of communities to BGP peers. (Disable the default by using an export policy to delete communities.)

✔ Uses route preference more so than local preference. (Junos OS software has no concept of weight.)

✔ By default, prefers all BGP-received routes over IGP internal routes. (Modify the default at the protocol, group, or neighbor level, or you can also use an import policy to modify the route preference on a per-route basis.)

✔ By default, enables deterministic MED. (Disable the default if you want the router to mimic the Cisco IOS nondeterministic MED behavior in order to provide compatibility with Cisco IOS routers.)

To get around this "no re-advertise" limitation, IBGP requires a *full mesh* configuration — that is, every router within your network must be configured as an internal peer to every other router in your network, regardless of whether they're physically connected via a link. This reason is why you see router 2 configured as a neighbor to router 3 when they're not physically linked.

BGP is now configured on your router.

Notice that the IBGP neighbor configuration differs slightly from the EBGP neighbor configuration (shown in Figure 13-3) in that the neighbor addresses for IBGP are *loopback addresses*. If a particular interface goes down within your network, the router may still be reachable via other routes provided by your IGP. You don't need to take down the IBGP session in this case. You peer with the loopback addresses because they're always up as long as the box is reachable. With EBGP, however, you generally peer with the interface you're directly connecting through. If that interface goes down, you have no other route to that host. So, in this case, you're better off taking the session down to prevent routing across that link.

Monitoring BGP

Perhaps you sometimes find it hard to tell whether BGP is really working. The key to finding out if the session you configured is established is the show bgp neighbor command, as shown in Listing 13-1.

Listing 13-1: Monitoring BGP with the show bgp neighbor Command

```
mike@router1> show bgp neighbor
Peer: 10.245.245.1+179 AS 200  Local: 10.245.245.3+3770 AS 100
Type: External    State: Established    Flags: <ImportEval Sync>
Last State: OpenConfirm  Last Event: RecvKeepAlive
Last Error: None
Options: <Multihop Preference LocalAddress HoldTime AddressFamily PeerAS
         Rib-group Refresh>
Address families configured: iso-vpn-unicast
Local Address: 10.245.245.3 Holdtime: 90 Preference: 170
Number of flaps: 0
Peer ID: 10.245.245.1     Local ID: 10.245.245.3      Active Holdtime: 90
Keepalive Interval: 30         Peer index: 0
NLRI advertised by peer: iso-vpn-unicast
NLRI for this session: iso-vpn-unicast
Peer supports Refresh capability (2)
Table bgp.isovpn.0 Bit: 10000
RIB State: BGP restart is complete
RIB State: VPN restart is complete
Send state: in sync
Active prefixes:              3
Received prefixes:            3
Suppressed due to damping:    0
Advertised prefixes:          3
Table aaaa.iso.0
RIB State: BGP restart is complete
RIB State: VPN restart is complete
Send state: not advertising
Active prefixes:              3
Received prefixes:            3
Suppressed due to damping:    0
Last traffic (seconds): Received 6    Sent 5  Checked 5
Input messages:  Total 1736   Updates 4    Refreshes 0   Octets 33385
Output messages: Total 1738   Updates 3    Refreshes 0   Octets 33305
Output Queue[0]: 0
Output Queue[1]: 0
```

The show bgp neighbor command shows a lot of information, most of
which isn't terribly relevant most of the time, but you do need to focus on
a couple of important fields in the output, especially when determining
whether a successful connection was established. Here, focus on only the
first four lines of output:

```
mike@router1> show bgp neighbor
Peer: 10.245.245.1+179 AS 200  Local: 10.245.245.3+3770 AS 100
Type: External    State: Established    Flags: <ImportEval Sync>
Last State: OpenConfirm  Last Event: RecvKeepAlive
Last Error: None
```

The basic part of determining whether a peering session is up is to identify the state of the session. In this case, the state is `Established,` which means the BGP configuration worked.

Other possible states include the following:

- ✔ `idle`: This is the starting point for BGP sessions prior to any messages being exchanged. If you see an idle state, you probably just need to wait until BGP begins sending messages.

- ✔ `connect`: `connect` indicates that BGP messages are being exchanged and BGP is waiting for the underlying TCP connection to be established. This state means that things are either in progress or they've stalled on the TCP side of things.

- ✔ `active`: The most misleading of the state names, `active` does not mean that the BGP session is active; it means that BGP is *actively* looking for its peer. A common cause for these types of issues is misconfiguration, so check your AS numbers and make sure that they're configured correctly.

- ✔ **OpenSent** and **OpenConfirm:** These are transition states while BGP is negotiating. If you see these states, just enter the `show bgp neighbor` command a second time and see whether the states have transitioned to `Established`.

Depending on the state value, you can use the peering information at the top of the output in Listing 13-1 to determine whether the peering address and AS number are configured correctly. Remember that the BGP configuration on both sides of the peering session must be correct to establish the session correctly, so if you're having problems, the issue may not reside on your router but with the peer it is trying to connect to.

Knowing why you can't ping

After you set up BGP between the two peering routers and among all your internal peers, similar to the topology shown in Figure 13-4, you may think that you can ping router 7 from router 4, despite the two routers residing in different ASs. Likewise, after the BGP session is up and running, you may be tempted to assume that you've finished configuring your network, but a simple `ping` command to any of the routers in the neighboring AS reveals that none of them are reachable.

Here is why you cannot `ping` from one AS to the other even though BGP is configured to run correctly between them.

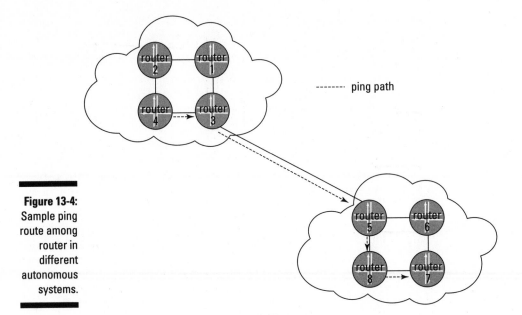

Figure 13-4:
Sample ping
route among
router in
different
autonomous
systems.

BGP differs from IGPs in that, by default, it doesn't share all the information about routes. OSPF's default behavior is to advertise all routes learned by OSPF to all OSPF neighbors and to import all routes learned by OSPF from those same neighbors. BGP, on the other hand, holds on to its routes and only exports them if they were learned through BGP. In this way, IGP routes are not sent to BGP peers.

For a ping between ASs, you must have a route to the destination AS. Examine the routing table in Listing 13-2 to see whether you have a BGP route to that host.

Listing 13-2: Checking a Routing Table for a Ping Route

```
sally@router2> show route
inet.0: 16 destinations, 16 routes (15 active, 0 holddown, 1 hidden)
+ = Active Route, - = Last Active, * = Both

10.5.0.0/16        *[Static/5] 6w0d 00:18:22
to 192.168.71.254 via fxp0.0
10.10.0.0/16       *[Static/5] 6w0d 00:25:57
to 192.168.71.254 via fxp0.0
10.13.10.0/23      *[Static/5] 6w0d 00:18:22
to 192.168.71.254 via fxp0.0
10.84.0.0/16       *[Static/5] 6w0d 00:18:22
to 192.168.71.254 via fxp0.0
10.150.0.0/16      *[Static/5] 6w0d 00:18:22
to 192.168.71.254 via fxp0.0
```

```
10.157.64.0/19     *[Static/5] 6w0d 00:18:22
to 192.168.71.254 via fxp0.0
10.209.0.0/16      *[Static/5] 6w0d 00:18:22
to 192.168.71.254 via fxp0.0
172.16.0.0/12      *[Static/5] 6w0d 00:25:57
to 192.168.71.254 via fxp0.0
192.168.0.0/16     *[Static/5] 6w0d 00:25:57
to 192.168.71.254 via fxp0.0
192.168.40.0/22    *[Static/5] 6w0d 00:18:22
to 192.168.71.254 via fxp0.0
192.168.64.0/21    *[Direct/0] 6w0d 00:25:57
via fxp0.0
192.168.71.246/32  *[Local/0] 6w0d 00:25:57
Local via fxp0.0
192.168.102.0/23   *[Static/5] 6w0d 00:25:57
to 192.168.71.254 via fxp0.0
207.17.136.0/24    *[Static/5] 6w0d 00:25:57
to 192.168.71.254 via fxp0.0
207.17.136.192/32  *[Static/5] 6w0d 00:18:22
to 192.168.71.254 via fxp0.0
```

In Listing 13-2, the interface address for router 5 is not in router 2's route table, meaning there is *no* route to that host, which verifies what you already know: You can't ping that interface.

Another way you can check on the route is to look at the BGP routes and see what route information BGP is sharing. A quick look at the `show route protocol bgp` output reveals that no BGP route exists:

```
user@router4> show route protocol bgp
```

```
inet.0: 16 destinations, 16 routes (15 active, 0 holddown, 1 hidden)
```

The question becomes how do you get BGP routes into the routing table?

Within your own network, the number of routes is relatively small or at least contained. If OSPF floods these routes to all other OSPF-enabled routers, it's probably not a big deal. And even OSPF has the ability to isolate routes through the use of areas to address the possibility of very large networks having tons of route advertisements.

So imagine BGP now. BGP connects networks to networks. If you were to take all the routes from your internal network and advertise them to your peering network, your peering network would have to track both its own internal routes and all of yours. Also, if a peer to your peer were to receive all the routes from both you and your peer — well, you can see this situation would get very bad, very fast.

Therefore, BGP requires you to explicitly state what you want to advertise and to whom. It brings sanity to what would otherwise be a chaotic world full of 220 thousand routes on every router.

Configuring routing policies that advertise routes

Getting BGP routes into the routing table is a matter of advertising. The default behavior of BGP is to accept all loop-free routes learned via BGP. You must configure routing policies to make sure that these routes are propagated through the network. Examine the topology in Figure 13-5.

Each link in the topology is a subnet to which the routers are connected. These subnets are included in the route table as static routes (direct routes, to be more precise: Chapter 5 covers static routes). If you can advertise those subnets to your internal neighbors, you'll have BGP routes to all your internal peers.

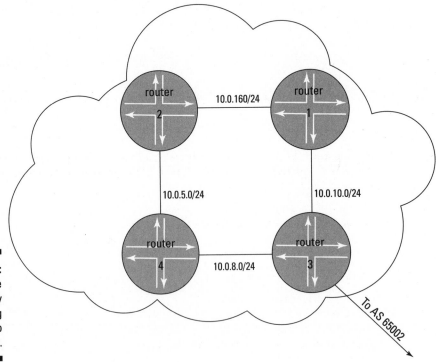

Figure 13-5: Sample topology advertising routes to another AS.

Configuring routing policy requires the definition of the policy and the application of that policy on either the inbound (import) control traffic or the outbound (export) control traffic.

In this case, you want to include static routes, so you use the `accept` action. This policy is named `ibgp-export` and has one term, `export-statics`, that advertises all static addresses with BGP:

```
[edit policy-options]
policy-statement ibgp-export {
    term export-statics {
        from protocol static;
        then accept;
    }
}
```

In this routing policy, you accept all routes that are static. Whether you accept them as you receive protocol control traffic or include them in your outbound protocol control traffic depends on *where* you apply the policy. In this example, you include the routes in your outbound BGP advertisements, so you need to apply the policy as an export policy for your IBGP group:

```
[edit protocols]
bgp {
    group my-guys {
        type internal;
        export ibgp-export;
        neighbor 192.168.14.1;
        neighbor 192.168.14.2;
        neighbor 192.168.14.4;
    }
}
```

Issuing a `show route` command reveals that BGP routes are now in the routing table, as shown in Listing 13-3, which, as you will see, I truncated slightly in order to fit it within these pages.

Listing 13-3: A Routing Table Showing BGP Routes

```
user@router2> show route

inet.0: 16 destinations, 16 routes (15 active, 0 holddown, 1 hidden)
+ = Active Route, - = Last Active, * = Both

192.168.14.1/24    *[BGP/100] 6w0d 01:56:10
to 192.168.14.3 via fe-0/0/0.0
192.168.14.2/24    *[BGP/100] 6w0d 01:56:10
to 192.168.14.3 via fe-0/0/0.0
192.168.14.4/24    *[BGP/100] 6w0d 01:56:10
```

(continued)

Listing 13-3 *(continued)*

```
to 192.168.14.3 via fe-0/0/0.0
192.168.64.0/21    *[Direct/0] 6w0d 02:03:45
via fxp0.0
192.168.71.246/32 *[Local/0] 6w0d 02:03:45
Local via fxp0.0
192.168.102.0/23    *[BGP/100] 6w0d 02:03:45
to 192.168.71.254 via fxp0.0
207.17.136.0/24    *[Static/5] 6w0d 02:03:45
to 192.168.71.254 via fxp0.0
207.17.136.192/32 *[Static/5] 6w0d 01:56:10
to 192.168.71.254 via fxp0.0
…
```

You can identify the BGP routes in Listing 13-3 by the content within brackets. Bracketed content indicates how the route was learned and specifies the local preference. The local preference is used to choose among routes to the same destination prefix. Lowest value wins, so (for example) a static route next hop (local preference 5) is used instead of a BGP (100) next hop (in some cases they share the same next hop, but that is not always true).

The *local preference* is used to decide which route to use if there are two routes to the same destination. For example, if a static route has a local preference of 5, and BGP has a local preference of 100, the router will use the static route because of the higher preference value (lower number).

After configuring the routing policy for your IBGP routers, you must configure the policy for your EBGP router. As it turns out, you can use a very similar policy and apply it on your external group:

```
[edit policy-options]
policy-statement ebgp-export {
    term export-statics {
    from protocol static;
    then accept;
    }
}
```

Now apply it to your external group:

```
[edit protocols]
bgp {
    group those-guys {
        type external;
        export ebgp-export;
        peer-as 65002;
        neighbor 10.0.26.2;
    }
}
```

The application of these two routing policies ensures that routes are shared within your IBGP mesh and that those routes will not be leaked via the EBGP connection between ASs, which is important because you don't want to flood (or, by extension, be flooded by) internal routes into a neighboring network. Issuing a `show route protocol bgp` command on each of the routers should reveal that only the expected routes are included in the route tables.

TIP

Consider setting up an aggregate route to represent your entire set of addresses. For example, if you have a lot of contiguous 192.168.x/24 addresses, configure an aggregate route and filter those routes. (For more details about route filtering, see Chapter 14.)

Using next-hop self

After seeing that the route table appears to have all the necessary routes, you probably now think that you can ping the routers in one AS from the other AS. However, that's not quite the case. Understanding why pinging still doesn't work requires a little explanation of how BGP routes are exchanged, along with a look at Figure 13-6.

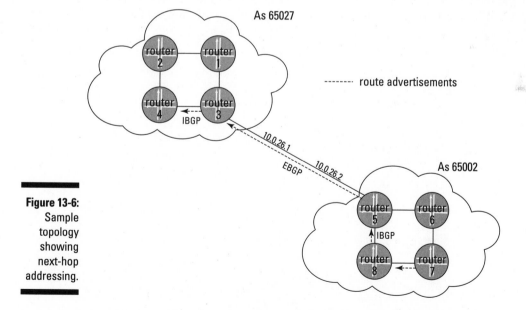

Figure 13-6:
Sample
topology
showing
next-hop
addressing.

When BGP shares a route via BGP messages, it includes next-hop information so that a router knows where to send traffic when forwarding to that particular destination. In Figure 13-5, shown earlier in this chapter, the peers that reside within AS 65502 send their routes through the gateway router 5.

When that route is passed to router 3 via EBGP, the advertisement includes the next-hop information tied to that EBGP link. Specifically, the interface address on router 5 (10.0.26.2) is marked as the next hop.

The problem is that when router 2 wants to send traffic to a peer within AS 65002, router 2 must know where the route 10.0.26.2/24 is. But how does it get this information? That address is not in the local AS 65027! And you really don't want to duplicate all internal addresses in every AS — that's why BGP was invented in the first place.

One easy way to ensure that a router has a route to the next-hop address is to set the next-hop address to one that the router already knows how to reach. The address 10.0.26.2 might not be in AS 65027, but the loopback address for router 3 is. In your AS, the routers all know each other's loopback addresses by virtue of OSPF. OSPF tells IBGP how to reach the loopback interface so that IBGP can establish its BGP session. So, if router 3 can set the next-hop address to one of its own addresses (such as the loopback), overwriting the previous address, then all the routers in your AS will be able to send traffic.

To overwrite the previous next-hop address and use the router's own loopback as the next-hop address, use a routing policy to set `next-hop self`:

```
[edit policy-options]
policy-statement ibgp-export {
    term export-statics {
        from protocol static;
        then accept;
    }
    term next-hop self {
        then {
            next-hop self;
        }
    }
}
```

The addition of a second term accomplishes this task. Routes are evaluated against the first term and accepted if they're static routes. Then those accepted BGP routes have the next-hop value set to the local router loopback address. When those routes are learned by other peers within your network, those peer routers will send traffic to the loopback address of your gateway router, because they know how to reach the loopback address. (The "self" option on router 3 basically says, "Use my loopback address as the next hop when you advertise this route inside AS 65027. Then when routers in AS 65027 have a packet for AS 65002, they send it to me. I have the AS 65005 next hop as 10.0.26.2, so all is well."

The alternative way to solve the problem of next-hop self is to ensure that you have a route to the peering subnet between your AS and the adjacent AS. If you run an IGP, the subnets are automatically advertised through that IGP to all your internal routers. If you run OSPF or another IGP *passively* on that link (meaning that you don't want to establish an adjacency and flood routes there), your routers will learn the 10.0.26.0/24 subnet. In many organizations, next-hop self or IGP passive is the preferred method for BGP next hops.

Pinging to the loopbacks

After you configure both EBGP and IBGP, the routing policies associated with each, and the next-hop information, it would be a shame if you couldn't ping a router in one AS from the other AS.

In Figure 13-7, notice that both router 2 and router 7 are in different ASs, but aren't directly connected. If your BGP configuration is correct, you should be able to find a route to router 7 from router 2.

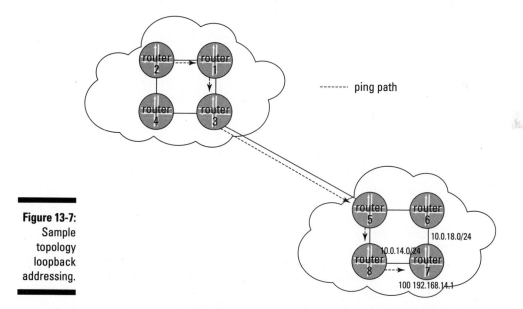

Figure 13-7: Sample topology loopback addressing.

To verify that the two are, in fact, reachable, issue a ping to the remote router, but look what happens when you issue the `ping` command:

```
user@router2> ping 192.168.14.1
PING 192.168.14.1 (192.168.14.1): 56 data bytes
ping: sendto: No route to host
ping: sendto: No route to host
ping: sendto: No route to host
```

Oops! This `ping` command was supposed to work. What happened? Remember that your routing policies were advertising static routes, which were essentially all the directly connected routes. You weren't advertising all the *loopback addresses* of the individual routers. So the routing table on router 2 contains only routes to the subnets connecting all the routers, not routes to all the loopbacks. (Yeah, this inter-AS routing is trickier than it looks . . . but it's all to prevent flooding every route into every AS, big and small.)

If you examine the routing table in Listing 13-4, you will see a route to the subnets for router 7's outbound interfaces. (Note that the routing table is truncated to fit on these pages.)

Listing 13-4:   Routing Table Showing Routes to Loopbacks

```
mike@router2> show route

inet.0: 16 destinations, 16 routes (15 active, 0 holddown, 1 hidden)
+ = Active Route, - = Last Active, * = Both


10.5.0.0/16        *[Static/5] 6w0d 01:56:10
to 192.168.71.254 via fxp0.0
10.0.14.0/24       *[BGP/100] 6w0d 02:03:45
to 192.168.14.1 via fe-0/0/1.0
10.0.18.0/24    *[BGP/100] 6w0d 02:03:45
to 192.168.14.1 via fe-0/0/1.0
...
```

As expected, routes go to the `10.0.14.0/24` subnet and the `10.0.18.0/24` subnet. A ping to either of the interfaces on those subnets should yield results like this:

```
mike@router2> ping 10.0.14.1
PING 10.0.14.1 (10.0.14.1): 56 data bytes
64 bytes from 10.0.14.1: icmp_seq=0 ttl=63 time=0.917 ms
64 bytes from 10.0.14.1: icmp_seq=1 ttl=63 time=0.429 ms
64 bytes from 10.0.14.1: icmp_seq=2 ttl=63 time=0.452 ms
```

In order to ping to the loopback addresses of the routers in the neighboring AS, you must configure a BGP routing policy to export those routes. In this case, you may want to advertise a single route aggregate for all the routes within the AS (see Chapter 14 for more on routing policies).

Configuring Route Reflection

Configuring BGP can be quite onerous, particularly with large numbers of peering sessions that must be configured manually. In fact, in a large network, the full-mesh requirement for IBGP can be a provisioning nightmare.

If you have 10 routers in your network, as shown in Figure 13-8, you have to configure an IBGP session between every pair of routers.

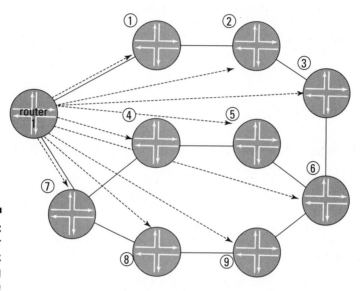

Figure 13-8:
A 10-router network illustrating route reflection.

--------- IBGP Session

Looking at Figure 13-8, you realize that you have to configure a session on each router to each other router. A formula reveals that you have 45 IBGP peering sessions that need configuring — $N*(N-1)/2$, where N is the number of routers in your network.

If you've been wondering why BGP wasn't used universally rather than IGPs, it's because IBGP configuration is difficult to maintain. Adding a single router to your network requires that you touch the configuration of every other router that is already in the network. This task is challenging at best and downright unmanageable for large networks.

BGP's answer to the IBGP pairing configuration nightmare that is the full mesh is called *route reflection*. Route reflection allows sharing of routing information among a group of router without having to send the exact same information to each of them individually. It's sort of like giving information to one person and having them distribute it to all their peers.

Route reflectors on large networks

IBGP comes with a significant restriction: IBGP peers should not re-advertise IBGP-learned routes to other IBGP speakers, which is why they all need to be fully meshed. If you can't re-advertise IBGP routes, you must be directly connected to the originator of the route, hence the full mesh requirement. Remember, IBGP has no dedicated loop prevention mechanism, and this is why you need route reflectors for large networks.

The concept of *route reflection* allows you to designate one or more of your routers as route reflectors. BGP relaxes the re-advertising restriction on these route reflectors, allowing them to accept and propagate IBGP routes to their clients. Figure 13-9 shows a 16-router topology.

Because of the IBGP full-mesh requirement, this topology would require 15 IBGP peering sessions per router, or 120 distinct IBGP sessions within the network. However, if you designate router 4 as a route reflector, you can start to minimize this requirement. For example, look at what happens in Figure 13-10 with the routers directly connected to router 4.

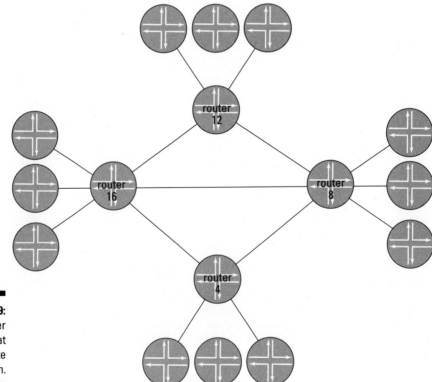

Figure 13-9:
A 16-router network that needs route reflection.

In this part of the topology, router 4 has three directly-connected routers. If just this part of the topology is running IBGP, you have to configure a full mesh between the 4 routers. However, if you designate router 4 as a route reflector, BGP only requires that every route reflector client have an IBGP connection to the route reflector (not to each other), as shown in Figure 13-11.

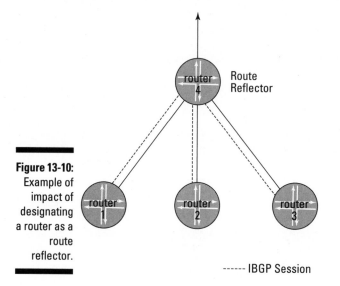

Figure 13-10: Example of impact of designating a router as a route reflector.

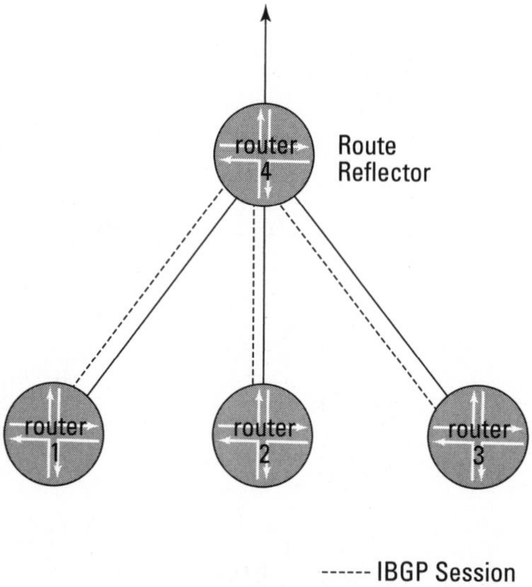

------ IBGP Session

Figure 13-11: Router 4 subnetwork with IBGP sessions and BGP routes.

------ IBGP Session

With the new configuration shown in Figure 13-11, the IBGP routes from routers 1, 2, and 3 are sent to the route reflector. Router 4, acting as the route reflector, re-advertises these routes to all of its clients. In this way, router 1 and router 2 are connected via IBGP, through their shared route reflector, router 4. This group of routers is called a *cluster,* and each cluster is uniquely identified by its *cluster ID* (a 32-bit number similar to an IP address).

Looking back at the original 16-router network, if you make similar route reflectors with routers 8, 12, and 16, you can create four route reflectors and reduce the number of IBGP sessions, as shown in Figure 13-12.

However, all 16 routers are still in the same AS, which means that IBGP has to fully connect all 16 routers. How do you do this?

Ultimately, you must have connectivity somewhere. That connectivity occurs at the route reflector level. The route reflectors must be fully meshed, meaning that you must have IBGP peering sessions between each of the four route reflectors.

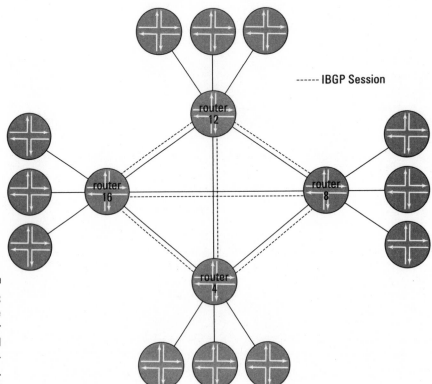

------ IBGP Session

Figure 13-12:
The
16-router
fully meshed
route reflec-
tor network.

Essentially, you have drastically reduced the number of IBGP sessions in your network. Where you previously needed 120 sessions to fully mesh your network, you now need only three sessions from each route reflector to its clients and an additional six sessions to fully mesh the route reflectors (for a total of 18 IBGP sessions).

Route reflector configuration

When you actually set up a router to act as a route reflector, the configuration of route reflectors must happen on both the route reflector and the client. In Figure 13-13, examine router 4's clients.

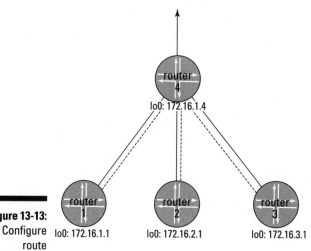

router
4
lo0: 172.16.1.4

router
1
lo0: 172.16.1.1

router
2
lo0: 172.16.2.1

router
3
lo0: 172.16.3.1

Figure 13-13: Configure route reflection in a router.

------ IBGP Session

On the route reflector side, the configuration requires only that you identify the routing cluster for which the router is the reflector:

```
[edit protocols]
bgp {
    group reflector-peers {
        type internal;
        cluster 172.16.1.1;
        neighbor 172.16.2.2;
        neighbor 172.16.3.3;
        neighbor 172.16.4.4;
    }
}
```

The configuration is identical to a normal IBGP configuration except that a cluster ID is specified.

Notice in this configuration that the cluster ID is configured to be identical to the router ID. Use this configuration as a best practice because with it, you can more easily track the originating cluster for routes that are advertised throughout your network.

On the client side, the configuration is identical to previous IBGP configurations except that you now have only a session configured between each client and the route reflector (not between each other):

```
[edit protocols]
bgp {
    group route-reflector {
        type internal;
        neighbor 172.16.1.1;
    }
}
```

Each client to the route reflector will have that route reflector configured as an internal peer.

You still have to configure the routing policy to ensure that routes are advertised as expected. The route reflector doesn't change that requirement. You, however, don't want to configure a next-hop-self policy on your route reflector because you don't want all your externally bound traffic to flow through the route reflectors. You want it to take the shortest path, which isn't generally through the route reflector. The exception to this rule is when the EBGP session from another AS is directly connected to your route reflector.

Dual route reflectors for backup

Basic route reflection is fairly straightforward, but comes with a basic drawback. If you have only a single route reflector and that route reflector fails, your routers will be separated from your network, which means that you inadvertently created a single point of failure for that part of your network. To solve this problem, you can choose to configure dual route reflectors (see Figure 13-14).

In this type of cluster, each client simply configures IBGP connections to both route reflectors. Each of the route reflectors configures its own cluster ID and forms peering relationships with its clients.

The two route reflectors themselves can interconnect in one of two ways: Either they can peer through a straight IBGP connection as per normal IBGP, or you can have each route reflector be a client to the other.

In the case where you have dual route reflectors, consider configuring each of them with exactly the same cluster ID. This configuration reduces the total number of routes that must be stored, and it tends to be far easier to understand when you depict the topology graphically (for example, the cluster has a single ID with two reflectors serving it).

route reflectors

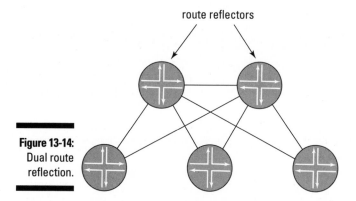

Figure 13-14:
Dual route
reflection.

Chapter 14

Working with Router Policies

In This Chapter

▶ Applying and validating routing policies

▶ Filtering your routes

▶ Aggregating routes

*A*s discussed in Chapter 10, a router gathers location information from routing protocols and stores it in routing tables. These routing tables are then whittled down to include only the best information, and that information is used in the forwarding table, which is ultimately responsible for where traffic is forwarded hop-by-hop through the network.

This assumes, of course, that all the information a router sends and receives is correct. The information learned by the routing protocols could be wrong. You're receiving information from your neighbors, but if your neighbors are doing something you do not want them to do (like sending you traffic that should go somewhere else), you need a way of controlling how information is imported into your router. And on the flip side of the coin, you need a way to prevent your router from doing things that neighboring routers might not like (like sending them a lot of traffic they can't use). Routing policies are the solution to monitoring, filtering, or even modifying what gets into and what comes out of your routing and forwarding tables.

This chapter starts by creating and validating the policies that tell the router what to do with receive routing information, how to use it, and how to pass it on. Then we'll see how you can filter the routes themselves (really, the route's attributes) so that some things can be emphasized and others ignored. Finally, we'll examine aggregate route in more detail and see why they are so helpful.

Constructing Routing Policies

Routing protocols allow routers to exchange information and figure out where every device in the network is located. When a routing protocol like BGP shares information about the BGP routes it knows, these routes are received by your router and stored in the routing table. The *routing table* represents the collective knowledge of all the routing information that your router has (IGPs such as OSPF contribute their share of information, too). And from that repository of routing knowledge, your router selects only the best routes. These best routes are used as the *forwarding table,* which provides the final word on all forwarding decisions.

As shown in Chapter 10, the best route to link-state protocols such as OSPF and IS-IS might be the one with the fewest hops, or the one with the most bandwidth, or the one that follows a multicast topology, and so on. BGP has a bewildering array of *attributes* that you can tweak to influence the AS path that a packet takes through a large network. This chapter is all about controlling the flow of this routing information, especially for BGP.

Routing policies are the constructs designed by administrators to control what goes into and what comes out of the routing table. That is, routing policies act as an inbound filter into the routing table and ultimately determine what information your router shares with other routers through outbound router advertisements. (See Chapter 10 for more information on router advertisements.)

To understand how to configure routing policies, you need to know the basic building blocks and components that make up policies:

✔ Terms

✔ Match conditions

✔ Match actions

✔ Default actions

✔ Application of routing policies

✔ Evaluation of routing policies

The following sections describe these building blocks and components in detail.

Working with terms

The building blocks that make up routing policies are called *terms.* Each term contains match conditions, a series of "if" statements that are compared to the routes under consideration. The match conditions are checked against the routing information. Based on the outcome of those checks, the router will take one or more actions, as illustrated in Figure 14-1. Terms can be strung together to form a routing policy.

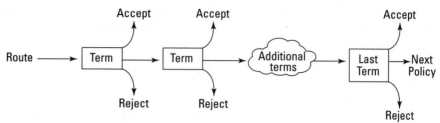

Figure 14-1:
Terms and
actions
needed to
create a
policy.

Assume that you apply a routing policy to filter incoming routing protocol information (most people just say "incoming routes," and that's what we do here). The routing policy is made up of several terms. As the route comes in, the policy is invoked. The first term in the policy is evaluated. If the route matches the conditions specified in the term, some kind of action is taken. If the route doesn't match, the second term in the policy is evaluated. That second term's conditions are checked, and if they match, an action is taken. If they don't match, the third term in the policy is evaluated, and so on until all terms have been examined.

If none of the terms of the policy are a match for the route in question, the next policy is evaluated, and so on until the default policy action is taken. It's important to realize that some default action is _always_ taken unless an earlier match condition applies. (For more information on the default action when there is no match, see the section, "Default actions," later in this chapter.)

To configure a routing policy, you must configure one or more terms within that policy. You handle configuration for policies within the `policy-options` configuration hierarchy:

```
[edit policy-options]
policy-statement my-sample-policy {
    term my-first-term {
        from {
            match-conditions;
        }
        then {
            action;
        }
    }
    term my-second-term {
        from {
            match-conditions;
        }
        then {
            action;
        }
    }
}
```

In this configuration skeleton, you configure a single routing policy called `my-sample-policy`. That policy has two terms, each of which has a match condition and a match action. If a route is evaluated against this policy and neither term matches, the default action is executed. Once an action is taken, the policy is no longer evaluated. So, if you have an action triggered in the first term, the second term never evaluates the second term.

Because the policy chain evaluation stops with any applied action, the *ordering of terms* is crucial to proper policy operation.

Note that we'll use this skeleton to construct some basic routing policies throughout this chapter.

Terms within a policy are evaluated in a top-down manner, so the order of the terms within your configuration counts. The challenge here is that whenever you add a new term to an existing policy, by default, these terms are appended to the terms that are already configured. More recently added terms are always evaluated after the terms initially configured. For example, examine the following policy configuration:

```
[edit policy-options]
policy-statement advertise-ospf-routes {
    term find-ospf {
        from {
            protocol ospf;
        }
        then {
            accept;
        }
    }
}
```

When applied as an input policy, this policy simply accepts all OSPF routes. To fine-tune this policy a little bit and accept all OSPF routes except those that originate from a particular area in your OSPF network, you need to add a term. Because terms are, by default, appended to existing terms, your configuration will be as follows:

```
[edit policy-options]
policy-statement advertise-ospf-routes {
    term find-ospf {
        from {
            protocol ospf;
        }
        then {
            accept;
        }
    }
```

```
        term reject-area-10 {
            from {
                protocol ospf;
                area 10;
            }
            then {
                reject;
            }
        }
    }
```

Here, you want all OSPF routes to be accepted unless they come from area 10. However, when a route comes in, the first term is evaluated. If the route is an OSPF route, it's accepted, regardless of its area of origin. No routes from area 10 are ever rejected, because the first term accepts all OSPF routes.

To add the `reject-area-10` term before the `find-ospf` term, you use the `insert` command. You configure the two terms exactly as you did in the preceding code, but when you're done, you insert the term where you want it:

```
user@host# insert policy-statement advertise-ospf-routes term reject-area-10
      before term find-ospf
```

The `insert` command moves the configuration for the `reject-area-10` term before the configuration to find all OSPF routes. The resulting configuration does what you want:

```
[edit policy-options]
policy-statement advertise-ospf-routes {
    term reject-area-10 {
        from {
            protocol ospf;
            area 10;
        }
        then {
            reject;
        }
    }
    term find-ospf {
        from {
            protocol ospf;
        }
        then {
            accept;
        }
    }
}
```

Match conditions

The whole point of routing policies is to take a particular route (and its corresponding attributes) and match it against some anticipated values. In this context, match conditions form the *if* part of an *if-then* construct. *If* a route matches the condition specified, *then* take some action. The match conditions, therefore, determine what your routing policies can detect.

Okay, so they called it "from-then" rather than "if-then." However, don't think of the *from* as being *received,* because that makes no sense for a routing information *export* policy (the export policy determines what routes will be advertised to neighbors). Think of the policy *from* as *out of all.* So, "from protocol ospf" means "out of all the routes that you look at (learned from OSPF, IS-IS, BGP, and so on) match the OSPF protocol routes only."

There are a number of match conditions, but only a subset of all the different conditions are typically used. Table 14-1 lists some of the more common match conditions. We'll look at only a few in detail.

Table 14-1	JUNOS Routing Policy Match Conditions	
Summary	*Configuration Keyword*	*Description*
Route metric	`metric`	Corresponds to the metric value associated with the route.
Route preference	`preference`	Matches on the route preference.
Interface name	`interface`	Identifies the interface through which a route was received.
Neighbor address	`neighbor`	Typically the peer from which a route was received.
Protocol	`protocol`	Typically the name of the protocol from which a route was learned.
Area ID	`area`	For OSPF routes, identifies the area from which a route was learned.
AS Path	`as-path`	For BGP routes, identifies the AS path associated with a particular route.

It's not enough to know what the match conditions are — you must also know how they're oriented. Routes can be evaluated based on where they come from as well as where they're going. For example, you can match on all routes that are learned through a particular neighbor or on all routes being exported to a particular neighbor.

To configure a match condition, you use the `from` keyword:

```
[edit policy-options]
policy-statement my-sample-policy {
    term my-first-term {
        from {
            protocol ospf;
        }
        then {
            action;
        }
    term my-second-term {
        from {
            neighbor 10.22.32.1;
        }
        then {
            action;
        }
}
```

In the preceding configuration, a routing policy skeleton contains a pair of match conditions. Read "from protocol ospf" as "out of all the routes, match the OSPF routes" and "from neighbor `10.22.32.1`" as "out of all the routes, match the routes learned from device `10.22.32.1`." If the first condition is met, then some action (yet to be specified) is taken. If it doesn't match, the second term is evaluated.

This last configuration is actually a little different than what you'll see on the router. Because you have only a single match condition, the router simplifies the configuration and collapses multiple lines into one, omitting the brackets:

```
[edit policy-options]
policy-statement my-sample-policy {
    term my-first-term {
        from protocol ospf;
        then {
            action;
        }
    term my-second-term {
        from neighbor 10.22.32.1;
        then {
            action;
        }
}
```

The preceding configuration is identical in meaning to the previous `my-sample-policy`, but it's streamlined a bit and matches what you'll see in the configuration file if you issue a `show configuration` command after creating the policy.

Applying a routing policy to all traffic

At times, you may want a routing policy to apply to all routing protocol traffic regardless of the match condition. That is, you need to "match all routes." In these cases, all you need to do is omit the `from` statement within the policy. If there is no `from` statement, Junos OS applies the match action to all traffic:

```
[edit policy-options]
policy-statement accept-all-routes {
```

```
   term accept-all {
      then accept;
   }
}
```

In this case, because there is nothing to match against, all routing protocol traffic is subject to the specified action. In this case, all routes are accepted for import or export, depending on how you apply the policy.

Match actions

Whereas the match conditions are the IF, the match *actions* are the THEN. (At least they called it THEN and not TO, or something even less intuitive.) When a particular match condition is met, the action associated with that term is executed. Table 14-2 lists the actions you can choose from.

Table 14-2	JUNOS Routing Policy Match Actions
Action	*Description*
accept	Accept or advertise the route.
reject	Reject or suppress the route.
next-term	Stop evaluating the current term in the policy and immediately go to the next term. In this case, no terminating action is executed, but all other actions are executed (meaning a route can be modified before passing to the next term).
next-policy	Stop evaluating the current term in the policy and immediately move to the next policy. In this case, no terminating action is executed, but all other actions are executed (exactly as the previous action).
modify	Several modifying actions manipulate values in the route, such as as-path, metric, preference, and so on. These actions are not terminating actions. The specified route attribute is modified as configured, and then any other match actions are executed (if more than one is configured for that particular term). If there are no terminating actions, the next term is evaluated (if one exists).
trace	Log the match to a trace file. This is useful for debugging routing policy.

About 95 percent of the time (if not more), you'll be able to do what you want using only `accept` and `reject`. These actions are called *terminating actions*, because when they're executed, the routing policy evaluation stops, and the decision about the route is made. You don't need to continue evaluating other terms in the policy or other policies in the chain.

Actions such as `next-term` and `next-policy` provide some sophisticated flow control capabilities, but you probably will not need them right away. (In fact, in many cases they just complicate figuring out exactly what the policy will do when you turn the policy loose.) Additionally, unless you're a service provider, modifying route attributes is probably not something you want to deal with. Although you can do some interesting things by modifying route attributes, such constructs are more widely used in carrier networks.

If match actions form the THEN part of the IF-THEN statement, it probably makes sense to configure them using the `then` statement within a policy:

```
[edit policy-options]
policy-statement my-sample-policy {
   term my-first-term {
      from protocol ospf;
      then accept;
   term my-second-term {
      from neighbor 10.22.32.1;
      then reject;
   }
}
```

Specifying multiple match conditions

If you specify multiple match conditions, the conditions act as a logical AND statement. For a route to be a match against the conditions, that route has to match all the conditions specified. For example, if you want to match on all routes learned through OSPF that had a metric of 20 ("out of all the routes, match those that were learned by OSPF and have a metric of 20"), you can use the following:

```
[edit policy-options]
policy-statement my-sample-policy {
   term my-first-term {
      from {
         protocol ospf;
         metric 20;
      }
      then {
         action;
      }
   }
}
```

Specifying more than one match action

As with match conditions, you can specify more than one match action. For example, you may want to modify a route metric so that it becomes the preferred route, and then you want to accept that route. In this case, you need both a modifying action and the accept terminating action. This configuration is as follows:

```
[edit policy-options]
policy-statement my-sample-policy {
    term my-first-term {
        from protocol ospf;
```

```
    then {
        metric 5;
        accept;
    }
  }
}
```

In this example, you match on all OSPF routes. Before accepting the route, you set the route metric to 5 (why it isn't "modify metric 5" is a mystery). Both match actions are executed in this case.

Notice that, just like with the match conditions, the configuration is collapsed when you have a single match action. In this example, the first term is evaluated. If the route is an OSPF route, the route is accepted. If the route isn't an OSPF route, the second term is evaluated. If the route has been learned from the neighbor 10.22.32.1, the route is rejected.

Note that this latest my-sample-policy does *not* reject OSPF routes learned from 10.22.32.1. The first term accepts all OSPF routes and the second one rejects everything learned from 10.22.32.1. Match conditions in the same term are evaluated as a logical AND, but policy terms are evaluated more like a logical OR in the order encountered. If you want something special to happen to OSPF routes learned from 10.22.32.1, this is *not* the way to do it. If you're now confused, at least you understand how delicate routing policy formulation can be.

Default actions

What if none of the terms in a match condition match? Examine this policy:

```
[edit policy-options]
policy-statement my-sample-policy {
    term my-first-term {
        from protocol bgp;
        then accept;
    }
}
```

In this example, if the route was learned via BGP, it's accepted. However, if you assume the route is rejected if it's not learned via BGP . . . well, you'd be wrong.

If a route doesn't match any of the configured terms, a *default action* is taken. The question becomes, "What is the default action?"

And as with any complex topic, the answer is, "It depends." The default action depends on where the routing policy is applied and what protocol is involved in the routing information.

Each routing protocol has its own default policy, so the default action depends on which protocol (or protocols) the policy is applied to. The default action also depends on whether the policy is applied to routes being imported (brought into the routing table) or exported (advertised from the routing table). Table 14-3 summarizes the default actions tied to some routing protocols.

Table 14-3	JUNOS Routing Policy Default Actions
Protocol	*Default Action*
RIP	Import: Accept all routes received on RIP-enabled interfaces. Export: Do not export any RIP routes.
OSPF	Import: Policies can't be used for imported routes. Export: Export all routes learned via OSPF and all direct routes associated with the OSPF-enabled interfaces.
BGP	Import: Accept all routes learned from BGP neighbors. Export: Export all active routes learned via BGP to all BGP neighbors.

Notice that the default action can only be `accept` (allow/advertise) or `reject` (disallow/suppress). The default action must be a terminating action to ensure that all routes reach some definitive conclusion. That is, all routes are eventually either accepted or rejected (this is a good thing).

Application of policies

The combination of two facts determines how a routing policy is applied:

✔ Policies are associated with routing protocols.

✔ Policies control either what is *imported into* or what is *exported out of* (advertised from) the routing table.

For example, assume that you want to apply a routing policy to advertise the routes the device learned from BGP with OSPF. (Use this policy carefully! BGP routing tables with all Internet routes can be huge!) Your first policy configuration might look like this:

```
[edit policy-options]
policy-statement my-sample-policy {
    term my-first-term {
        from protocol bgp;
        then accept;
    }
}


[edit protocols]
ospf {
    export my-sample-policy;
}
```

The policy now begins to take on some meaning. In fact, all policies just sort of sit there until you apply them somehow to a routing protocol. By applying the policy as an export policy for OSPF, you're saying that you'll advertise via OSPF all routes learned through BGP.

Import policies and OSPF

The reason you can't create import policies for OSPF (or IS-IS for that matter) is that OSPF is a *link-state protocol*, as mentioned in Chapter 10. Link-state protocols work by ensuring that every node within the network shares the exact same view of the link-state database. If you were to modify or filter inbound routes, you'd create a local copy of the link-state database that wouldn't necessarily match the shared view of the database. If the databases aren't identical, you can't be sure that you've avoided putting routing loops in the topology.

If a route doesn't match any of the terms' conditions, the default action will kick in. Because this default action is dependent on the routing protocol and direction (either received or advertised routing information), it can be less than obvious what will happen to routes that don't match your criteria. To avoid confusion, you can explicitly configure a final action that will be executed if a route doesn't match any of your terms:

```
[edit policy-options]
policy-statement my-sample-policy {
    term my-first-term {
        from protocol static;
        then accept;
    term my-second-term {
        from neighbor 10.22.32.1;
        then reject;
    }
    then reject;
}
```

In this example, a final action is configured to reject all routes. If a route doesn't match any of the terms, the final action is evoked, and the route is rejected. This final action is evaluated before the default action for whatever protocol this policy is applied against. So now you can clearly specify what default action to take without worrying about whether the policy is applied to OSPF or BGP traffic, to inbound or to outbound routes. Note that the final action is not bound to a specific term, but the policy itself, so the final action applies to all routes that do not match any of the terms.

If the route is not learned via BGP, it is not automatically rejected. If the route doesn't match the term's conditions, the route is subjected to the default action. Because the policy is applied to OSPF, the default export behavior is to accept all routes learned via OSPF. If you're not sure about the default action in a specific case, refer to Table 14-3. This behavior means that an OSPF route, even though it doesn't match the term, will be accepted because of the default action.

To apply the same policy to explicitly import all received BGP routing information into your routing table, you simply change how the policy is applied:

```
[edit protocols]
bgp {
    import my-sample-policy;
}
```

By changing only how the policy is applied, the entire meaning of the policy is altered.

When you're creating policies, don't get too wrapped up in the words "accept" and "reject." Accept doesn't necessarily mean that your routing table will be accepting the routes: When applied as an export policy, you're advertising the routes. Conversely, reject doesn't imply that your routing table will be rejecting routes: When applied as an export policy, reject will suppress the route, but not make it disappear from your router. The behavior depends on whether the routing policy is applied on the inbound side (as an import policy) or on the outbound side (as an export policy).

Evaluation of routing policies

When constructing routing policies, you need to understand how they're evaluated. Multiple policies strung together are called a *policy chain*. Figure 14-2 depicts the basic flow for policy evaluation in a policy chain.

Figure 14-2: The flow for policy evaluation in a policy chain.

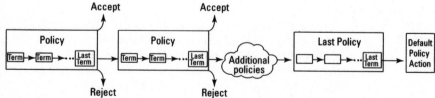

Just as with policy terms, the order of policy configuration makes a difference. As a route comes in, it's evaluated against the first policy in the chain. The match criteria in the first term in the first policy are checked. If a match occurs, the corresponding match action is taken. If no match exists, the second term is evaluated, and so on. If there is no next term in the policy, the next policy in the chain is evaluated. If there are no matches in any of that policy's terms, the evaluation continues until no policies are remaining, at which point the default action is taken.

Configuring Route Filters

The fundamental purpose of routing policies is to prevent certain routes from being either accepted into your routing table or advertised to some adjacent router. Sometimes, matching specific routes or a set of routes is useful. To do so, you use a *route filter*.

Route filters match on specific IP addresses or ranges of prefixes. Much like other routing policies, they include some match criteria and then a corresponding match action. The basic configuration resembles the following:

```
[edit policy-options]
policy-statement my-route-filter {
    term router-filter-term {
        from {
            router-filter prefix/prefix-length match-type;
        }
        then {
            actions;
        }
    }
}
```

This basic configuration outline matches a route against the specified filter. If the route matches, the defined action is taken. If it doesn't, the next term or policy is evaluated. As with other policies, if no match occurs, the protocol default action executes.

An important difference between route filters and other policy match conditions is how multiple filters are handled. If you have more than one match condition, the conditions are treated as a logical AND, meaning all of them must be true for it to be considered a match. With route filters, the presence of multiple filters represents a logical OR, meaning it's a match if the route matches any of the configured filters.

Prefixes and prefix lengths

If you want to effectively create route filters, you need to make sure that you understand *route prefixes* and *prefix lengths*. An IPv4 address in dotted decimal notation is really just a shorthand way of representing a 32-bit address. For example, the address 192.168.32.4 represents the following 32-bit address:

```
11000000 10101000 00100000 00000100
```

So, when you add a prefix length to this IP address, you're specifying the number of significant digits in the expanded 32-bit address to include. If you want to match a prefix length of 24 (192.168.32/24, for example), you're really identifying the first three octets in the address. Usually, the prefix covers the network address portion of the IP address (the rest of the bits form the host address), but not always. The fewer bits the prefix includes, the more network addresses that are covered. A prefix like 10/8 covers more than 16 million networks, whereas 192.168.32/24 covers only 254.

For more descriptions of how IPv4 addressing works in a router, see Chapter 10.

Match types

The combination of a route prefix and prefix length along with the type of match determines how route filters are evaluated against incoming routes. Table 14-4 shows the half-dozen match types to be aware of.

Table 14-4	JUNOS Route Filter Match Types
Match Type	*Description*
Exact	Matches if the prefix-length is equal to the route's prefix length.
Orlonger	Matches if the prefix-length is equal to or greater than the route's prefix length.
Longer	Matches if the prefix-length is greater than the route's prefix length.
Upto	Matches if the route shares the most significant bits in the prefix-length and the route's prefix length falls between the prefix-length and the configured upper limit.
prefix-length-range	Matches if the route shares the most significant bits in the prefix-length and the route's prefix length falls within the specified range.
Through	Route falls between the lower prefix/prefix-length and the upper prefix/prefix-length.

In Figure 14-3, each tree represents a set of addresses. For this particular picture, the top node within each tree represents the address 192.168/16 (about 66,000 network routes). Each set of nodes below the top node represents longer prefix lengths. In other words, as you traverse downward on the tree, the addresses become more specific. (More significant bits are specified.)

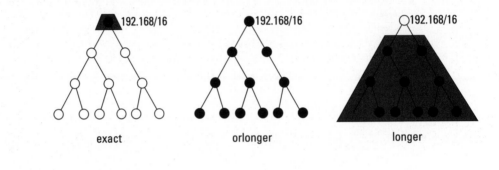

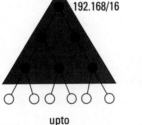
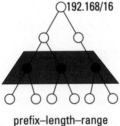
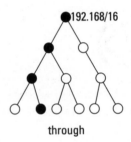

Figure 14-3: A topology showing the different types of matches.

Here's what the different match types mean:

- ✔ The exact match type means that only a route with the same prefix and same prefix length will match. It has to be an exact match, so only the 192.168/16 route is highlighted.

- ✔ The orlonger match indicates that any route that starts with 192.168 and has a prefix length of 16 or greater will match. In other words, any route that is more specific than 192.168/16 is a match, which is why all the routes are highlighted.

- ✔ The longer match type is the same as the orlonger match type, except that it doesn't include any exact matches. So the only difference is that the top node isn't included.

- ✔ If you use the upto match type, you must specify the upper limit for the prefix-length. For example, you'd configure 192.168/16 upto /24 to highlight all the addresses between 192.168/16 and 192.168/24.

✔ The `prefix-length-range` match type allows you to specify the significant bits of an address and then bound addresses with those significant bits between two prefix lengths. In this case, you can ensure that all addresses begin with 192.168, but you want to match only on addresses that have prefix lengths between 20 and 24.

✔ The final match type is `through`. This match type essentially creates a list of exact matches between the starting node and the ending address. All addresses between the two are considered matches. The term `0/0 through 0/32` covers every possible all-0 network address (usually, you'd want to reject these bogus address forms).

Match actions

The match actions available to route filters are identical to those available for other routing policies. You can accept routes, reject routes, modify attributes that belong to a route, or perform flow control type functions. By far, the most common actions to use with route filters are `accept` and `reject`.

Typically, you want to block bad routes and advertise good routes, which you do using `accept` and `reject`.

Once you know how to construct a route filter, you need to know the routes you want to filter. Although you may not want some routes for any number of reasons, nobody wants the following routes in their routing tables:

✔ `0.0.0.0/0`: Nobody wants the default route advertised through their network. Advertising that route can change the default route for all routers that accepted the advertisement.

✔ `127/8`: Don't route traffic to local loopback addresses, which is an internal address and not a next hop.

✔ `1/8, 2/8, 5/8, 7/8`, and `23/8`: The addresses in these ranges haven't been allocated by IANA (the organization that hands out IP addresses to Internet users). Because they shouldn't be in use, you need to filter them.

Routes that should never be present in any routing table have taken on an interesting name. These types of routes are called *Martian addresses*, perhaps because they're "out of this world." The Junos OS software has a set of Martian addresses that are automatically blocked from appearing in your routing table:

✔ `0.0.0.0/8`

✔ `127.0.0.0/8`

✔ `128.0.0.0/16`

✔ 191.255.0.0/16

✔ 192.0.0.0/24

✔ 223.255.255.0/24

✔ 240.0.0.0/4

If you want to configure your router so that it doesn't accept these unallocated routes, you need to create the route filter and then apply it to your protocols. Here's how you create the filter:

```
[edit policy-options]
policy-statement filter-unwanted-routes {
    term bad-routes {
        from {
            route-filter 1.0.0.0/8 orlonger;
            route-filter 2.0.0.0/8 orlonger;
            route-filter 5.0.0.0/8 orlonger;
            route-filter 7.0.0.0/8 orlonger;
            route-filter 23.0.0.0/8 orlonger;
        }
        then reject;
    }
}
```

In this example, you specify the routes that you want to make sure never get into your routing table. Notice that the default route and loopback routes aren't included in this list because they're considered Martian routes and are blocked by default. Also, it's worth noting that 0.0.0.0/8 doesn't include the default route (0.0.0.0/0). Additionally, you can add or delete routes from the Martian table as needed. (But do so at your own peril — if things go wrong, who's going the check the Martian table first?)

Now you must apply this policy to your router. Because you're trying to prevent your router from importing these known "bad" routes from your neighboring routers, you want an import policy.

You can't apply import policies to OSPF or IS-IS, but you usually have a great deal of control over an IGP. BGP routes, which come from another AS, are another story. You want to apply the policy as an import policy for your BGP routes:

```
[edit protocols]
bgp {
    import filter-unwanted-routes;
}
```

Reserved addresses

A number of reserved address ranges are used for internal or "private" addressing. RFC 1918 defines these addresses:

✔ 10/8

✔ 172.16/12

✔ 192.168/16

These addresses are reserved, and you should not be receiving route advertisements from other networks containing them. However, they're not automatically filtered because you'll likely want to use these addresses to address your own gear. (And without them, writing books like this would be a lot harder!)

It does make sense, though, to ensure that your peering networks aren't advertising these addresses to you and that you're not sharing these addresses unintentionally with them — so you should configure route filters on the border routers that peer with other networks. Configure a single policy to reject these routes and apply that policy as both an import and export policy with your external BGP peers:

```
[edit protocols]
bgp {
    group external-peers {
        import filter-reserved-addresses;
        export filter-reserved-addresses;
    }
}
```

Now, this policy will neither accept nor advertise unwanted routes. Being a good network citizen and policing your own actions is generally a good thing.

Configuring an Aggregate Route

As the number of devices connected to the Internet grows so, too, does the number of IP addresses assigned to those devices. And the more IP addresses, the more routes your router must maintain. Even worse, as the number of routes increases, so does the time it takes to look up next-hop values. Transit time for traffic is dependent, at least in part, on the number of routes that are in each router's routing table. For example, examine Figure 14-4's topology of interconnected networks.

In Figure 14-4, notice the depiction of three separate networks. Each network has been allocated a /16 prefix. A /16 prefix equates to 2^{16} different addresses ($2^{16} = 65,535$). So, if the entire Internet were to include only these three networks, each device would require 3×2^{16} routes in its routing table, a large amount of stored data, not to mention the huge amount of time it would take to look up next hops.

You might think that every device in AS 3 needs a route to every device on AS 17. Everything has to go through the one border router in the figure anyway. It is sufficient to provide a route only to the border router for AS 3, which sends the traffic to AS 17, and the border router in AS 17 knows how to route within its own domain.

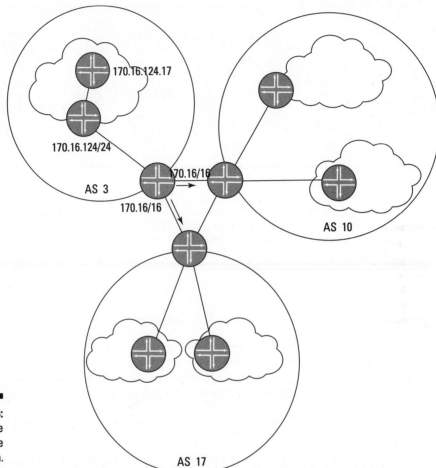

Figure 14-4:
An example
of route
aggregation.

In fact, if the gateway router for AS 3 advertises only a summary of all the routes that fall within its domain, the number of routes it needs to advertise could be reduced from 2^{16} to 1. As that route is propagated through the rest of the Internet, each device that wants to send traffic to a device in AS 3 needs to know only how to get to the border or gateway router.

This type of route summarization is called *route aggregation*. And if everyone plays nicely, the overall size of routing tables can remain relatively small, even when the total number of devices is quite large.

Aggregate routes must first be configured, and then they must be advertised. Examine the aggregate route shown in Figure 14-5.

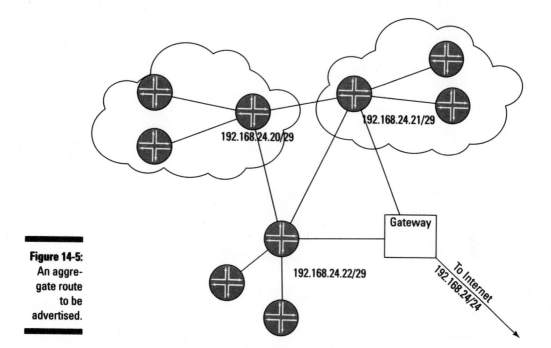

Figure 14-5:
An aggre-
gate route
to be
advertised.

If Figure 14-5 were your network, you'd want to configure an aggregate route on the gateway router and advertise that route to your peering network. In this case, the aggregate route is 192.168.24/24.

To configure this aggregate route, simply identify it as an aggregate within the `routing-options` hierarchy:

```
[edit routing-options]
aggregate {
    192.168.24.0/24;
}
```

Now all you have to do is advertise this route to your neighbor. Route advertisements are controlled through routing policy, of course. You're peering with your neighbor through a BGP connection, and because it's an advertisement, you want an export policy:

```
[edit policy-options]
policy-statement advertise-aggregate {
    term find-aggregate {
        from protocol aggregate;
        then accept;
    }
}
```

```
[edit protocols']
bgp {
    export advertise-aggregates;
}
```

This policy matches and accepts all aggregate routes. The policy is applied as an export policy, which means that BGP will send these aggregate routes to all BGP peers.

Here's another way to look at it. Suppose that you had to route packages to each of the fifty states in the United States. There are ten of you all together. You have to tell the others what states you can reach. And you realize that all of your states begin with the letter M: Minnesota, Michigan, and so on. In fact, you have all of those states, and none starting with any other states. If it takes five minutes to write to each other "router," you could send "I know how to reach Michigan. Send anything for Michigan over here!" and "I know how to reach Massachusetts. Send anything for Massachusetts over here!" and so on. Or you could just create a single aggregate route and say "Anything with an M, send it here!" That's the power of an aggregate.

Chapter 15

Enabling Class of Service

In a basic IP network, all traffic is treated the exact same way. Packets and frames come into your routers and switches, and packets and frames go out of your routers and switches. It really doesn't matter what kind of packets or frames they are or what their transport requirements are.

As you see in this chapter, you can use *class of service* to group similar types of traffic into classes and treat each class of traffic in a specific way, granting preference to traffic that is less tolerant to jitter, delay, and packet loss. Essentially, class of service lets you determine which traffic in your network is a first class passenger and which traffic has to ride economy.

It was once common in networking to call the provision of service levels on a network Quality of Service (QOS or QoS). This implied that applications could tell the network almost any value they needed: a delay of 25 milliseconds or 26 milliseconds. To keep things simpler, service providers established fixed services *classes* such as "best effort," "voice," or "gold," and called this practice COS or CoS. However, now with mobility, in spite of the popularity of classes, the term QoS seems to be making a comeback.

Because service classification is more commonly understood and performed at the packet level, this chapter considers how routers use class of service (CoS). It's not that other types of devices don't use CoS at the frame or message level, but we don't have the time or space to talk about all of those, too.

Knowing What Pieces a COS Configuration Requires

The basic idea behind CoS is that you examine traffic entering your network to determine what type of traffic it is. Once you know the type of traffic (voice traffic, data traffic, traffic tied to a particular customer, and so on), you can mark that traffic at the packet layer accordingly. As those packets flow through your network, each router can then identify the traffic and make decisions on how to handle it based on its type. In this manner, all of your delay-sensitive traffic can be forwarded faster, or your critical traffic may be less likely to be dropped in times of congestion.

CoS is how you control jitter and delay in your network. In this chapter, we explain exactly what jitter and delay are, beginning with the following definitions:

- *Jitter* is the variation in delay over time. The primary contributor to jitter is the variability of queuing/scheduling delay over time.

- *Propagation delay* is the time it takes for signals to traverse a link — basically the speed of light.

- *Switching delay* is the time difference between receiving a packet on an incoming interface and the queuing of the packet in the scheduler of its outbound interface.

- *Serialization delay* is the time taken to clock a packet onto a link.

- *Scheduling/queuing delay* is the time difference between enqueueing the packet of the outbound interface scheduler and the start of clocking the packet onto the outbound link.

Figure 15-1 shows the different components that make up a CoS implementation on a Junos OS router.

Here is what each component does:

- **Classifier.** A *classifier* examines incoming traffic and assigns a *forwarding class* and *loss priority* based on one or more fields in the packet header. These forwarding classes are then assigned to input *queues*.

- **Policers.** Input *policers* ensure that the incoming bandwidth for each traffic flow is within its configured constraints. If a particular traffic flow exceeds its allocated bandwidth, the router can drop the packets within the flow or mark it such that it's eligible to be discarded should congestion occur. If a traffic flow violates the bandwidth set for it, everything that is in violation does not go into another queue, because this practice could lead to out-of-order packets. Instead, you have the option to drop the traffic or tag it so that it can be dropped, if necessary.

✔ **Scheduler.** On the outbound side of the equation, flows are assigned to output queues. These queues are serviced by the router based on how they're mapped to a *scheduler*. The scheduler basically dictates which queues get preferential treatment and which queues are forced to wait before they're serviced.

✔ **Drop profile.** As these queues fill up, they may still overflow. If a queue overflows, packets are dropped as per the configured *drop profile*.

✔ **Router rewrite.** When the packet is ready to exit the router and head to the next hop along the way to its destination, the router can *rewrite* the bits in the header associated with CoS so that the next router can examine the header and process the packet based on a new set of CoS rules.

This entire description isn't meant to describe how CoS works; instead, it's meant to give you an idea of what pieces are required within a CoS configuration so that you can better understand each of them as they're described in a bit more detail in the following sections.

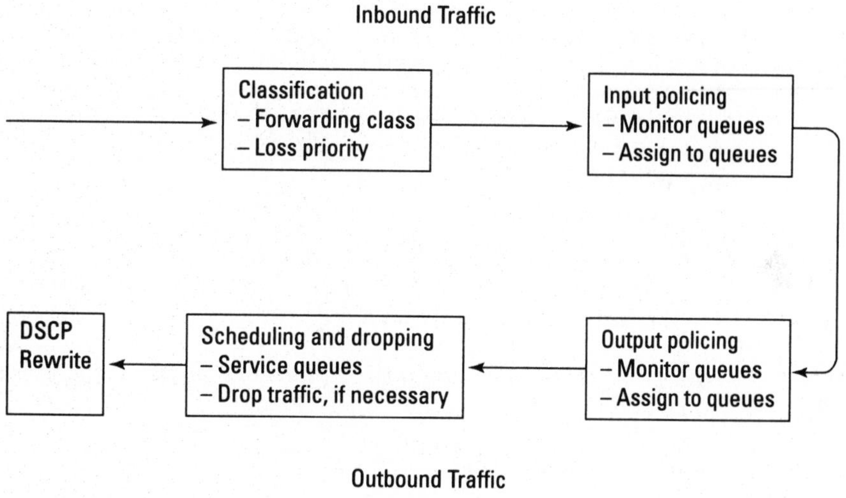

Inbound Traffic

Figure 15-1: CoS flow on a router.

Outbound Traffic

Classifying Inbound Traffic

If your router is going to examine packets to figure out whether they're first-class passengers or regular economy-class passengers, you have to know where in the packet this information is stored. There are two fundamental ways to classify traffic, depending on how you set up your network:

✔ Assume that all CoS settings in a packet are correctly set to conform to your network's CoS implementation, in which case you need only look at the CoS values in the packet's header.

✔ Assume that the packet's CoS settings aren't set in accordance with your network's CoS implementation, in which case you need another way to determine what type of traffic the packet is carrying.

For example, look at Figure 15-2, a typical edge-core network for a couple of different areas of primary concern when it comes to CoS.

At your network's core, traffic is being passed from routers you control to other routers you control. In this case, you can be fairly certain that the configuration on those boxes will conform to whatever CoS rules you've established within your network. So when you classify traffic, you basically need to look only at CoS values that you've set within a packet's headers. This type of classification is known as *behavior aggregate (BA) classification*.

At the edge of your network, traffic is coming to your routers from devices that you don't control. It's anybody's guess how the CoS values are set. Although it would be nice to imagine a world where everyone classified traffic the same way, the reality is that this uniformity is seldom the case. In this scenario, you may want to classify the traffic based on where it came from, not solely on the CoS values in a packet's headers. So, in this case, you need to look at more than just the CoS field; you need to look at the source and destination address of the packet, or maybe the source and destination ports. This type of classification requires looking at multiple fields within the packet header, so it has been aptly labeled *multifield (MF) classification*.

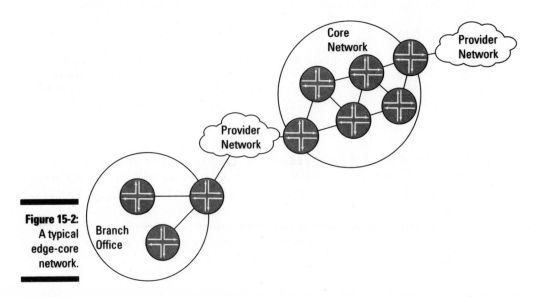

Figure 15-2: A typical edge-core network.

Using all the bits in DSCP

DSCPs are 8-bit fields within the packet header — the last 2 bits in the field are used for Explicit Congestion Notification (ECN). When a router's outbound buffers are full, it sets the ECN bits to let the downstream node know that congestion is on the link. Without going into specifics, the two routers essentially use the information to throttle back traffic on the link.

The DSCP replaces the Type of Service (ToS) field, which used to be the primary field used

for CoS implementation. The major difference between the two is that the ToS field really uses only the IP Precedence bits (3 bits that identify the type of forwarding to be used for the packet). Conversely, the DSCP uses 6 bits in the field to identify both the type of forwarding as well as the packet loss priority (PLP). As such, it provides more granularity in how a packet is classified and is thus the more common choice in today's networks.

Differentiated Services Code Points (DSCP)

The most common way to look at the IP packet header when classifying traffic for use with a CoS implementation is to interpret the header "type of service" bits as the Differentiated Services Code Point (DSCP). This field has 8 bits, the first 6 of which are important to CoS. Although you can look at traffic other ways, especially at the frame level, DSCP is the most popular and powerful choice for CoS these days, so we focus on DSCP in this chapter.

Forwarding classes

The DSCP's 6 bits identify two important pieces of the CoS puzzle: the forwarding class and the packet loss priority. The combination of these pieces makes up what is called the *per-hop behavior* (PHB), which basically describes what happens to packets for any particular hop in its path.

Here are the five classes of traffic:

- **Best effort (be):** Best effort forwarding is the base forwarding for all traffic. Basically, the router does its best to forward the traffic. If congestion develops on the router (its buffers are full, for example), this traffic is likely to be dropped.

- **Expedited forwarding (ef):** Expedited forwarding is essentially first-class travel for packets in the router. The router provides priority services for this traffic, and it ensures that packets in this forwarding class are the last to be delayed or dropped during times of congestion.

As packets come in, if the total bandwidth doesn't exceed the allocated bandwidth for this class, the traffic is considered *in-profile*, and the packet is forwarded normally. If the total bandwidth exceeds the allocation, the traffic is considered *out-of-profile*. The router will basically do whatever it can to forward the traffic using available bandwidth from the other classes. If there is no available bandwidth, packets can be dropped, though they'll be the last packets subjected to this horrid fate.

Expedited forwarding is what you use for mission-critical traffic that can't be dropped or have excess jitter or delay (think voice traffic).

✔ **Assured forwarding (af):** Assured forwarding is pretty similar to expedited forwarding. Assured forwarding is kind of like passengers flying business class (that is, they get lots of perks, but not quite the first-class treatment).

As packets come in, they're either in-profile or out-of-profile (just like ef packets). Packets that are in-profile are forwarded normally. The difference is that whereas ef packets are automatically queued up for forwarding if they're out-of-profile, af packets can be subjected to a random early detection (RED) drop profile. Packets in the af class can be assigned a drop precedence (using the PLP bit), and they're randomly dropped to ease congestion.

Assured forwarding is used for applications that need better than best-effort forwarding but aren't quite mission-critical (typically applications such as PeopleSoft, SAP, or Oracle).

✔ **Network control (nc):** Network control traffic includes packets like routing protocol hello messages or keepalives. Packets in this class are forwarded with lower priority, meaning they're more subject to delay. However, these packets are less likely to be discarded. Because the loss of these packets can cause network-wide events (like routing adjacencies flapping), delaying delivery is much better than dropping the packet completely.

✔ **Class selector (cs):** CS values enable backward compatibility with the older IP Precedence scheme. The Class Selector codepoints are of the form xxx000. The first three bits are the IP precedence bits. Each IP precedence value can be mapped into a DiffServ class. If a packet is received from a non–DiffServ-aware router that used IP precedence markings, the DiffServ router can still understand the encoding as a Class Selector codepoint.

Each of these forwarding classes has at least one PLP associated with it. The combination of forwarding class and PLP is identified by the bit pattern in the DSCP. So when you want to either match on or assign one a particular PHB (that is, you want to specify how a packet is to be handled), you need to specify the specific bit pattern.

Code point aliases

Memorizing bit patterns of forwarding classes can be painful. A better way is to use *code point aliases*. When determining your CoS policy, instead of specifying the bit pattern, you can define the alias name that represents the bit patters. Such aliases are called code point aliases.

Put simply, use code point aliases, not bit patterns. If you assign English phrases or words to a particular pattern, it's far easier to go back and understand the configuration at a later date. Try looking at 101110; you know immediately that it refers to expedited forwarding. Additionally, if you create a set of rules that you apply to a particular pattern and that pattern changes, changing the definition of the alias is far easier.

To simplify things even more, some well-known bit patterns already have aliases built into the software. Table 15-1 lists the common DSCP aliases along with the corresponding bit patterns, forwarding classes, and PLP values.

Table 15-1   Behavior Aggregate Classification Aliases

Code Point Alias	Forwarding Class	PLP	Bit pattern
ef	expedited-forwarding	low	101110
af11	assured-forwarding	low	001010
af12	assured-forwarding	high	001100
af13	assured-forwarding	high	001110
af21	best-effort	low	010010
af22	best-effort	low	010100
af23	best-effort	low	010110
af31	best-effort	low	011010
af32	best-effort	low	011100
af33	best-effort	low	011110
af41	best-effort	low	100010
af42	best-effort	low	100100
af43	best-effort	low	100110
be	best-effort	low	000000
cs1	best-effort	low	001000

(continued)

Table 15-1 *(continued)*

Code Point Alias	Forwarding Class	PLP	Bit pattern
cs2	best-effort	low	010000
cs3	best-effort	low	011000
cs4	best-effort	low	100000
cs5	best-effort	low	101000
nc1/cs6	network-control	low	110000
nc2/cs7	network-control	low	111000
other	best-effort	low	(none)

The combinations in Table 15-1 aren't exhaustive, but they represent the well-known patterns that you can leverage in your classification of traffic. If you want to add a pattern that isn't already present, you can configure that pattern and name it whatever you want:

```
[edit class-of-service]
code-point aliases {
    dscp {
        my-dscp-alias 110001;
    }
}
```

Using this configuration, you can assign a name to a particular DSCP bit pattern. Every time you want to match on that bit pattern in the rest of the CoS configuration, you need to reference only the alias name.

Configuring BA classifiers

Once you match packets to a particular DSCP value, you have to configure the router to match these values. In this context, matching the values constitutes classifying the traffic. That is, once you match the DSCP values, you should know how you want to treat that traffic.

To configure the classification portion of the CoS implementation, you want to create logic that says

```
If traffic has a dscp value that matches some pattern,
    Then send that traffic to a particular queue and
    assign a particular loss priority
```

The first part of this logic is straightforward. You need to be able to match the DSCP value of incoming traffic to some values that you want to use to govern how that traffic is forwarded. The second part of the logic is really how you want to treat the traffic after it's been classified.

Forwarding classes

Imagine that a router is like an airline counter. People walk up to the counter expecting to be serviced. But all people aren't equal to the airline. The airline may service its first class passengers in one line, its frequent flyers in yet another line, and finally the remainder of its passengers in still another line. Depending on the type of customer each person represents, people filter themselves into one of the various lines.

The important detail in this example is that two things are going on:

✔ Passengers are filtering themselves based on the type of ticket they hold.

✔ The airline is telling them which line corresponds to their particular type.

A router behaves the same way. Traffic that comes in is evaluated to determine what type of traffic it is — is it first class, frequent flyer, or regular — by looking at the DSCP values for the packet. Then the router tells those packets where to go. In the latter case, where to go equates to which outbound queue to use.

When classifying traffic, you must match the traffic and assign that traffic to a queue. The assignment of traffic to a queue is done through forwarding classes. Forwarding classes simply map traffic that is matched to a queue.

Queues

The branch routers (J-series routers) support up to eight different queues, numbered 0 through 7. By default, the first four of these queues are used by the four forwarding classes described earlier:

✔ **Queue 0** — best effort: Any packet without a DSCP value set is forwarded in this queue. This is the default for all non–network-control traffic.

✔ **Queue 1** — expedited forwarding: Note that no predefined schedulers are associated with this queue. If you want to use this queue, you need to explicitly configure the forwarding class and then configure the scheduler to be used.

✔ **Queue 2** — assured forwarding: Note that no predefined schedulers are associated with this queue. If you want to use this queue, you need to explicitly configure the forwarding class and then configure the scheduler to be used.

✔ **Queue 3 —** `network control`: Network control traffic is forwarded using this queue. Remember that this queue is serviced with a low priority, but traffic isn't dropped from this queue. The `low` here means packet loss priority, which is the drop probability bit (with local significance to the device). If the PLP is low, it's less likely to be dropped during congestion than those having a high priority marking.

Although the default action is to use these queues for the specified forwarding classes, you can still use these queues for other things. In fact, you may want to define different actions for even these four forwarding classes, assigning traffic to different queues.

So the real question here is, "How do you use these in a real network?"

Imagine that the network has the different types of traffic shown in Table 15-2 with the corresponding sensitivities to delay and jitter.

Table 15-2	Types of Network Traffic			
Traffic Type	**Applications**	**Forwarding Class**	**Queue**	**Forwarding Class Name**
Voice	Real-time voice calls	expe-dited-forward-ing	4	cos_voice
Video	Streaming video	assured-forward-ing	5	cos_video
Business critical apps	Sales apps, Oracle, etc.	assured-forward-ing	6	cos_buscrit
Noncritical apps	Data sniffers	best-effort	7	cos_non-crit

With these types of applications, you may want to create your own queues and then allocate a certain percentage of available bandwidth to these types of applications. Traffic that doesn't fall into these categories can use the default queues for transit. To use these queues, you have to assign them to forwarding classes, which are then used to forward traffic:

```
[edit class-of-service]
forwarding-classes {
    queue 0 best-effort;
    queue 1 expedited-forwarding;
    queue 2 assured-forwarding;
```

```
    queue 3 network-control;
    queue 4 cos-voice;
    queue 5 cos-video;
    queue 6 cos-buscrit;
    queue 7 cos-noncrit;
}
```

This configuration defines eight queues into which packets can be distributed. The assumption is that each of these queues will be allocated some percentage of the total bandwidth. (See the section "Scheduler configuration," later in this chapter.)

Queues 0 through 3 represent the default queues. You don't need to explicitly configure them. They're configured here for illustrative purposes only. You could even configure your own queues in place of these if you wanted to separate, say, certain other applications or signaling traffic.

Linking forwarding classes to classifiers

The logic you're trying to configure is

```
If traffic has a dscp value that matches some pattern,
   Then send that traffic to a particular queue and
   assign a particular loss priority
```

The DSCP values characterize traffic, and the forwarding classes (and corresponding queues) allow you to classify that traffic so that you can treat it appropriately. To pull these two pieces together, you configure BA classifiers, referencing defined forwarding classes:

```
[edit class-of-service]
classifiers {
   dscp dscp-classifier {
      forwarding-class cos-voice {
         loss-priority low code-points ef;
      }
      forwarding-class cos-video {
         loss-priority high code-points cs1;
         loss-priority low code-points af31;
      }
      forwarding-class cos-buscrit {
         loss-priority low code-points af41
      }
      forwarding-class cos-noncrit {
         loss-priority high code-points cs5;
         loss-priority low  code-points af13;
      }
   }
}
```

This configuration creates your match conditions, and it assigns traffic that meets those conditions to one of the specified forwarding classes, which, in turn, maps to a particular outbound queue.

Specifically, this configuration specifies that any traffic that has a DSCP value of ef (corresponding to a bit pattern of 101110) should be given a loss-priortyof low and assigned to the forwarding class called cos-voice. Basically, you're saying that any traffic that is marked as expedited forwarding is voice traffic, and that traffic shouldn't be dropped, so you're giving it a low loss priority. That traffic is then being assigned to the voice forwarding class, which corresponds to queue 5 on the router. Essentially, you're dumping all your voice traffic into a single queue with the expectation that you'll allocate a certain percentage of your total bandwidth to that traffic.

This configuration also classifies video traffic. In the case of video, you want to minimize delay and jitter because it impacts video quality, but the nature of the traffic is such that it's not as critical to your business as the voice traffic on your network. In this case, you want to assign it to an assured forwarding class.

In fact, your network may have multiple sources of video. Imagine that video streaming from one server is being used to send live stock data to a number of different branches in your company. Because decisions are made based on that data, you want to make sure that stream is uninterrupted. Meanwhile, another video stream is sending training or other corporate information that is less critical. Although you want that stream to be uninterrupted, if you're forced to choose between that one and the streaming stock quotes, you want to preserve the stock quotes. So this configuration sets a loss priority of high on the training video and a low loss priority on the stock quotes. During times of congestion, the training video is more likely to be impacted, thus preserving the higher priority stock quotes.

For these forwarding classes, no scheduler is defined yet. You must explicitly configure a scheduler in the Junos OS before the forwarding classes become useful. Schedulers assign route resources to the forwarding classes; without resources, a forwarding class remains just a concept. See the section "Scheduler configuration," later in this chapter, for information on configuring schedulers and scheduler maps.

Linking classifiers to traffic

After you create a classifier that matches types of traffic based on the DSCP value, it then assigns that traffic to a forwarding class that corresponds to some queue on the router.

Classifiers must be linked to one or more flows of traffic before they're useful. The traffic itself flows through interfaces. You must link your newly configured classifiers to the interfaces on the router through which the traffic is flowing.

You have a couple of options here. You can apply your classifiers to all, some, or one of the interfaces on your router. (Applying them to none of the interfaces doesn't make a lot of sense, so we don't include that option.) Even on the interfaces, you can apply your classifiers to all, some, or one of the logical interfaces (units). To make this process a bit easier, Junos supports wildcards.

In this case, you have only a single classifier, so it's easy enough to configure it on all interfaces:

```
[edit class-of-service]
interfaces {
    all {
        unit * {
            classifiers {
                dscp dscp-classifier;
            }
        }
    }
}
```

In this configuration, you're applying the `dscp-classifier` to all interfaces. Notice that you must specify which unit you're applying it to. In this case, you're using the wildcard (asterisk) to indicate that it's to be applied to all units on all interfaces. If you want to apply the `dscp-classifier` to only unit 0 on all interfaces, you can replace the asterisk with a 0.

If you configure several classifiers and want to apply them on different interfaces, you can use the asterisk wildcard with the interface name. For example, if you know that your video traffic travels only on Gigabit Ethernet interfaces, and you've configured a classifier to handle only video, you can have a configuration that resembles this:

```
[edit class-of-service]
interfaces {
    ge-* {
        unit * {
            classifiers {
                dscp dscp-video-classifier;
            }
        }
    }
}
```

In this configuration example, the wildcard indicates that all Gigabit Ethernet interfaces should use the specified voice classifier on all units.

Take care when you apply one classifier to many interfaces. In this example, all interfaces share a single classifier, and they're contending for the same classifier. What you want to do is configure the `per-unit-classifiers` statement so that each unit has its own classifier treatment.

Controlling Outbound Traffic

After you've effectively identified the inbound traffic on your router and classified it into one of your forwarding classes, you then want to control the outbound flow of that traffic.

Traffic enters the router, and based on a packet's DSCP value, it's assigned to a forwarding class, which identifies the outbound queue into which it's sent. (Oh, yeah, it's routed to the proper next hop too — sometimes you overlook the basics when you discuss a new feature.)

You may want to control various properties of the outbound queue, including

✔ Total bandwidth assigned to the queue

✔ Total buffer memory assigned to the queue for storing outbound packets

✔ Priority of the queue (the order in which the queue is serviced)

Scheduler configuration

Before you can get into tweaking the various operating parameters of the outbound traffic, you have to understand the underlying mechanism used to configure these parameters.

There are two major components to the scheduler configuration:

✔ **Schedulers:** Define the properties of the outbound queues. Once they're tied to individual interfaces and forwarding classes, all traffic matching a particular forwarding class is treated as per the definitions in the scheduler.

✔ **Scheduler maps:** Associate a forwarding class with a scheduler. Scheduler maps are then tied to interfaces, thereby configuring the hardware queues, packet schedulers, and RED processes that operate according to the mapping.

In other words, schedulers and their maps associate resources with forwarding classes and queues. In this example, you have four customized forwarding classes, each of which requires a scheduler to be explicitly configured. To create the schedulers, configure the following:

```
[edit class-of-service]
schedulers {
    cos-sched-voice;
    cos-sched-video;
    cos-sched-buscrit;
    cos-sched-noncrit;
}
```

This configuration simply creates the schedulers. No properties are associated with these schedulers yet. That's what the maps do.

After creating the schedulers, you want to associate each forwarding class with one of the schedulers:

```
[edit class-of-services]
scheduler-maps {
    forwarding-class cos-voice scheduler cos-sched-voice;
    forwarding-class cos-video scheduler cos-sched-video;
    forwarding-class cos-buscrit scheduler cos-sched-buscrit;
    forwarding-class cos-noncrit scheduler cos-sched-noncrit;
}
```

This configuration maps each of the forwarding classes from the previous examples to its corresponding scheduler.

You're using four of the predefined forwarding classes. Although these forwarding classes didn't need to be explicitly configured, only two of them had default schedulers associated with them. By default, only the best-effort traffic associated with queue 0 and the network-control traffic associated with queue 3 have schedulers (and the resources they represent) associated with them. If you want to use either the expedited or the assured forwarding classes, you must explicitly configure a scheduler and related resources for those.

Shaping outbound traffic

The most common forwarding resource you'll want to control is the bandwidth allocated for a particular application. For example, say that your video traffic is critical to your business, but you don't want it consuming all of your networking resources. You still need bandwidth to handle your voice, business applications, and even network control traffic. So it makes sense to cap the amount of bandwidth available to the video streams, in which case shaping becomes valuable. As you might expect, in the Junos OS, this resource-handling is all configured through the scheduler.

Examine the types of traffic on your network and consider these underlying assumptions about bandwidth consumption:

- ✔ **Voice traffic:** The most critical traffic for this particular network. Because this business is predicated on communication between employees and customers, voice calls can never be dropped. This traffic needs to be forwarded at all costs.

- ✔ **Video traffic:** Because of the dependence on streaming stock quotes, this traffic is critical to the business. However, you don't want this traffic consuming all available bandwidth, so you want to cap it at 40 percent of the available bandwidth.

> ✔ **Business critical applications:** These applications are critical to the business and must receive some amount of assured bandwidth. These applications can't exceed 30 percent of the total bandwidth.
>
> ✔ **Noncritical applications:** Noncritical applications don't have a demonstrable impact on business, so they should be treated as best-effort tasks. Because they're not business-impacting, they should not consume more than 10 percent of the available bandwidth.

Given these requirements, you must configure a number of different parameters. The configuration is done within the specified schedulers that are mapped to the forwarding classes to which this traffic is tied.

Configuring strict-high scheduling

Voice traffic is delay-sensitive, so you want to ensure that voice packets in your network are serviced with minimum delay. To do so, you must configure strict priority queuing, which basically means that the voice packets will be processed before anything else is processed.

To configure the strict-priority queuing:

```
[edit class-of-service]
schedulers {
   cos-sched-voice {
      priority strict-high;
   }
}
```

This configuration simply assigns the `strict-high` priority to the voice traffic. The scheduler map associates this scheduler with a forwarding class so that it can be used to service voice traffic.

Capping a transmission rate

Say, for example, that you want to cap the total bandwidth consumption for video traffic at 40 percent of the available bandwidth on a given interface. To specify the maximum percentage of total bandwidth that a particular forwarding class can use, configure a transmit rate:

```
[edit class-of-service]
schedulers {
   cos-sched-video {
      transmit-rate percent 40;
   }
   cos-sched-buscrit {
      transmit-rate percent 30;
   }
   cos-sched-noncrit {
      transmit-rate percent 10;
   }
}
```

TIP

Preventing queue starvation

With strict priority queuing configured, your voice packets will be serviced as soon as they enter the router. There is actually a problem with this approach, though. If enough voice traffic enters the box, you could effectively starve the other queues because the voice traffic will always be serviced first instead of those queues. To prevent starvation of your other queues, you may want to configure an outbound policer that defines a limit for the amount of traffic the queue can service.

To address this issue, you actually want to configure two separate policers. The first policer identifies the bandwidth limit for the voice traffic. If total voice traffic exceeds 256kpps or the traffic bursts exceed 15kpps, you want to flag the traffic as out-of-profile. As you recall, traffic that is out of profile is sent using available bandwidth from the other queues (if available bandwidth exists). Otherwise, it's dropped.

The second policer sets an upper limit. If the total voice traffic exceeds the upper threshold (set here at 512kpps) or the burst size exceeds 30kpps, you want to discard the packets, regardless of congestion on the interface.

Examine the following firewall policers:

```
[edit]
firewall {
    policer voice-excess-policer {
        if-exceeding {
            bandwidth-limit 256k;
            burst-size-limit 15k;
        }
        then out-of-profile;
    }
    policer voice-upper-limit-policer {
        if-exceeding {
            bandwidth-limit 512k;
            burst-size-limit 30k;
        }
        then discard;
```

```
    }
}
```

After creating the policers, you have to tie them to the voice forwarding class. Essentially, you want to make sure that all traffic identified as part of the cos-voice forwarding class is policed with the previously configured firewalls.

```
filter voice-filter {
    term upper-limit {
        from {
            forwarding-class cos-
        voice;
        }
        then {
            policer voice-upper-
        limit-policer;
            next term;
        }
    }
    term excess {
        from {
            forwarding-class cos-
        voice;
        }
        then {
            policer voice-excess-
        policer;
        }
    }
    term accept {
        then accept;
    }
}
```

This configuration first evaluates the traffic against the upper limit. If the traffic exceeds the upper limit, you want to discard it, so you should check that condition first. If the traffic isn't discarded, the excess bandwidth policy is evaluated. If the forwarding class exceeds the allocated bandwidth, the traffic is flagged as out of profile and is accepted. It will be forwarded with available bandwidth (if any exists) or dropped.

TIP

Creating second-rate traffic

You will notice that the examples of schedulers include specific schedulers for various types of traffic that you might see in your network. But where does the generic traffic go? Consider configuring a default forwarding class and associating with it a default scheduler. Any traffic that is `best-effort`, but at least somewhat notable, can be classified into this forwarding class.

And when it comes to ensuring that this second-class traffic gets serviced, you can configure the scheduler to use up whatever bandwidth is left on a particular interface. Basically, you're saying that you don't want a dedicated piece of

the pie; you just want to use whatever is available at the time.

To configure this default scheduler:

```
[edit class-of-service]
schedulers {
    cos-sched-default {
        transmit-rate remainder;
    }
}
```

The `remainder` keyword specifies that this scheduler is to use whatever is left over after the other schedulers have carved out their pieces.

This configuration sets the maximum transmission rate at the specified percentage. If the total throughput on a link is 1.5 Mbps, setting a transmit rate of 40 percent means that the forwarding class can, at most, consume 600 Kbps.

Setting up outbound buffers

The whole point behind constraining the total bandwidth allocated to specific forwarding classes is that you want to prevent a single application or traffic flow from consuming an interface's entire set of resources. Well, if bandwidth is the most important resource to cap, *buffer size* is a close second.

In this context, *buffers* refer to the available memory on an interface card available for queuing packets before they're sent downstream. Essentially, after the router performs the next-hop lookup, it sends the packets to the interface where it's stored in memory. The interface then services its queues based on the relative priority of each queue. While it services those queues, packets being sent by the router for eventual transmission are stored up.

During periods of *congestion* (defined here as times when the total rate of queuing packets exceeds the rate of transmission), these buffers begin to fill. When they're completely full, any new packets being sent to the interface can be dropped because there is no place to store them.

Because some traffic may be less critical (or because you can tolerate drops of some types of traffic more than others), you may want to guarantee a slice of the buffer pie. Also, similar to capping the transmit rates, you may want to prevent a particular forwarding class or traffic flow from consuming all available buffer space.

The configuration to shape the outbound buffers closely resembles the configuration to shape outbound traffic:

```
[edit class-of-service]
schedulers {
    cos-sched-video {
        transmit-rate percent 40;
        buffer-size percent 40;
    }
    cos-sched-buscrit {
        transmit-rate percent 30;
        buffer-size percent 10;
    }
    cos-sched-noncrit {
        transmit-rate percent 10;
        buffer-size percent 10;
    }
    cos-sched-default {
        transmit-rate remainder;
        buffer-size remainder;
    }
}
```

The deeper the buffer, the more delay that can occur. In a well-functioning network, buffer memory usage will be low most of the time. Buffers are really intended to absorb bursts of traffic.

Configuring priority scheduling

Each scheduler is assigned a priority. By extension, because each queue is linked to a scheduler, each queue has a priority associated with it. When packets are sent to an outbound interface for transmission, they're stored in queues, as defined by their forwarding class. Junos services these queues based on their priority. If you want to ensure that a particular queue is serviced ahead of others, configure a higher priority for that queue's scheduler.

For example, the video traffic in your network may be high priority. The business-critical traffic in the network may be important but somewhat lower in priority than the video traffic, and the noncritical traffic may be lower still. Finally, the default traffic may be of the lowest priority. To reflect this prioritization in the configuration:

```
[edit class-of-service]
schedulers {
   cos-sched-voice {
      priority strict-high;
   }
   cos-sched-video {
      transmit-rate percent 40;
      buffer-size percent 40;
      priority high;
   }
   cos-sched-buscrit {
      transmit-rate percent 30;
      buffer-size percent 10;
      priority medium-high;
   }
   cos-sched-noncrit {
      transmit-rate percent 10;
      buffer-size percent 10;
      priority medium-low;
   }
   cos-sched-default {
      transmit-rate remainder;
      buffer-size remainder;
      priority low;
   }
}
```

When you configured the scheduler to handle voice traffic, you configured the priority as strict-high, despite not having yet introduced the notion of priority scheduling — and that was really just an instance of this same concept.

Once you set these priorities, Junos uses them to determine the order in which queues are serviced. On a particular physical interface, the output queues are serviced as follows:

1. **All high-priority queues currently in profile are serviced.**

   In profile means that the traffic fits within the allocated bandwidth for that particular queue. Multiple high-priority queues are serviced in weighted round-robin fashion. High-priority queues include strict-high priority queues, which are considered to always be in profile.

2. **All medium-high priority queues currently in profile are serviced.**

   Again, multiple queues of the same priority are serviced in weighted round-robin fashion.

3. **All medium-low priority queues in profile are serviced.**

4. **All low-priority queues in profile are serviced.**

5. **All high-priority queues that are currently out of profile and are not rate-limited are serviced.**

   Multiple queues are serviced in weighted round-robin fashion.

6. **All medium-high priority queues currently out of profile are serviced.**

7. **All medium-low priority queues currently out of profile are serviced.**

8. **All low-priority queues currently out of profile are serviced.**

Massaging BA Classifiers for Core Transit

This entire chapter is predicated on one assumption: the DSCP values have been set correctly before the packets enter your router. If the DSCP values are uniformly applied across an entire network, it's pretty straightforward. You can trust that the configured forwarding classes match the type of traffic that is inbound, and all your CoS configuration just works.

The problem is that at the edge of your network, you're exceedingly unlikely to receive packets that consider your particular CoS implementation. As an example, do you typically ask your peering networks what DSCP values they use? Probably not. Similarly, they have no idea what you use. So any traffic that is passed over that boundary needs to be classified independent of the BA classifiers.

The big question is how to do it. The answer is *multifield classifiers*. MF classifiers work very similarly to BA classifiers in that they examine the packet's header and based on the contents therein, assign the packet to a forwarding class. The difference is that MF classifiers examine more than just the CoS bits in the header.

If you accept the premise that your neighboring networks don't know or don't care what CoS bits are set in packets that are sent to your network, you have to find a different way to match traffic. You can do so in two easy ways:

✔ Look at where the traffic is from.

✔ Look at where the traffic is heading.

Matching traffic based on the source address

In many cases, the source address of a packet tells you what type of packet it is. For example, imagine that you have an application server with the address 192.168.66.77. Any packet that has that source address in its header can be classified the same way. In this case, you basically assign those packets to the forwarding class tied to that application or set of applications.

For this scenario, assume that inbound traffic has a source address of 192.168.66.77, and that traffic from this host is to be classified with the other business-critical applications grouped into the `cos-buscrit` forwarding class. Configure a firewall filter that matches on the source address:

```
[edit firewall]
filter mf-classifier {
    interface-specific;
    term assured-forwarding {
        from {
            source-address 192.168.66.77;
        }
        then {
            forwarding-class cos-buscrit;
            loss-priority low;
        }
    }
}
```

This configuration matches all traffic with a source address matching the specified source. Any traffic that meets those conditions is then assigned to the `cos-buscrit` forwarding class, and its PLP is set to `low`.

You must then apply the filter to an interface. Because you're matching on inbound traffic, you want the configuration to be an *input filter*.

```
[edit interfaces]
t1-0/0/1 {
    unit 0 {
        family inet {
            filter input mf-classifier;
        }
    }
}
```

All inbound traffic on the specified interface will be matched.

Instead of using the `filter input` statement, try using the `input-list` statement:

```
[edit interfaces]
t1-0/0/1 {
    unit 0 {
        family inet {
            filter input-list mf-classifier;
        }
    }
}
```

If you use the `input-list` statement, you can add multiple firewall filters to the same interface if you ever need to. Otherwise, you can configure only one filter per interface at a time.

Matching traffic based on destination port

In addition to being able to match traffic based on where it originates, you can often determine the type of packet (and therefore the proper packet classification) based on the destination port. For example, some applications use well-known ports. SIP is an excellent example. SIP traffic uses the port 5060, so you should be able to match packets based on their destination port. Any packet with a destination port of 5060 can be classified with the other SIP traffic.

In this example, all voice traffic (including signaling) is being handled as part of the `cos-voice` forwarding class.

```
[edit firewall]
filter voice-mf-classifier {
   interface-specific;
   term expedited-forwarding {
      from {
         destination-port 5060;
      }
      then {
         forwarding-class cos-voice;
         loss-priority low;
      }
   }
}

[edit interfaces]
t1-0/0/0 {
   unit 0 {
      family inet {
         filter input-list voice-mf-classifier;
      }
   }
}
```

This configuration defines another input filter that matches on the destination port. Traffic matching the specified port is classified as voice traffic and uses the `voice forwarding` class defined previously.

Setting DSCP values for transit

Being able to match on the source and destination addresses certainly solves the problem where you don't know that the DSCP values have been set in accordance with your CoS implementation. However, if the values aren't set correctly upon entering your network, you must be able to set them so that the rest of your BA classifiers within your network will function as expected.

A typical CoS implementation includes this functionality at the edge routers via the DSCP rewrite capabilities. Essentially, you match on the destination address or port or whatever field you're using to identify traffic. Then based on the type of traffic you know it to be, you configure the router to overwrite the existing DSCP value and use the value that corresponds to the type of traffic you're matching on. When the packet is forwarded to the next hop within your network, that next router can simply look at the DSCP value and treat the packet accordingly.

To configure DSCP rewrites, you simply specify what code points you want associated with a particular forwarding class. This configuration is pretty straightforward; you simply configure the code points you want to match on for a particular forwarding class. Then you explicitly write those values upon ingress into your network.

Here's where you define the DSCPs to match on:

```
[edit class-of-service]
classifiers {
   dscp dscp-classifier {
      forwarding-class cos-voice {
         loss-priority low code-points ef;
      }
      forwarding-class cos-video {
         loss-priority high code-points cs1;
         loss-priority low code-points af11;
      }
      forwarding-class cos-buscrit {
         loss-priority low code-points af13;
      }
      forwarding-class cos-noncrit {
         loss-priority high code-points cs5;
         loss-priority low  code-points af43;
      }
   }
}
```

To configure rewrites that match the values the rest of your network is keying on:

```
[edit class-of-service]
rewrite-rules {
   dscp rewrite-dscps {
      forwarding-class cos-voice {
         loss-priority low code-points ef;
```

```
        }
    forwarding-class cos-video {
        loss-priority high code-points cs1;
        loss-priority low code-points af11;
    }
    forwarding-class cos-buscrit {
        loss-priority low code-points af13;
    }
    forwarding-class cos-noncrit {
        loss-priority high code-points cs5;
        loss-priority low  code-points af43;
    }
  }
}
```

Now you need to apply these rewrite rules to an interface:

```
[edit class-of-service]
interfaces t1-0/0/1 {
   unit 0 {
       rewrite-rules dscp rewrite-dscps;
   }
}
```

All traffic on the specified interface that is assigned to one of the forwarding classes will have its DSCPs rewritten to match the expected DSCP values for the rest of the network. Basically, you use a firewall filter to assign traffic to a forwarding class, and then you use the DSCP rewrite functionality to mark the traffic for subsequent CoS processing within your network.

Chapter 16

Using Multi-Protocol Level Switching

Routing protocols are about making your network functional. They allow you to send traffic across the network, and they even allow you to tune your network in some small measure to control how traffic is sent.

Multi-Protocol Label Switching (MPLS) builds on top of that foundation and really grants you a different level of control over how your network transports traffic. By converting your routed network to something closer to a switched network, MPLS offers transport efficiencies that simply aren't available in a traditional IP-routed network. These efficiencies are then augmented with traffic engineering functionality that makes MPLS still more effective. Combined, the switching and traffic engineering capabilities have made something that was once used only in service provider networks one of the emerging technologies in the enterprise.

This chapter attempts to demystify some of these powers, explaining in plain English both how MPLS operates and how you configure it in the Junos OS to get more out of your network.

Packet-Switched Networking

MPLS is part new technology, part throwback to older technologies. Its power is really in how it marries both new and old to get the best of both worlds.

Routing works by choosing the best next hop router-by-router across a network. Each packet is routed independently, and even if the packet in question is the second part of a fragment, the packet gets the whole router header examination and destination lookup treatment, even though 99 percent of the time, the packet is going to exactly the same place.

MPLS was originally used by service providers to address the situation shown in Figure 16-1. Why route each packet hop-by-hop, when it is immediately obvious at the first router on the left that the packet has to make its way to the router on the right.

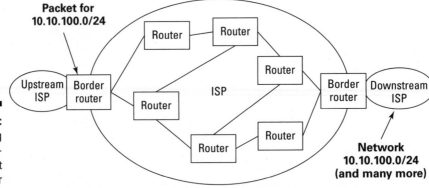

Figure 16-1:
Routing
hop-by-
hop is not
needed for
transit
traffic.

The Border Router knows right away, thanks to BGP, that the packet for 10.10.100.0/24 must exit at the other border router.

Routing is effective for networks that are resilient and that have widely dispersed destinations, but switching is more effective for networks with stable paths and a set of limited destinations. Also, paths provide a convenient way to apply CoS parameters to a packet flow, because the path that packets follow should have consistent bandwidth and delay parameters.

To understand how MPLS leverages both new and old, you must have a firm grasp on the following topics:

- ✔ Label switching
- ✔ Label-switched paths
- ✔ Label-switching routers
- ✔ Labels
- ✔ Label operations
- ✔ Establishing label-switched paths

Label switching

As already mentioned, packets enter a router, the router examines the header, and then the router sends the packet to the next hop based on the ultimate destination address.

In a label-switched network, the operation is different. Packets aren't forwarded on a hop-by-hop basis. Instead, paths are established for particular source-destination pairs. Look at the network topology in Figure 16-2.

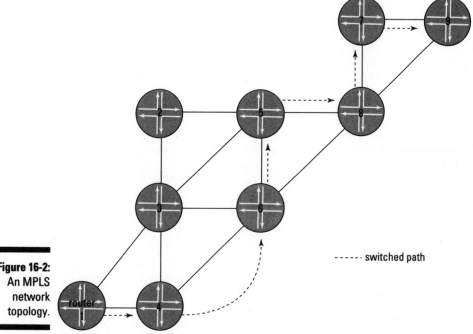

Figure 16-2:
An MPLS
network
topology.

- - - - - switched path

If the topology in Figure 16-2 represents an IP-routed network, traffic from router 1 is forwarded to router 4, which then makes its own forwarding decision, and so on, until the packets arrive at router 9.

In a label-switched network, a path from router 1 to router 9 is created so that all traffic from router 1 to router 9 takes the same deterministic path. Because a preset path exists, individual routing nodes don't need to do a forwarding lookup on the packets as they enter the router. Instead, each node must keep information only on the paths that have been established through it (so switching tables tend to be much smaller than routing tables). As packets from that flow enter a router, the router can switch the packets on to a predefined path toward its destination through the network.

Put simply, if router 4 knows that for all traffic from router 1 to router 9, the next stop along the way is router 6, it can just forward the packets to that predetermined hop without ever looking up the route in its routing table.

Label-switched paths

The predetermined paths that make MPLS work are called *label-switched paths* (LSPs). Routers in an MPLS network exchange MPLS information to set up these paths for various source-destination pairs. So in Figure 16-2, information is exchanged through the network to establish the path from router 1 to router 9.

What is important here is that every router along the LSP from router 1 to router 9 must have the same view of the LSP. If a switched path is to have any real efficiencies over typical IP routing, every router on the LSP must be able to switch the packet forward.

MPLS is often called a layer 2.5 technology because it shares both routing (layer 3) and switching (layer 2) characteristics. The fact that paths are preset makes MPLS behave quite like a layer 2 protocol. However, MPLS's capability to use signaling protocols, which themselves rely on routing knowledge for LSP establishment and traffic engineering and adjust on the fly, definitely makes it more layer 3ish. (Standard layers are a wonderful way to understand networks . . . except when things like MPLS and tunnels complicate things.)

Label-switching routers

The routers that make up an LSP are called *label-switching routers* (LSRs), and they come in a few flavors:

- ✔ **Ingress router:** The router at the entry point of an LSP. The ingress router is the only place where normal IP traffic can flow into an MPLS LSP. The inbound router receives IP traffic. When it determines that to reach its destination it must go thru an LSP, the inbound router encapsulates the traffic with an MPLS header and forwards it to the next hop in the LSP.

- ✔ **Transit router:** Any router in the middle of an LSP. Transit routers simply switch MPLS packets to the next hop in the LSP, using the incoming interface where the packet came in from as well as the MPLS header to determine where to send the packet.

✔ **Penultimate router:** The second-to-last router in the LSP. The penultimate router is the router before the last hop in an LSP. Because the last hop in an LSP doesn't need to switch the packet forward to another transit router, it has no need for the MPLS headers. It's the responsibility of the penultimate router to remove the MPLS header before sending it on to the last hop in the LSP. Note that having the penultimate router remove the MPLS label before sending it on to the egress router is optional.

✔ **Egress router:** The exit point for the LSP. The egress router receives IP traffic from the penultimate router. It does a normal IP lookup, and it forwards the traffic using normal IP routing.

Note that the traffic on the LSP from router 1 to router 9 doesn't have to originate at router 1. Imagine that router 1 is connected to a server. That server is running an application that is being used by someone accessing the network somewhere beyond router 9. Just because the entire traffic flow extends beyond the two endpoints of the LSP doesn't mean that the traffic doesn't use the LSP.

In this case, normal IP routing is used to pass the traffic to router 1. Router 1 does a normal lookup as though the packet were a normal IP packet. The lookup reveals that the destination for this traffic is router 9, and that destination is associated with an LSP. In other words, the next hop is the whole LSP, not just the next hop router. Router 1 then forwards the packet along as per the LSP definition, and each subsequent router treats the packet as an LSP packet. In this case, router 1 represents the starting point for the LSP. As such, router1 is the *ingress router*.

Examining the path again, router 9 is the last router in the LSP. So when the packet arrives at router 9, there is no LSP to follow. Therefore, router 9 does a normal IP lookup on the packet, and it forwards the packet as an IP packet. And because router 9 is the last router in the LSP, it's the *egress router*.

All the routers between router 1 and router 8 are *transit routers*. They're responsible for ushering the MPLS traffic along to the next hop in the LSP. The second-to-last router in the LSP (router 8, in this example) is the *penultimate router*. The penultimate router is typically responsible for stripping the MPLS headers off the packets (known as penultimate hop popping, or PHP). (For more information on PHP, see the upcoming section "Label operations.")

Labels

As packets are forwarded in a label-switching framework, MPLS routers encapsulate the packets with special headers called *labels*. A label basically tells the router which LSP it belongs to. The router can then use the ingress port and the LSP information to determine where the next hop in the LSP is (see Figure 16-3).

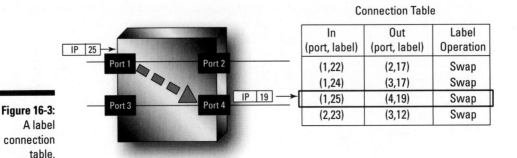

Connection Table

In (port, label)	Out (port, label)	Label Operation
(1,22)	(2,17)	Swap
(1,24)	(3,17)	Swap
(1,25)	(4,19)	Swap
(2,23)	(3,12)	Swap

Figure 16-3:
A label
connection
table.

In Figure 16-3, the MPLS packet arrives via port 1. The router examines the label and sees that it has a numeric identifier that associates the packet with a particular LSP. Based on the input port and the label value, the router can look up in its MPLS routing table where the next hop in the LSP is. In this case, the lookup reveals that the outbound port is port 4. The packet forwards the traffic out the correct port, and the process repeats at the next LSR.

Label operations

An LSR's responsibilities extend beyond just looking at the label and forwarding the packet to wherever it needs to go. LSRs are also responsible for managing and assigning the label on the packet.

For example, when the packet arrives at the ingress router for a particular LSP, that ingress router is responsible for examining the packet so that it can send the packet through the LSP. However, it must also add the MPLS label so that the next hop in the LSP can process the packet correctly. The act of adding an MPLS label is called *pushing*. The following three label operations form the basis of all MPLS forwarding:

- ✔ **Push:** Adds a new MPLS label to a packet. When a normal IP packet enters an LSP, the new label is the first label on the packet.

- ✔ **Pop:** Removes the MPLS label from a packet. This is typically done at either the penultimate or the egress router.

- ✔ **Swap:** Replaces the label with a new label. When an LSR performs an MPLS lookup, that lookup yields the LSP next hop information as well as the numeric identifier for the next segment in the LSP.

Two other label operations — *multiple push* and *swap and push* — are really just extensions of the first three operations. Because you're unlikely to need these operations, we don't describe them in detail here. Suffice it to say that they perform multiple operations at once.

Label stacking

You can actually add labels to packets that already have labels (known as *label stacking*). Examine the topology in the figure.

This topology has an LSP defined between router 1 and router 11. But router 4 and router 8 also have an LSP between them. In this scenario, you have an LSP containing an LSP. So as IP traffic enters the first LSP, the ingress router adds an MPLS label. That label is used to switch the packet through to router 4.

Router 4 is an ingress router for an LSP. As the ingress router, it pushes a new label to the packet. That label is used to switch the packet forward to router 8. Router 8, the egress router for the LSP, removes the label and forwards the packet based on the original label, which is exactly what Layer-3 VPNs do.

In the context of a single network, label stacking may not be that interesting, but imagine

now that network boundaries appear around the LSPs.

The topology is the same except that now carrier networks are identified. You want to switch a packet from the branch office (router 1) to headquarters (router 9). That path traverses your own network as well as a carrier network. You want to switch the packet through your network, so you use an LSP and push your own label to the packet.

Meanwhile, the carrier wants to switch all your traffic through an LSP. So as the packet enters the carrier network, the carrier can add its own label and switch the packet through its transit network. When the packet is handed back to your headquarters, the label has been removed, and you can continue switching the packet to the eventual destination (router 9 in this example).

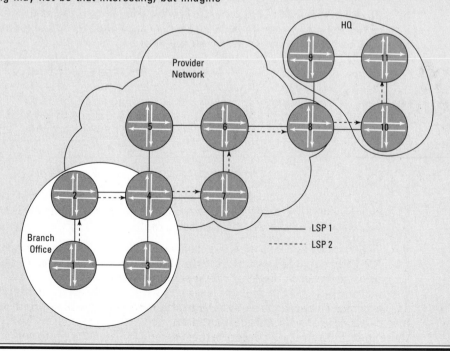

Establishing Label-Switched Paths

You can create MPLS LSPs in one of two ways:

✔ **Static configuration:** Static LSPs are a lot like static routes. You basically have to explicitly configure every LSR in an LSP manually. Because no protocols dynamically signal the LSP for you, the load on the LSRs is reduced. However, if you have changes in the topology, the paths can't adapt to the new network. As a result, topology changes create routing black holes.

The lack of dynamic update is a significant drawback and one that should not be overlooked. We recommend using dynamic LSPs wherever feasible.

✔ **Dynamic setup:** Dynamic LSPs use signaling protocols to establish themselves and propagate LSP information to other LSRs in the network. You configure the ingress router with LSP information that is transmitted throughout the network when you enable the signaling protocols across the LSRs. Note that you have to configure the signaling protocols on all of the LSRs. If only a subset of routers is able to exchange information, the LSP isn't established.

Because the LSRs must exchange and process signaling packets and instructions, dynamic LSPs consume more resources than static LSPs. However, dynamic LSPs can avoid the network black holes of static LSPs by detecting topology changes and outages and dynamically establishing new LSPs to move around the failure.

Signaling Protocols

You need to be aware of two primary types of MPLS signaling protocols, both of which the Junos OS supports:

✔ **Label Distribution Protocol (LDP):** LDP is a fairly simple signaling protocol that behaves much like one of the IGPs (OSPF and IS-IS). LDP runs on top of an IGP configuration, which means you have to get OSPF or IS-IS running first. Moreover, you must configure LDP on the exact set of interfaces as your IGP.

After you configure both your IGP and LDP on an interface, LDP begins transmitting and receiving LDP messages on that interface. LDP starts off by sending LDP discovery messages to all the LDP-enabled interfaces. When an adjacent router receives the discovery message, it establishes a TCP session with the source router.

When the LDP session is established, the routers maintain adjacencies much in the same way that OSPF routers maintain adjacencies. When the topology changes, those changes generate LDP messages that allow LDP to set up new paths.

LDP is fantastic in that it's so simple and just works. However, because of its simplicity, it lacks some of the more powerful traffic engineering features that RSVP boasts. For this reason, the major application for LDP-signaled LSPs is in support of Layer 3 VPNs. Suffice it to say that LDP lacks any real traffic engineering capabilities.

✔ **Resource Reservation Protocol (RSVP):** RSVP is a bit more complex than LDP and offers traffic engineering features that aren't available with LDP-signaled LSPs.

RSVP works by setting up unidirectional paths between an LSP ingress router and an egress router. In the configuration, you specify what the bandwidth requirements are for an LSP. After you configure these paths and enable RSVP, the ingress router sends a path message to the egress router. The path message contains the configured information about the resources required for the LSP to be established.

When the egress router receives the path message, it sends a reservation message back to the ingress router in response. This reservation message is passed from router to router along the same path as the original path message (in opposite order, of course). Once the ingress router receives this reservation message, an RSVP path is established that meets the required constraints.

All the LSRs along the path receive the same path and reservation messages, which contain the bandwidth reservation requirements. If they have the available bandwidth (that is, if no other higher-priority RSVP LSP has reserved bandwidth), they're included in the LSP. If a router doesn't have available bandwidth, it generates its own reservation message, and a new route that doesn't include the offending router is found. If no route can be found, the LSP isn't established.

The established LSP stays active as long as the RSVP session stays active. RSVP maintains activity through the continued transmission and response to RSVP path and reservation messages. If the messages stop for three minutes, the RSVP session terminates, and the LSP is lost.

Configuring RSVP-Signaled LSPs

Imagine that you have a network where you're carrying a lot of voice traffic. You want to make sure that voice traffic gets forwarded along a path that has enough bandwidth to support the load without congestion. And because voice packets can't be received out of order, you want the entire voice flow to travel over the same path, as shown in Figure 16-4.

In this topology, you have a source of voice traffic (router 1) that is aggregating all your voice flows from various branch sites. You want to transport this data to headquarters, which requires sending the traffic through router 5 and off through the network and eventually to your headquarters.

You want to ensure that you have reserved bandwidth for all your flows, so you're going to use RSVP as your LSP signaling protocol. To configure the LSP across your network, you must

✔ Enable MPLS and RSVP on your router.

✔ Enable RSVP and RSVP on your transit interfaces.

✔ Configure your IGP to support traffic engineering.

✔ Set up an LSP from the ingress to the egress router.

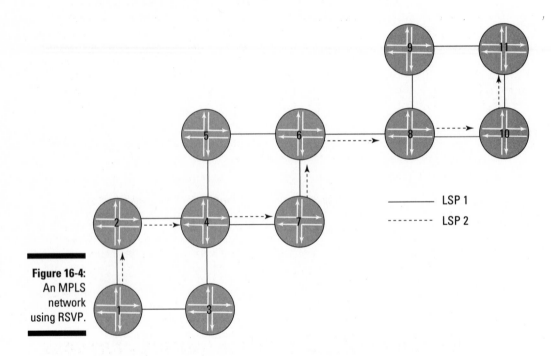

Figure 16-4:
An MPLS
network
using RSVP.

Enabling MPLS and RSVP

Assuming that you've already set up your IGP and other routing protocols, the first thing you need to do to establish an RSVP LSP across your network is to enable both MPLS and RSVP on your routers.

You have to enable MPLS and RSVP across all the routers in your network, not just the ingress and egress routers. RSVP works by sending path messages and ensuring that all routers within an LSP can meet the bandwidth requirements for that particular path.

To enable these protocols:

```
[edit protocols]
rsvp {
    interface all;
}
mpls {
    interface all;
}
```

This configuration is pretty straightforward. By enabling the protocols on all interfaces, you avoid having to explicitly add each interface, which has the added benefit of making it easy to swap new interfaces in and out.

If you're using management interfaces, you don't want to run the signaling protocols across those LAN interfaces. You can prevent MPLS and RSVP from running on those interfaces by explicitly excluding them using the `disable` statement:

```
[edit protocols]
rsvp {
    interface all;
    interface fe-0/0/0.0 {
        disable;
    }
}
mpls {
    interface all;
    interface fe-0/0/0.0 {
        disable;
    }
}
```

Enabling MPLS on your transit interfaces

After enabling MPLS and RSVP on your router, you must configure your transit interfaces. Refer to the network topology in Figure 16-4, earlier in this chapter.

Which router pops the MPLS label matters

The MPLS label on a switched packet is popped by either the egress router or the penultimate router, depending on your configuration.

Picture a network that has a single peering connection with a provider network. Many (if not all) flows from the network to any site outside the network likely will flow through the same gateway. If you've configured LSPs in your network, many of them will have the same egress router.

If you use ultimate hop popping (where the egress router pops the MPLS labels), all those

flows and all those packets need to be processed by a single router. If you have a lot of LSPs with a lot of traffic, this step can be resource-intensive.

If you decide to use penultimate hop popping, you essentially terminate the LSP one hop earlier. The MPLS labels are popped by the routers that connect to the egress router, rather than all of them being popped by the same egress router. You can effectively divide and conquer when it comes to label popping, which helps avoid running out of resources during heavy loads.

You must enable MPLS on all the interfaces called out in the topology. To enable the protocols on a transit interface:

```
[edit interfaces]
fe-1/0/1 {
    unit 0 {
        family inet {
            address 10.0.24.1/24;
        }
        family mpls;
    }
}
```

Configuring an LSP

After you have MPLS and RSVP turned on and ready to go, the only thing you need to do is to configure your LSP from router 1 to router 5. To configure an RSVP LSP, you must create an LSP on router 1 that points to router 5:

```
[edit protocols]
mpls {
    label-switched-path router1-to-router5 {
        to 10.0.0.5;
    }
}
```

Within the MPLS configuration, creating an LSP is as easy as naming it and identifying the remote loopback address of the router you want to use as your egress router for the LSP.

Creating an LSP that mirrors itself on the egress router is generally a good idea so that you can support bidirectional communication. In this case, you need to also configure on router 5:

```
[edit protocols]
mpls {
    label-switched-path router5-to-router1 {
        to 10.0.0.1;
    }
}
```

Verifying the LSPs

After configuring something, you need to make sure that it works as expected. To verify the LSP configuration, use the show mpls lsp extensive command. If you issue the command from router 1, expect to see two separate LSPs, as shown in Listing 16-1 (the one to router 5 and the one from router 5).

Listing 16-1:   Output from the show mpls lsp extensive Command

```
user@router1> show mpls lsp extensive
Ingress LSP: 1 sessions

10.0.0.5
  From: 10.0.0.1, State: Up, ActiveRoute: 1, LSPname: router1-to-router5
  ActivePath: (primary)
  LoadBalance: Random
  Encoding type: Packet, Switching type: Packet, GPID: IPv4
  *Primary                 State: Up
    Computed ERO (S [L] denotes strict [loose] hops): (CSPF metric: 20)
10.1.13.2 S 10.1.36.2 S
    Received RRO (ProtectionFlag 1=Available 2=InUse 4=B/W 8=Node
10=SoftPreempt):
          10.1.13.2 10.1.36.2
    6 Dec 13 11:50:15 Selected as active path
    5 Dec 13 11:50:15 Record Route:  10.1.13.2 10.1.36.2
    4 Dec 13 11:50:15 Up
    3 Dec 13 11:50:15 Originate Call
    2 Dec 13 11:50:15 CSPF: computation result accepted
    1 Dec 13 11:49:45 CSPF failed: no route toward 10.0.0.6[6 times]
  Created: Mon Dec 13 11:47:19 2004
Total 1 displayed, Up 1, Down 0

Egress LSP: 1 sessions
```

(continued)

Listing 16-1 *(continued)*

```
10.0.0.1
  From: 10.0.0.5, LSPstate: Up, ActiveRoute: 0
  LSPname: router5-to-router1, LSPpath: Primary
  Suggested label received: -, Suggested label sent: -
  Recovery label received: -, Recovery label sent: -
  Resv style: 1 FF, Label in: 3, Label out: -
  Time left: 127, Since: Mon Dec 13 11:50:10 2004
  Tspec: rate 0bps size 0bps peak Infbps m 20 M 1500
  Port number: sender 1 receiver 39136 protocol 0
  PATH rcvfrom: 10.1.13.2 (so-0/0/2.0) 28709 pkts
  Adspec: received MTU 1500
  PATH sentto: localclient
  RESV rcvfrom: localclient
  Record route: 10.1.36.2 10.1.13.2 <self>
Total 1 displayed, Up 1, Down 0

Transit LSP: 0 sessions
Total 0 displayed, Up 0, Down 0
```

The output does indeed show two separate LSPs to which router 1 is a member. The first LSP is the ingress LSP for which router 1 is the ingress router. The second LSP is the egress LSP from router 5.

Placing Constraints on Packet Forwarding

When RSVP creates the paths for its LSPs, it uses information learned from the underlying IGP configuration. Basically, if OSPF has the shortest route from A to B, RSVP will establish an LSP across that path. At times, however, you may want to dictate your own path. For example, you may know that in terms of hops, one path is shorter, but when you talk about actual latency and link speed, a different path is preferable. In these instances, you want to put constraints on the path taken through your network.

Routing LSPs based on these constraints is called *constraint-based routing*. You may want to constrain the path that an LSP takes in a few different ways:

✔ Reserve bandwidth so that guaranteed bandwidth appears along the path.

✔ Specify a particular node in the network through which the LSP will pass.

✔ Identify the exact path for the LSP.

Reserving bandwidth on an LSP

One of the best parts about RSVP is that you can specify a minimum bandwidth that must be supported on each transit router in the LSP. This specification helps ensure that you have enough allocated bandwidth from ingress to egress, especially for traffic that is particularly sensitive to latency or drop.

For example, imagine that you're streaming video across your network that you're using to conduct simulations in multiple branch offices. For the simulation to work well, every site must receive the same feed with the same timing. You may want to ensure that the LSPs you're using to stream the video across your MPLS core all have enough bandwidth to support the rather high requirements for your media. In this case, you can use RSVP to guarantee the bandwidth along the path from source to egress router.

To configure this bandwidth constraint, you can build off your basic MPLS configuration. In the previous MPLS example, you configure an RSVP LSP and verify that it is operating. Taking that LSP, add to it such that the bandwidth requirement is 5MB:

```
[edit protocols]
mpls {
    label-switched-path router1-to-router5 {
        to 10.0.0.5;
        bandwidth 50m;
    }
}
```

The simple inclusion of the bandwidth statement adds that value to the reservation messages that each transit router must respond to. If a router in the network doesn't have the required bandwidth (either because its interfaces don't support that much throughput or because bandwidth has already been allocated to other LSPs), RSVP won't use that router in the LSP. Instead, it sends messages to other routers until it finds a path that meets the bandwidth requirements. Although this path may not be the shortest in terms of hops or overall latency, you'll know that each path segment can support the required bandwidth.

Verifying bandwidth on an LSP

It's important to check that your RSVP-signaled LSP has the appropriate bandwidth allocation. How can you tell that your RSVP-signaled LSP has the appropriate bandwidth allocation? If you want to look at the characteristics, you use the show rsvp interface command:

```
user@router1> show rsvp interface
RSVP interface: 4 active
                 Active Subscr- Static      Available   Reserved   Highwater
  Interface State resv  iption BW           BW          BW         mark
  fe-0/0/0.0 Up       2   100% 155.52Mbps   155.52Mbps  50Mbps     0bps
  fe-0/0/1.0 Up       0   100% 155.52Mbps   155.52Mbps  0bps       0bps
  fe-1/0/1.0 Up       0   100% 155.52Mbps  .155.52Mbps  0bps       0bps
```

In this example, router 1 has three interfaces with RSVP enabled. When you look at the reserved bandwidth on the router, you need to know what bandwidth reservation really means. If you have umpteen flows through a particular interface, what you really want to do is limit some or all of those flows to a specific piece of the overall capacity on the link.

So when you look at RSVP sessions and the bandwidth tied to them, what you're seeing with the `show rsvp interface` command is the total sum of all allocated bandwidth on *all* the LSPs for which this router is an LSR. The totals can be extremely helpful in ensuring that your allocated bandwidth is in line with what you want it to be. If the allocated bandwidth exceeds 100 percent, the LSPs with a reserved bandwidth specified won't use that router as a transit router.

Explicitly configuring an LSP route

When you use RSVP (or even LDP) to signal an LSP, the basic configuration uses the underlying IGP to calculate the LSP route. That is, the LSP travels whatever route the IGP selects. In some cases, however, you may want traffic to pass through a particular node. (Note that this option is available only if you're using RSVP as your signaling protocol.) Examine the topology in Figure 16-5.

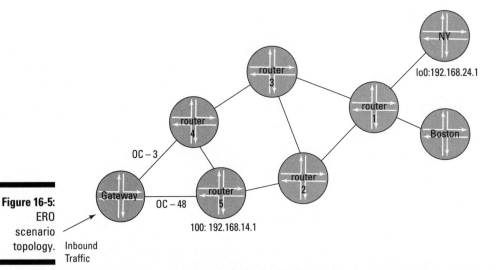

Figure 16-5: ERO scenario topology.

Inbound Traffic

This particular topology has a single ingress point and a single egress point in the MPLS core. Traffic that comes from the corporate headquarters is passed to different branch sites. Maybe the site in New York has more latency-sensitive traffic than the traffic destined for Boston (such as stock trades, for example). You may want to make sure that the New York traffic takes the faster route while the Boston traffic takes the road less traveled.

In the absence of any explicit configuration, if you're using an LSP to route traffic across your MPLS core, the traffic headed to both destinations will take the same path.

Configuring a static route

To make sure that traffic is separated in a particular way, the solution is actually a combination of old and new. First, you want to set up static routes that basically say that if the traffic is destined for New York, then use a particular route.

Static routes are configured under the `routing-options` hierarchy. From the gateway router, do the following:

```
[edit routing-options]
static {
    route 192.168.24.1 {
        next-hop 192.168.14.1;
    }
}
```

This configuration is just the standard static route configuration. It defines a static route for all traffic destined for New York, and it sets the next-hop address to route through router 2.

Configuring an explicit route

If you want, you can set up an LSP for traffic that includes router 3 so that traffic destined for New York uses the faster path. To do so, you must explicitly specify that the LSP is to use router 3. This constraint is called an *explicit route object* (ERO).

To configure an ERO that forces the LSP to use router 3, you first have to set up the LSP. On the gateway router, do the following:

```
[edit protocols mpls]
label-switched-path ny-traffic {
    to 192.168.20.1;
}
```

You must first enable MPLS and RSVP on the appropriate interfaces. After you've set up the LSP, you have to associate it with a particular path. In this case, we want to specify that the path goes through router 3. To configure the explicit route, use the `path` statement:

```
[edit protocols mpls]
path to-router3 {
    10.0.18.1 loose;
}
label-switched-path ny-traffic {
    to 192.168.20.1;
    primary to-router3;
}
```

This configuration does two things: defines a path and applies that path. The path (called `to-router3`) specifies a particular IP address through which the LSP must traverse toward its destination. Because the path is loosely constrained (configured with the `loose` statement), the only requirement is that the LSP pass through that address. It doesn't matter which interface is used, what path is used to get to that point, or what path is used from that point to the destination.

When RSVP sets up this LSP, it uses the underlying IGP to route from the ingress point to the ERO (router 3, in this case) before continuing to its final destination over the established LSP. RSVP uses the IGP to route from the ERO to the LSP egress point.

In this example, the address used for the path constraint is a specific interface address for router 3. By specifying the interface address, you can pretty much dictate how the traffic will flow through the network. That is to say that traffic will be routed to that interface en route to the final destination. If you use the loopback address of router 3 instead of a particular interface address, you have less control over the path the inbound traffic will take. Traffic is routed to router 3, but it may arrive on any interface. However, your IGP should know the shortest path to reach this loopback interface.

The *primary* statement is what ties the LSP to the path you created. When you apply the path to the LSP, you want to apply it as the primary path so that all traffic on this LSP uses the path. You can configure secondary paths, which would then be used if the primary path is not available (if, for example, an ERO in the primary path was not reachable).

Linking the route to the LSP

After you've configured a static route and created an LSP, the next task is to make sure that all traffic destined for New York travels through the LSP you just created. What you're really doing is specifying that all New York-bound traffic use the LSP as its next hop and allow all forwarding decisions after that to be made based on the LSP.

To link the route to the LSP, use the `lsp-next-hop` statement with the static route configuration:

```
[edit routing-options]
static {
    route 192.168.24.1 {
        lsp-next-hop ny-traffic;
    }
}
```

When traffic comes in with a destination address of 192.168.24.1, the router associates that traffic with the LSP, and it forwards the traffic to the next hop in the LSP.

Verifying traffic using the LSP

The easiest way to verify the path is by using the `traceroute` command. Examine the topology in Figure 16-6 to see the expected path:

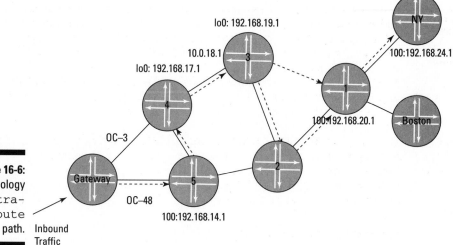

Figure 16-6: A topology with `traceroute` path.

Here's how it looks:

```
user@gateway> traceroute new-york
traceroute to new-york (192.168.24.1), 30 hops max, 40 byte packets
 1  router5 (192.168.14.1)  0.869 ms  0.638 ms  0.536 ms
    MPLS Label-100004 CoS=0 TTL=1 S=1
 2  router4 (192.168.17.1)  0.869 ms  0.638 ms  0.536 ms
    MPLS Label-100004 CoS=0 TTL=1 S=1
 3  router3 (192.168.19.1)  24.968 ms  0.727 ms  0.363 ms
    MPLS Label-100004 CoS=0 TTL=1 S=1
 5  router1 (192.168.20.1)  24.968 ms  0.727 ms  0.363 ms
 6  new-york (192.168.24.1)  24.968 ms  0.727 ms  0.363 ms
```

In the output, you want to verify that traffic is passing through the ERO (router 3). You also want to verify that MPLS labels are being used. Typically, it's probably enough for you to verify that an MPLS label is in use. If you want to get more detailed, you can start to check the MPLS labels against the expected label values.

Explicitly configuring an entire LSP path

In some cases, you may want to have a bit more control over the path an LSP takes. For example, you may want to do the following:

- ✔ Ensure that the very first hop in an LSP is a specific router.

- ✔ Make sure that traffic flows from router 1 to router 2 to router 3, in that order.

- ✔ Bound a path at a couple of points, allowing the routers to decide how to get between those points.

Figure 16-7 shows these scenarios.

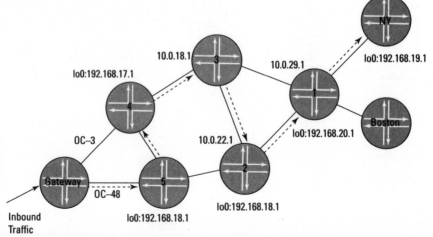

Figure 16-7: Exerting more control over an LSP path.

Imagine that you want traffic in the LSP to travel from the ingress point directly to router 3. From router 3, you want to make sure that it passes through router 5, but you don't care how it gets to router 5. And then from router 5, you want to make sure that the traffic passes through router 7 before being forwarded to the egress point for the LSP.

Configuration for this type of more constrained LSP is handled through the path configuration:

```
[edit protocols mpls]
path to-router3 {
    10.0.18.1 strict;
    10.0.22.1 loose;
    10.0.29.1 loose;
}
```

The strict keyword indicates that traffic has to flow directly to that router. It can't go through any other router in the LSP en route to that router. If you specify two strict addresses in a row, it means that traffic has to flow directly through those two routers without any path deviations in the middle.

Then, after traffic flows through 10.0.18.1, it can take any path and any number of hops (to be determined by the underlying IGP) to 10.0.22.1. From there, the traffic passes through any number of hops to 10.0.29.1, and eventually the traffic is forwarded to the LSP egress router.

Again, to verify the path, use the traceroute command:

```
user@gateway> traceroute new-york
traceroute to new-york (192.168.24.1), 30 hops max, 40 byte packets
 1  router5 (192.168.14.1)  0.869 ms  0.638 ms  0.536 ms
    MPLS Label-100004 CoS=0 TTL=1 S=1
 2  router4 (192.168.17.1)  0.869 ms  0.638 ms  0.536 ms
    MPLS Label-100004 CoS=0 TTL=1 S=1
 3  10.0.18.1 (10.0.18.1)  24.968 ms  0.727 ms  0.363 ms
    MPLS Label-100004 CoS=0 TTL=1 S=1
 4  10.0.22.1 (10.0.22.1)  0.869 ms  0.638 ms  0.536 ms
    MPLS Label-100004 CoS=0 TTL=1 S=1
 5  10.0.29.1 (10.0.29.1)  24.968 ms  0.727 ms  0.363 ms
 6  new-york (192.168.24.1)  24.968 ms  0.727 ms  0.363 ms
```

Chapter 17

Operating and Troubleshooting Your Network

*W*hen networks were new, they broke all the time. But when they did break, the problem was easy to find and usually could be fixed quickly. Today, networks don't really break: They get "sick." The network is still functioning, but parts of it are not doing what they are supposed to. Often, the root problem is difficult to isolate, and the fix may not work in all cases at all times.

Even the definition of just what a network is has changed over time. Everything is connected; we know that. So instead of fretting about what's a network or Internet or subnet, you can just say, "A network is all of the servers, clients, routers, switches, and other devices that I am responsible for." Add them all up, and you have the global public Internet.

In this chapter, we look at the things you can do when your network is not functioning as it should. We show you how to find the root cause of a problem (or problems) and minimize the risk to your network by making incremental and controlled changes. You see how congestion can be addressed with the process of Traffic Engineering. Along the way, we explore a series of general procedures that can be used to investigate troubles.

Identifying the Cause of Problems

Operations monitoring is the baseline for troubleshooting. Only if you are watching the essential layers and nodes in the network can you hope to effectively identify the cause of problems when they arise. It is one thing to address connectivity and protocol issues, but without a firm grasp of what should be connected and how the protocols should operate, the network is visible only when it is malfunctioning.

Imagine driving a car without a fuel gauge, a low oil indicator, or even a speedometer. It's possible you might drive around until the car stopped and then, *first,* try putting gas in it to see if it will start again. But if the engine had seized because there is no oil, you would be wasting your time. Even if the car runs, without a speedometer, you might wonder why the police keep stopping you and giving you tickets.

That's what it's like to have a network without adequate operation and monitoring tools.

One of the most valuable troubleshooting tools you have is the ability to say, "Show me a good one." When someone complains that things are wrong, it's important to know what's right. Unless you have set up ways to monitor and operate your network in good times, you'll be hard-pressed to zoom right to the trouble area in bad times.

Some people may imagine that their network is too small to expend resources on keeping elaborate event tracking logs, and that if things go wrong, the root cause will be obvious. However, these people are wrong. Instead, small networks need resources and event tracking as much as, if not more than, larger ones because any network, even a small one, is a very complicated thing and small networks tend to have smaller staffing.

Here are the essential Junos tools for network monitoring, all of which we cover in the following sections:

- ✔ System logging (syslog)
- ✔ SNMP polling
- ✔ SNMP traps
- ✔ CLI show commands

System logging

You need to monitor system logs, change logs, and interactive commands to establish a basis for troubleshooting when problems occur (and they will). Logs also help to correlate network events with configuration changes. The syslog file can also flag certain events as identify, notify, or alarm. You can store these syslog files locally on the device's hard drive or a flash drive, or you can send syslog messages to a remote or centralized syslog server.

The severity hierarchy in the Junos OS is

- ✔ Debug
- ✔ Info
- ✔ Notice
- ✔ Warning
- ✔ Error
- ✔ Critical
- ✔ Alert
- ✔ Emergency

Here's how it looks:

```
user@router>set system syslog user * any emergency
user@router>set system syslog file syslog-messages any notice
user@router>set system syslog file messages authorization info
user@router>set system syslog file interactive-commands interactive-commands any
user@router>show system syslog
user * {
    any emergency;
}
file syslog-messages {
    any notice;
    authorization info;
}
file interactive-commands {
    interactive-commands any;
}
```

The configuration above performs three essential syslog functions:

- ✔ Logs any emergency level messages or higher. The ability to apply levels this way cuts down on the configuration size.

- ✔ Logs any info level authorization attempts (or any notice level messages or higher). These are stored in the configured file named `syslog-messages` and stored in the default `/var/log` directory on the router.

- ✔ Logs any interactive commands issued by users on the router. The log file `interactive-commands` is also stored in `/var/log`.

The wildcard * symbol applies the configuration stanza that follows to all users (or interfaces when used there, and so on).

SNMP polling

SNMP is a poll-and-response device management protocol ("Are you OK?" "Yep.") that can also have a managed device send unsolicited messages called *traps* to a management console. First, we deal with the poll-and-response aspects of SNMP.

As essential as SNMP might be, it is *not* enabled by default in Junos — you must explicitly configure SNMP!

The following configuration allows read-only polling from a specific client (host address 172.17.110.10) and establishes an SNMP community string of mysnmp (the community string is a simple passphrase and not a secure password, but it will do here).

```
user@router>set snmp community mysnmp authorization read-only
user@router>set snmp community mysnmp clients 172.16.110.10/32
user@router>show snmp
community mysnmp {
    authorization read-only;
    clients {
                                172.16.110.10/32;

    }
}
```

SNMP traps

Polling is essential for monitoring a network, but frequent polling can add load to the device and the network. In stable networks, much of the information gathered by polling is redundant. So mature networks rely more on traps: SNMP messages sent in response to a condition on the managed device.

We introduced SNMP traps in Chapter 7. Configuring traps is a similar operation to configuring SNMP polling. You use the trap-groups keyword and flags, however.

You must configure an additional SNMP community and SNMP server to use traps in the Junos OS. You can trap one or all of the following events:

- ✔ Authentication (failures to authenticate an activity)
- ✔ Chassis (all chassis or environmental notifications)
- ✔ Configuration (changes to the configuration)
- ✔ Link (all link transitions such as up or down)
- ✔ Remote operations (remote access to the router)
- ✔ RMON alarm (alarms concerning remote monitoring)

✔ Routing (notifications sent by routing protocols)

✔ Services (notifications regarding the routers application services)

✔ SONET/SDH alarms (standard alarms for WAN links)

✔ Startup (system warm and cold starts)

✔ VRRP events (notifications for the Virtual Router Redundancy Protocol)

Unlike syslog levels, SNMP traps are specific to each type of event. If you want to capture all types of traps, you must configure them all.

The following configuration traps all authentication, chassis, configuration, link, routing, and startup alarms (we handle Ethernet link events in the section, "Issues at Layer 1 and Layer 2" later in this chapter). Traps are sent to the SNMP client with community `mytraps`.

```
user@router>set snmp trap-group mytraps targets 172.16.110.10
user@router>set snmp trap-group mytraps categories authorization
user@router>set snmp trap-group mytraps categories chassis
user@router>set snmp trap-group mytraps categories configuration
user@router>set snmp trap-group mytraps categories link
user@router>set snmp trap-group mytraps categories routing
user@router>set snmp trap-group mytraps categories startup
user@router>show snmp trap-group mytraps
categories {
            authentication;
            chassis;
            configuration;
            link;
            routing;
            startup;
}
targets {
            172.16.110.10;
}
```

CLI show commands

When it comes to monitoring the network, the most essential CLI commands are `show interfaces brief` and `show interface detail`. For example, if you suspect that Gigabit Ethernet interface `ge-0/0/0` is down, a simple `show` command reveals its status (which is indeed "Down"):

```
user@router>show interfaces ge-0/0/0 brief
Physical interface: ge-0/0/0, Enabled, Physical link is Down
  Link-level type: Ethernet, MTU 1514, Speed 1ge, Loopback: Disabled
  Source filtering: Disabled, Flow control: Enabled
  Device flags    : Present Running Down
  Interface flags : Hardware-Down SNMP-Traps Internal: 0x4000
  Link flags      : None
```

On the other hand, to see a lot more detail about the interface's queues, input-output byte counts, and the same for packet counts, you can use the show interfaces ge-0/0/0 command to add this information:

```
user@router>show interfaces ge-0/0/0 detail
Physical interface: ge-0/0/0, Enabled, Physical link is Down
  Link-level type: Ethernet, MTU 1514, Speed 1ge, Loopback: Disabled
  Source filtering: Disabled, Flow control: Enabled
  Device flags    : Present Running Down
  Interface flags : Hardware-Down SNMP-Traps Internal: 0x4000
  Link flags      : None
  CoS queues      : 4 supported, 4 maximum usable queues
  Hold-times      : Up 0 ms, Down 0 ms
  Current address : 00:05:85:02:a4:00, Hardware address: 00:05:85:02:a4:00
  Last flapped    : 2010-12-15 14:30:58 PST (1w2d 23:03 ago)
  Statistics last cleared: Never
  Traffic statistics:
    Input bytes   :                0                0 bps
    Output bytes  :                0                0 bps
    Input packets :                0                0 bps
    Output packets:                0                0 bps
  IPv6 transit statistics:
    Input bytes   :                0
    Output bytes  :                0
    Input packets :                0
    Output packets:                0
  Egress queues: 4 supported, 4 in use
  Queue counters:     Queued packets  Transmitted packets  Dropped packets
    0 best-effort                  0                    0                0
    1 expedited-fo                 0                    0                0
    2 assured-forw                 0                    0                0
    3 network-cont                 0                    0                0
  Active alarms   : LINK
  Active defects  : LINK
```

Implementing Controlled Change

In the early days of networks, changing *anything* was a source of anxiety and tension. Adding new links, routes, applications . . . in short, any hardware or software at all . . . imperiled network stability and introduced a new number of unknowns into the network. Therefore, network changes were "requested" and introduced at fixed intervals, usually over a weekend so that if things went haywire, the old network state would be restored by Monday.

The more essential the network to the organization, the longer the interval between changes. Small companies changed weekly or monthly. Banks changed only every quarter or so, and some critical networks operated on even longer change schedules.

No network could function that way today, but these early practices emphasized the useful idea of *controlled change* into networks.

Controlled change does not necessarily mean batching up changes and making them at once, although this is still sometimes done. Controlled change means that if there is a network problem, you don't just wildly plunge in and start changing configurations and operational parameters. The emphasis is on *control*.

Similar to "Show me a good one," the basic idea behind controlled change is often, "Can I make the problem move somewhere else?" or the opposite of, "What do two instances of the problem have in common?" As a simple, non-network example, imagine that you have a monitor that inexplicably blanks out when a portion of the web page is blown up to full screen mode. You wonder what is at fault, the monitor (hardware) or the browser (software). Instead of making haphazard changes, you try a different browser to see if the same result occurs, and it does — still blank in full screen mode. Now you check the monitor settings . . . the problem disappears when "Use Hardware Acceleration" is turned off. Someone enabled an unsupported feature, resulting in the blank screen.

Controlled change troubleshooting requires careful thought, cautious record keeping, and a methodical mind. But it can save a great deal of time in the long run.

Understanding Traffic Engineering

Congestion is an issue with any network. Unlike the strictly local concept of flow control (no sender should send faster than a receiver can handle), congestion is a global property of the network (no sender is sending fast . . . there's just too much traffic on this part of the network). Experience with early networks quickly showed that avoiding congestion is much better than trying to alleviate it.

The art of trying to anticipate natural points of congestion in a network and trying to deal with them ahead of time is called *traffic engineering*. A little traffic engineering can go a long way toward avoiding network congestion.

The universal sign of congestion in a network is when users complain that the network is slow. The problem is that slow to users can mean anything from "The response wasn't instantaneous" to "I pressed Enter yesterday, and I'm still waiting."

Tools available in the Junos OS for traffic engineering include the following:

- Load balancing on multiple, equal-cost routes
- Features built into routing protocols such as Open Shortest Path First (OSPF)
- Specific switching mechanisms such as Multiprotocol Label Switching (MPLS)
- Interface monitoring for traffic slowing

Troubleshooting Your Network

In many cases with layered architectures, a problem at one layer shows up first at a higher layer. So, a report of an unreachable service at the application layer may be caused by a problem delivering packets at the network layer (perhaps because of bad routing table information).

Think of how often a failure in a complex device like an automobile is traceable to a small fundamental unit of the whole, such as the oil reservoir or a loose wire. A small change at this micro-level, like a change to cable on a network, can have an enormous effect on the "layers" above like the engine and steering, or a network server. So much so that in many cases, it's best to start at the bottom and work your way up.

Common causes of network failure

Studies have shown that network failures are most often caused by one of the following:

- Cable dig-ups ("backhoe fade")
- Non–dig-up cable failures (aerial wires, electronics)
- Other network equipment causes (heat, cold)
- Network node failures (including configuration errors)
- Device internals
- Power supply failures

The point is not only that these things can go wrong (and if unsteady power causes the node to fail, which category does it belong in?), but that the greatest risk to a network is along the paths of the links that make up the network, which is why it is common today to deploy routers and other key pieces of network equipment in *quads:* four devices mesh-connected by six links. No single link or device failure in a quad failure will disrupt service.

Issues at Layer 1 and Layer 2

In the old days, when network links occupied huge racks in raised-floor computer rooms, you didn't have to decorate for the holidays — you just turned off the lights and watched the modem's blinking red and solid green lights flash and shine. Today, our computers are not in a computer room with the network equipment. Instead, that equipment is safely locked up and the risks minimized (the kind of thing we were referring to in the earlier section, "Implementing Controlled Change").

The lights on the link endpoints were Layer 1 (physical layer) indications of function. Today, networks rely on traps and other cues to detect changes and failures at Layer 1. The real troubleshooting today begins at Layer 2, with the sending and delivery of frames as a stream of bits over a network link such as Ethernet.

The most important transport for the modern network at Layer 1 and Layer 2 is Ethernet. Once confined to LANs exclusively, the Ethernet frame (which is *not* the same as the IEEE 802.3 frame) has become a popular transport for WAN links and other types of links as diverse as ATM and DSL. Ethernet is an international standard, and the alarms and warnings from other transport types such as DS-1 and SONET/SDH have been ported more or less wholesale into Ethernet.

Network people often blur the distinctions between Ethernet and what are called "IEEE 802.3 LANs" at the physical and frame layers. When these people say Ethernet, they usually mean, "I'm sending Ethernet II formatted frames over a physical network that complies with IEEE 802.3 committee standards." In other words, the *frame* is the important thing for Ethernet today.

Ethernet is no longer a simple LAN connectivity method. Today, especially at multi-gigabit speeds, Ethernet is often used as a WAN link replacement. Distances that once required SONET/SDH (the international standards for WANlinks) now are frequently spanned with Ethernet. In order to make Ethernet more appropriate for WAN deployment, many WAN topologies (such as self-healing Ethernet rings) and WAN monitoring methods (such as link-level alarms and frame delay measurements) are now included in the Ethernet standards family. For example, IEEE 802.3ah describes Ethernet link fault management.

Ethernet, and all LANs, have their own globally unique addressing scheme at Layer 2. This is the MAC address, and consists of a 48-bit field used as a source and destination in every Ethernet frame. The first 24 bits form a manufacturer's code and the last 24 bits is a serial number, although MAC card manufacturers are free to use these bits any way they like, as long as they are unique. IP addresses used in the packet at Layer 3 for source and destination are mapped to frame source and destination MAC addresses at Layer 2.

The Ethernet troubleshooting tools now include a complete set of standards for operations, administration, and maintenance (OAM). Ethernet OAM falls into two major categories:

 ✔ Simple link fault management (LFM)

 ✔ More complex connectivity fault management (CFM)

You don't have to enable Ethernet LFM or CFM in Junos, but you must configure them.

LFM operates at the Ethernet frame level and sets thresholds for frame error counts and other link-level events. Once triggered, LFM can create a syslog entry, declare the link down (and unusable), send a critical event trap to a management system, or all of the above. LFM operates on a link-by-link basis and is suitable for networks with many point-to-point Ethernet links.

The more complicated CFM is an end-to-end Ethernet management system that requires coordinated setup across a domain (a *domain* is the set of links and nodes that one organization is responsible for). A router can be a member of more than one *maintenance domain,* and these domains are given distinct names during CFM configuration. Maintenance domains, which are often nested, are assigned a level from 0 to 7, where lower numbers are closer to the network core and higher numbers are closer to the user end points. The maintenance domain consists of a number of *maintenance associations* (MAs) that stitch together the path that CFM frames follow across the network. A key aspect of the MAs is the configuration of level boundaries — for example, where Level 5 becomes Level 7 as a frame makes its way outward from the network core to the user site. These boundaries are established by configuring CFM *maintenance end points*, or MEPs.

MEPs can be with *up MEPs* or down *MEPs,* depending on whether the Ethernet link takes the frame closer to the core (down) or closer to the user (up). Naturally, a path in the down direction will be mirrored by a path in the up direction, and a link-tracing function in CFM keeps everything straight.

A full discussion of Ethernet LFM and CFM capabilities in Junos is impossible here, but because porting WAN link-style alarms (such as Loss of Signal or Loss of Frame) to Ethernet is important, we'll explore them by walking you through a few examples.

When an Ethernet interface is configured in LAN mode (instead of WAN mode) in the Junos OS, LFM, and CFM are not supported.

Example: Configuring IEEE 802.3ah–compliant LFM on a point-to-point Ethernet link

LFM provides the following functions on a point-to-point Ethernet link:

- ✔ Unidirectional or bidirectional detection of physical link failures
- ✔ Loopback for remote port diagnostics
- ✔ Error reporting and recording for link layer frame and symbol errors

In this example, you configure LFM to run on a Gigabit Ethernet link between a customer edge (CE) router and a provider edge (PE) router, as shown in Figure 17-1. If the link fails, LFM detects the fault, and the interfaces on both ends are marked `Link-Layer-Down`. Other subsystems, such as routing, will react to the outage. The LFM PDU interval is set to 1000 milliseconds (the default: the range is from 100 to 1000 milliseconds). Higher values mean faster reaction times, but they add traffic to the link. The LFM lost PDU threshold is set to 3 (also the default: the range is from 3 to 10 PDUs). Lower values react faster but do not tolerate transient conditions well. The configuration also allows both sides to put each other into loopback if the other end requests this action. Both sides must be configured to allow this negotiation and acceptance to take place.

Figure 17-1:
Configuring
Ethernet
LFM with
remote
loopback on
a span.

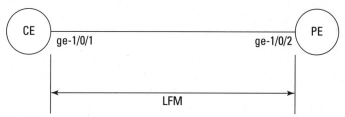

Configuration for the CE router

```
user@CE_router>set interfaces ge-1/0/1 unit 0 family inet address 10.11.11.1/24;
user@CE_router>set protocols oam ethernet link-fault-management interface
        ge-1/0/1 pdu-interval  1000
user@CE_router>set protocols oam ethernet link-fault-management interface
        ge-1/0/1 pdu-threshold 3
user@CE_router>set protocols oam ethernet link-fault-management interface
        ge-1/0/1 negotiation-options allow-remote-loopback
user@CE_router>show protocols oam etherent link-fault-management
interface ge-1/0/1 {
            pdu-interval 1000;
            pdu-threshold 3;
            negotiation-options {
                allow-remote-loopback;
            }
}
```

Configuration for the PE router

```
user@PE_router>set interfaces ge-1/0/2 unit 0 family inet address 10.11.11.2/24;
user@PE_router>set protocols oam ethernet link-fault-management interface
        ge-1/0/2 pdu-interval 1000
user@PE_router>set protocols oam ethernet link-fault-management interface
        ge-1/0/1 pdu-threshold 3
user@PE_router>set protocols oam ethernet link-fault-management interface
        ge-1/0/2 negotiation-options allow-remote-loopback
user@CE_router>show protocols oam etherent link-fault-management
interface ge-1/0/2 {
    pdu-interval 1000;
    pdu-threshold 3;
    negotiation-options {
        allow-remote-loopback;
    }
}
```

Note: The interval and threshold parameters do not have to match in both directions, but this practice results in more predictable bidirectional behavior.

If the link fails, the status of the interface changes to declare the link failed:

```
user@router> show oam ethernet link-fault-management brief
Interface: ge-1/0/1
Status: Fail, Discovery state: Send Any
Peer address: 00:90:69:72:2c:83
Flags: Link-Layer-Down
Remote loopback status: Disabled on local port, Enabled on peer port
Remote entity information:
Remote MUX action: discarding, Remote parser action: loopback
Discovery mode: active, Unidirectional mode: unsupported
Remote loopback mode: supported, Link events: supported
Variable requests: unsupported
```

Example: Configuring IEEE 802.3ag–compliant CFM on a point-to-point Ethernet link

CFM provides the following functions on a point-to-point Ethernet link:

- ✔ Link health and continuity check, including neighbor discovery for adjacencies

- ✔ Linktrace protocol for path discovery (similar to traceroute, but using source and destination MAC addresses)

- ✔ Loopback protocol for fault isolation (similar to ping)

CFM is based on a series of nested administrative domains numbered 0 through 7. Core operators, edge service providers, and customer links are mapped to these maintenance domains. This approach allows the administrative domains to perform troubleshooting and management functions across their maintenance domain without breaching security in other areas of the network. Outer domains closer to the network edges are assigned higher level numbers than inner domains closer to the network core.

In a CFM maintenance domain, each instance of CFM is a maintenance association. The MA consists of a mesh of maintenance endpoints that share basic characteristics. As we noted earlier, MEPs can be either up MEPs or down MEPs, depending on the level of the domain on each side of the link. A link from a Level 5 to Level 7 domain is an up MEP on the Level 5 interface but is a down MEP on the other interface. By convention, a link connecting domains at the same level is a down MEP.

Note: Configured customer CFM levels must be greater than service provider CFM levels. That way, the number is a general measure of the "depth" of the network the network manager is looking at.

Figure 17-2 shows a rather complicated network with three CFM levels: core (Level 3), provider (Level 5), and customer (Level 7). However, note that a simpler network may need only LFM.

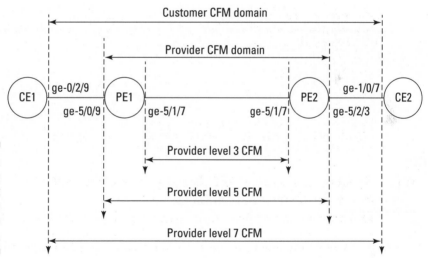

Figure 17-2: Configuring Ethernet CFM across multiple domains.

The configuration shows only the relevant Ethernet OAM parameters. Although it seems long, the configuration establishes only a few parameters for the `customerCE` maintenance domain and associated MEPs. Both sites match parameters for the interval at which continuity checks are carried out (1 second) and the MEP direction (down from Level 7 to Level 5), and both establish auto-discovery for paths between MAC addresses.

Configuration on CE1:

```
user@CE1-router>protocols oam management connectivity-fault-management
      maintenance-domain customerCE level 7
user@CE1-router>protocols oam management connectivity-fault-management
      maintenance-domain customerCE maintenance-association
      customer-site-CE1 continuity-check interval 1s
user@CE1-router>protocols oam management connectivity-fault-management
       maintenance-domain customerCE maintenance-association
       customer-site-CE1 mep 700 interface ge-0/2/9.0 direction down
user@CE1-router>protocols oam management connectivity-fault-management
      maintenance-domain customerCE maintenance-association customer-site-CE1
      mep 700 interface ge-0/2/9.0 auto-discovery
user@CE1-router>show protocols oam management connectivity-fault-management
maintenance-domain customerCE {
    level 7;
    maintenance-association customer-site-CE1 {
        continuity-check {
interval 1s;
        }
        mep 700 {
            interface ge-0/2/9.0;
            direction down;
            auto-discovery;
        }
    }
}
```

Configuration on CE2:

```
user@CE2-router>protocols oam management connectivity-fault-management
      maintenance-domain customerCE level 7
user@CE2-router>protocols oam management connectivity-fault-management
      maintenance-domain customerCE maintenance-association customer-site-CE2
      continuity-check interval 1s
user@CE2-router>protocols oam management connectivity-fault-management
      maintenance-domain customerCE maintenance-association customer-site-CE2
      mep 800 interface ge-1/0/7.0 direction down
user@CE2-router>protocols oam management connectivity-fault-management
      maintenance-domain customerCE maintenance-association customer-site-CE2
      mep 700 interface ge-1/2/7.0 auto-discovery
user@CE2-router>show protocols oam management connectivity-fault-management
maintenance-domain customerCE {
    level 7;
    maintenance-association customer-site-CE2 {
        continuity-check {
interval 1s;
        }
        mep 800 {
            interface ge-1/0/7.0;
            direction down;
            auto-discovery;
        }
    }
}
```

CFM on the two provider routers, PE1-router and PE2-router, is a bit more complicated because you must configure two sets of interfaces and MEPs (`provider-outer` and `provider-inner`). Aside from the maintenance domain and MEP names and directions, the interfaces all use a 1 second continuity check interval and auto-discovery of paths.

Configuration on PE1

```
user@PE1-router>protocols oam management connectivity-fault-management
        maintenance-domain provider-outer level 5
user@PE1-router>protocols oam management connectivity-fault-management
        maintenance-domain provider-outer maintenance-association
        provider-outer-site-PE1 continuity-check interval 1s
user@PE1-router>protocols oam management connectivity-fault-management
        maintenance-domain provider-outer maintenance-association
        provider-outer-site-PE1 mep 100 interface ge-5/0/9.0 direction up
user@PE1-router>protocols oam management connectivity-fault-management
        maintenance-domain provider-outer maintenance-association
        provider-outer-site-PE mep 100 interface ge-5/0/9.0 auto-discovery
user@PE1-router>protocols oam management connectivity-fault-management
        maintenance-domain provider-inner level 3
user@PE1-router>protocols oam management connectivity-fault-management
        maintenance-domain provider-inner maintenance-association
        provider-inner-site-PE continuity-check interval 1s
user@PE1-router>protocols oam management connectivity-fault-management
        maintenance-domain provider-inner maintenance-association
        provider-inner-site-PE mep 100 interface ge-5/1/7.0 direction down
user@PE1-router>protocols oam management connectivity-fault-management
        maintenance-domain provider-inner maintenance-association
        provider-inner-site-PE mep 100 interface ge-5/1/7.0 auto-discovery
user@PE1-router>show protocols oam management connectivity-fault-management
maintenance-domain provider-outer {
    level 5;
    maintenance-association provider-outer-site-PE {
        continuity-check {
            interval 1s;
        }
        mep 100 {
            interface ge-5/0/9;
            direction up;
            auto-discovery;
            }
        }
    }
maintenance-domain provider-outer {
    level 3;
    maintenance-association provider-outer-site-PE {
        continuity-check {
            interval 1s;
        }
        mep 100 {
```

```
            interface ge-5/1/7;
            direction down;
            auto-discovery;
            }
        }
    }
}
```

Configuration on PE2

```
user@PE2-router>protocols oam management connectivity-fault-management
     maintenance-domain provider-outer level 5
user@PE2-router>protocols oam management connectivity-fault-management
     maintenance-domain provider-outer maintenance-association
     provider-outer-site-PE continuity-check interval 1s
user@PE2-router>protocols oam management connectivity-fault-management
     maintenance-domain provider-outer maintenance-association
     provider-outer-site-PE mep 200 interface ge-5/2/3.0 direction up
user@PE2-router>protocols oam management connectivity-fault-management
     maintenance-domain provider-outer maintenance-association
     provider-outer-site-PE mep 200 interface ge-5/2/3.0 auto-discovery
user@PE2-router>protocols oam management connectivity-fault-management
     maintenance-domain provider-inner level 3
user@PE2-router>protocols oam management connectivity-fault-management
     maintenance-domain provider-inner maintenance-association
     provider-inner-site-PE continuity-check interval 1s
user@PE2-router>protocols oam management connectivity-fault-management
     maintenance-domain provider-inner maintenance-association
     provider-inner-site-PE mep 200 interface ge-5/1/7.0 direction down
user@PE2-router>protocols oam management connectivity-fault-management
     maintenance-domain provider-inner maintenance-association
     provider-inner-site-PE mep 200 interface ge-5/1/7.0 auto-discovery
user@PE2-router>show protocols oam management connectivity-fault-management
maintenance-domain provider-outer {
    level 5;
    maintenance-association provider-outer-site-PE {
        continuity-check {
            interval 1s;
        }
        mep 200 {
            interface ge-5/2/3;
            direction up;
            auto-discovery;
            }
        }
    }
maintenance-domain provider-outer {
    level 3;
    maintenance-association provider-outer-site-PE {
        continuity-check {
            interval 1s;
        }
        mep 200 {
```

```
            interface ge-5/1/7;
            direction down;
            auto-discovery;
            }
        }
    }
}
```

Now you can examine the continuity check message (CCM) status (and other events) on the interface:

```
user@host> show oam ethernet connectivity-fault-management interfaces
      ge-0/2/9 detail
Interface name: ge-0/2/9.0, Interface status: Active, Link status: Up
  Maintenance domain name: customer, Format: string, Level: 7
   Maintenance association name: customer-site1, Format: string
    Continuity-check status: enabled, Interval: 1s, Loss-threshold: 3 frames
    MEP identifier: 700, Direction: down, MAC address: 00:90:69:0b:4b:94
    MEP status: running
    Defects:
     Remote MEP not receiving CCM : no
     Erroneous CCM received : yes
     Cross-connect CCM received : no
     RDI sent by some MEP : yes
    Statistics:
     CCMs sent : 76
     CCMs received out of sequence : 0
     LBMs sent : 0
     Valid in-order LBRs received : 0
     Valid out-of-order LBRs received : 0
     LBRs received with corrupted data : 0
     LBRs sent : 0
     LTMs sent : 0
     LTMs received : 0
     LTRs sent : 0
     LTRs received : 0
     Sequence number of next LTM request : 0
     1DMs sent : 0
     Valid 1DMs received : 0
     Invalid 1DMs received : 0
     DMMs sent : 0
     DMRs sent : 0
     Valid DMRs received : 0
     Invalid DMRs received : 0
    Remote MEP count: 1
     Identifier   MAC address        State    Interface
       800        00:90:69:0b:7f:71 ok       ge-5/0/9.0
```

The advantage of CFM compared to LFM is the ability to monitor and trouble-shoot the network end-to-end with CFM, rather than merely registering failed links as with LFM.

Issues at Layer 3

Layer 3 issues concern packets, of course. Generally, the higher up in the protocol stack an issue lies, the more things that can be wrong with it. At the routing layer (one early name for Layer 3), routes to a given destination can be absent, can loop, or can send packets into a black hole.

Inside the router network are tools to examine the functioning of the protocols themselves, such as the `show route protocol ospf` or `show bgp summary` operational mode commands. You can use these commands to gain insight into the operation of the OSPF and BGP routing protocols, respectively.

However, as you've already seen, issues at Layer 3 are often caused by Layer 2 happenings. Even so, you can rely on the SNMP polling and traps and Ethernet OAM to capture problems at the network router link level. Now, take a look at a problem that is actually an issue at the packet layer. Here, you use a typical end user tool — traceroute — to isolate the router causing the problem, as shown in Figure 17-3.

Figure 17-3:
Using traceroute to find an outage.

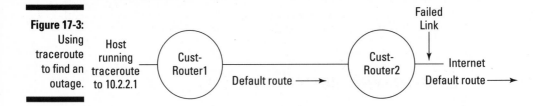

Traceroute sends a packet hop-by-hop from one router to another until the destination host is reached. If a packet arrives at a router that has no route to the destination, a *destination unreachable* ICMP message is sent back to the originator.

When using traceroute, remember that the problem usually lies *not* at the last hop to respond to the traceroute, but *beyond* the last responding device. The example in the figure shows why.

When all is well, the destination is normally five hops away from the source host. A change in the responder's network address is an indication that the packet has moved from one major portion of the network to another (from customer network to service provider network, for example).

In the following, notice how the routers normally respond to a traceroute (file this one under "show me a good one," of course) on the way to Dest-Host:

```
user@host>traceroute 10.2.2.1
traceroute to 10.2.2.1 (10.2.2.1), 30 hops max, 40 byte packets
1 192.168.10.1 (192.168.10.1) 2.617 ms 1.690 ms 2.851 ms (Cust-Router1)
2 192.168.10.6 (192.168.10.6) 3.386 ms 3.370 ms 5.570 ms (Cust-Router2)
3 172.16.11.1 (172.16.11.1) 13.513 ms 3.905 ms 5.060 ms (Prov-Rtr1)
4 172.16.44.2 (172.16.44.2) 3.778 ms 5.237 ms 5.413 ms (Prov-Rtr2)
5 172.16.44.27 (172.16.44.27) 10.867 ms 12.568 ms 5.991 ms (Dest-Host)
```

Now, watch what happens if the link — the only link, by the way — between the customer router (Cust-Router2) and the service provider router (Prov-Rtr1) fails:

```
user@host>traceroute 10.2.2.1
traceroute to 10.2.2.1 (10.2.2.1), 30 hops max, 40 byte packets
1 192.168.10.1 (192.168.10.1) 1.983 ms 2.440 ms 2.414 ms (Cust-Router1)
2 192.168.10.6 (192.168.10.6) 2.883 ms !H 4.136 ms !H 2.114 ms !H
```

The !H indicates that you are getting ICMP host unreachable messages from the second router. It may look like this Cust-Router2 device is the problem, but notice that the packets have made their way to Cust-Router2 and back without any trouble at all. No, the issue is *beyond* this last hop, on the link between the customer and the service provider. There is no useful route to the destination on Cust-Router2, so the !H is issued.

End-to-end considerations

Sometimes the issue is *not* the network at all, but what happens when the bits arrive at the destination. (Sometimes you say, "The trouble is leaving here just fine!")

End-to-end issues show up at Layer 4 and above (Layer 4 used to be called the "end-to-end layer" in many protocol stacks). Once it's verified that the segment or datagram inside the packets inside the frames has made its way across the network as a stream of bits, you're no longer looking at pure network problems.

Part V
The Part of Tens

The 5th Wave   By Rich Tennant

"Yes, JUNOS has an automated 'Help'
function. Why?"

In this part . . .

If the "Part of Tens" were IPv6-enabled, it would be a "Part of Ten Thousands." You get a quick reference of the top-ten most helpful commands, the keys to migrating from one network to a Junos network, and the rundown on other places you can go for more information.

Chapter 18

Ten Most Used Junos Commands

In This Chapter

▶ Breaking down common commands by category

▶ Showing a few commands that you'll use repeatedly

*Y*ou'll likely use a few commands in Junos OS repeatedly while administering your network. In this chapter, we list the top ten categories of usage and some of the more useful commands within each type of administration.

Show Me the Version and Version Detail

show version: Lists which version of Junos OS is running on your device. It also shows the hostname of the device and the Juniper model number. *Use:* Lets you check which version of Junos OS is running on the device. Check that all components of the Junos operating system are at same version level.

show version detail: Shows the version of all Junos processes running on the device. *Use:* Lets you check that all Junos processes are at same version level.

Show Me the Chassis Hardware and Chassis Hardware Detail

show chassis hardware: Displays hardware inventory of the device and components installed in the device. Shows version, Juniper part number, serial number, and description of each component. *Use:* Lets you perform hardware inventory to track components in your possession and provide information to customer support when a component fails.

`show chassis hardware detail:` Displays version, part number, and serial number for all memory installed on device components. *Use:* Provides you with an inventory of memory components.

Show Me and Confirm My Configuration

`configure:` Accesses configuration mode. *Use:* Allows an administrator to modify the configuration running on the device.

`show configuration:` Displays the configuration currently running (active) on the device. *Use:* Lets you verify that the configuration is as you expect it to be.

`commit confirmed:` Activates configuration changes, but returns to previous configuration automatically if you don't actively accept the new configuration. *Use:* When you're committing a configuration that you think may lock you out of the device or otherwise disrupt access to the device, use this command to guarantee that you'll be able to log in to the device.

Back Up and Roll Back My Configurations

`request system snapshot:` Backs up the device's file systems, including configurations. *Use:* Lets you archive all the directories and files on the device so that you can restore them if necessary.

`rollback:` Returns to the previously active device configuration. *Use:* If a newly committed configuration doesn't work as expected, use this command to return to the previous good configuration.

`file list detail /config and file list detail /var/db/config:` Lists the backup configuration files on the device. *Use:* Shows you when the previous configuration files were saved (committed).

Show Me the Interfaces in the Device

show interfaces terse: Lists all interfaces (network cards) present in the box and shows whether they're operational (up or down) and lists IP addresses of each interface. This command shows one interface per line, so it's easily scannable. *Use:* One of the first steps in tracking down a network problem is to make sure that all installed and configured interfaces are up and running and to check that IP addresses are properly configured.

Give Me More Detail About the Interfaces

show interfaces: Multiline output per interface lists properties of the physical (hardware) interface, including MAC address and hardware MTU, and of the logical (unit or subinterface) interface, including protocol MTU configured protocol addresses. *Use:* Adds more detail when tracking down network problems.

show interfaces *interface-name*: Multiline output for a single physical interface. Shows both physical and logical interface information. *Use:* Narrows down output to a single interface of interest.

show interfaces detail, show interfaces detail *interface-name*, **show interfaces extensive, and show interfaces extensive** *interface-name*: Show increasingly more detailed information about all interfaces or about a specific interface. The detail version adds interface statistics, and the extensive version adds error counters. Output is long, so you generally specify an interface name. *Use:* Adds more detail when tracking down network problems.

Show Me Something About Routing

show route: Lists the entries in all the device's routing tables. *Use:* Lets you check which routes the device knows about, and see which ones the device has calculated to be the best ones (the active routes). Check that the device has a route to a specific destination. Variants include the following:

✔ **show route inet.0:** Lists all IPv4 routes.

✔ **show route inet.61:** Lists all IPv6 routes.

✔ **show route detail:** Adds route preference, next hop, and other information.

✔ **show route *protocol*:** Lists all routes learned by the specified routing protocol.

✔ **show route forwarding-table:** Lists the entries in all the device's forwarding tables. *Use:* Lets you check which active routes are actually being used to forward traffic from the device toward network destinations.

show rip neighbor: Lists the RIP routers (neighbors) in the network. *Use:* Shows you the device interfaces on which RIP neighbors can be reached, along with the neighbors' IP addresses and distance (metric, or hop count) to the neighbors.

Give Me More Detail About Routing

show isis interface: Lists the device's interfaces running IS-IS. *Use:* Lets you verify that IS-IS is configured on the desired interfaces.

show isis adjacency: Lists the IS-IS routers (adjacencies) in the network. *Use:* Shows you the device interface on which IS-IS routers can be reached.

show ospf interface: Lists the device interfaces running OSPF. *Use:* Lets you verify that OSPF is configured on the desired interfaces.

show ospf neighbor: Lists the IS-IS routers (neighbors) in the network. *Use:* Shows you the device interface on which OSPF neighbors can be reached.

show bgp neighbor: Lists the BGP routers to which this device is connected. *Use:* Shows you which neighbors the device has established peering sessions with.

show bgp summary: Lists BGP group, peer, and session state information. *Use:* Helps you determine whether a BGP session has been established.

show route protocol bgp: Lists the routes learned from BGP. *Use:* Lets you confirm that the device is learning routes from only desired neighbors.

Show Me Something About Switching

show Ethernet-switching interfaces: Lists information about the switched Ethernet interfaces. *Use:* Enables you to find out the name, state, VLAN membership, and other details about each configured Ethernet interface.

show vlans: Lists the configured VLANs. *Use:* Lets you check configuration of the default and other VLANs.

show virtual-chassis status: Lists the role and member ID assignments in a virtual-chassis configuration. *Use:* Lets you see status, interfaces, and other data about the interconnection of platforms in a virtual chassis configuration.

show spanning-tree bridge: Lists configured or calculated Spanning Tree Protocol parameters. *Use:* Shows you bridge domain configuration and status.

show spanning-tree interface: Lists configured or calculated interface-level Spanning Tree Protocol (STP) parameters. *Use:* Lets you verify that STP is configured on the desired interfaces.

Show Me Details for Maintenance

show log messages: Lists the system log messages in the default syslog file messages. *Use:* The syslog family monitors all system-wide operations on the device and records them to syslog files. This command displays time-stamped entries so that you can see what has occurred on the device and when it occurred. Useful for tracking down device, network, and traffic flow problems.

show system uptime: Lists how long a device has been up and running. *Use:* Shows you the last time that the device was powered on, restarted, or rebooted.

Chapter 19

Ten Migration Tools

When it comes time to deploy your Junos-based devices, you may want to know what resources and tools are available to ease your migration. Fortunately, as a Juniper Networks customer, you have access to many tools that can help you save time and lower the risks of missteps. In this chapter, we share our favorites with you.

Junosphere Labs

A common first step of any migration is to model the new network in some way. Junosphere Labs, a cloud-based service offered by Juniper Networks, allows you to virtually build your network at scale. Using the services, you can model and test your new network prior to deployment without the full cost of a physical lab model — an option that isn't even feasible for large-scale networks.

Junosphere Labs offers a configurable network of virtual routers running Junos OS. Thus, you aren't just emulating the routing and control functions of your network; with Junosphere Labs you are actually testing routing and control as they will run in your Junos-based network.

Junosphere Labs offers an optional feature, known as Junosphere Connector, to connect your virtual network with physical network elements, either in your lab or in your production network (such as to access route tables), hence expanding the possibilities for testing. The service also includes optional virtual machine images for Junos Space and CentOS, letting you support UNIX network-monitoring tools and a variety of third-party test equipment in your virtual network. (Refer to Chapter 1 for more on Junos Space and visit www.centos.org for more on the Centos operating system.)

Use Junosphere Labs to ease your migration by testing how your new network will run, especially under the stress of various network and security events. You may also want to confirm interoperability with your existing network and integration with your operational systems, validate operational tools, test deployment and cutover procedures, and gain operational experience. After your new network is up and running, you can use Junosphere Labs to model changes, explore new features, and qualify software upgrades, as well as to update scenario planning in order to assess the security and availability characteristics of your network under the most recent set of considerations.

Juniper has plans to expand Junosphere Labs to add many more capabilities. Visit www.juniper.net/junosphere for the latest on the service.

Juniper Documents

Juniper publishes various documents that can help you in planning and deploying your new network:

✔ **Network configuration examples:** Provide complex multi-platform configuration examples for many advanced technologies and solutions. Examples include Class of Service, management, MPLS, routing, security, switching, IPv6, data center, VPLS, and VPNs. View the complete listing at www.juniper.net/nec.

Juniper posts the remaining documents across its website in its Solutions and Product pages, but you can find most of these documents by searching the document database of the Support team at www.juniper.net/customers/csc/documentation/techdocs.

✔ **Design Guides and Reference Architectures:** Describe how Juniper recommends designing the deployment of a solution that includes Juniper and/or Juniper partner products.

✔ **Application Notes:** Are "how to" documents describing an interesting or innovative application of a Juniper product or solution with detailed network design descriptions, architectures, and reference designs.

✔ **Implementation Guides:** Give network and system administrators important information about how to configure, verify, and start the operation of a Juniper Networks solution within their network infrastructure.

Juniper Networks Books

Juniper publishes a series of books focused on helping you to get your network up and running. These "Day One" books give you just what you need to get started on a new project. Many focus on migration topics, such as a book written specifically to help in migrating your network from the EIGRP routing protocol to the OSPF routing protocol. You can view the latest available titles and download them for free at www.juniper.net/dayone.

You might then consider heading to www.juniper.net/books for additional titles on a wide variety of networking and security topics.

Translators

A set of translators are available to convert configurations from other operating systems to Junos. Users paste their existing configuration into one of the translators, which translates the configuration and provides output suitable for downloading to a device running Junos. Juniper recommends that you review all output from the tools, but the tools can give you a good running start, typically translating 80 percent or more of your configuration.

Here are the two most popular translators:

- ✔ **IOS to Junos (I2J):** Translates full IOS configurations for Cisco 65xx, 75xx, and 12xxx platforms into Junos OS configurations. I2J supports interfaces, routing protocols, routing policy, packet filtering, and system commands. EX Series Ethernet Switch features include VLAN, RVI, Access Port, Trunk Port, STP, LAG, Voice VLAN, IP Source Guard, AutoQoS, 802.1x, Port Security, RADIUS Server, DHCP Snooping & DAI, and AAA Authentication.

- ✔ **ScreenOS to Junos (S2J):** Provides conversion of ScreenOS configuration files to Junos OS configuration files for SRX Series Services Gateways branch and datacenter platforms. S2J supports interfaces, protocols, policies, zones, route, NAT, user authentication, flow, HA, security, and other system commands.

Juniper customers with a support login can access the tools at https://migration-tools.juniper.net/tools/index.jsp. Find out how to use the I2J tool in a freely available eTraining module by selecting the Training link on the I2J tool page.

Installation Guides and Training

Juniper provides installation guides for its products in the Technical Documentation section of its website. These guides provide useful information and valuable tips for safely installing your new hardware. To find them, go to www.juniper.net/techpubs, navigate to your specific device, and click the Install tab. If you want to download a guide for use onsite, you can find a downloadable pdf file in the right-hand nav in the "download" section on many of the device pages. For a few of the products, the installation steps are covered in the product's hardware guide.

Additionally, online training on installation is available for many products. These self-paced courses describe preinstallation considerations and the installation process and also include detailed demonstrations. Because the Juniper course listing is now large, it's a bit harder to find these valuable resources than it used to be. Visit https://learningportal.juniper. net/juniper/user_courses.aspx. In the Delivery Modality drop-down box, select eLearning, change nothing else, and press Enter. Your search will find all the install courses, as well as other useful online training.

J-Web

J-Web (refer to Chapter 5) assists in the migration of individual devices by providing a set of configuration wizards that you can use to configure, secure, and run your device right out of the box.

For example, non-technical users can use the wizards to set up a branch office SRX Series device in less than five minutes. The Console Configuration Wizard walks you through setting up a basic system, user interface, and management configuration. You can then access other wizards to configure firewall policies, NAT, and IPSec VPNs. To find out more, go to www.juniper. net/dayone and download the *Day One: Configuring SRX Series with J-Web* book.

Junos Space Applications

The Junos Space portfolio includes a set of management applications that may streamline the deployment of your new network. (Refer to Chapter 1 for an introduction to Junos Space). This tool brings together a set of management applications with a simple Web 2.0 user interface for commissioning new devices in the network.

One example is Ethernet Design, which automates the configuration, visualization, monitoring, and administration of a large switch network. The tool offers automation schemes and Juniper best-practice templates that provide predefined port profile configurations by port type, security, class-of-service, and Spanning Tree Protocol (STP) settings to enable rapid and accurate deployments across multiple network elements.

Custom Commands

Junos automation provides a rich set of tools that ease the transition to Junos for network and security administrators. (Chapter 3 introduces Junos automation.) Junos automation lets you instruct the Junos OS to execute a sequence of tasks and commands tailored to your needs.

For example, with this toolset, you can customize operational commands and automate configuration changes. You could customize `show` output to familiar display listings so that the CLI screen appears familiar to new users. Or you can request confirmation for commands that might have a big impact on your network, such as the command `clear bgp neighbor`, which restarts all BGP peering sessions. (Refer to Chapter 13 for more about BGP.)

As a second example, you may want to allow new users to change a small part of the configuration, but only through guided, tailored entries to the CLI. With this type of custom automation, you can let new users with less expertise change the configuration, but only in a limited and controlled way. Consider a provisioning script that can ask relevant questions for a new connection and then automatically commit the needed configuration. With this type of automation, inexperienced users can safely provision new customers, where the automation scripts assure that the users are following established configuration guidelines, even for complex services such as those requiring advanced policy settings.

To get started, download *This Week: Applying Junos Automation* at `www.juniper.net/dayone` and then visit the Juniper script library at `www.juniper.net/automation` for many examples and templates.

Professional Services

Juniper and its partners provide a variety of professional services to directly assist in your migration with offerings such as assessment and analysis, design and planning, project implementation, network configuration services, conversion services, quick-start services, and start-up services. Visit `www.juniper.net/us/en/products-services` to discover more about the available consulting and professional services.

Chapter 20

Ten Help Resources

In This Chapter

▶ Finding help online

▶ Getting help from a live person

*I*f you still have a few more questions about using Junos OS, you can turn to many places for assistance. In this chapter, we provide our top-ten list of go-to sources to find more about software operations, training, and support — all the extra details that you may need to help you configure and operate Junos OS in your own network deployments.

Using the Command-Line Interface Help Commands

Are you looking for more background on how a particular feature works? You don't need to turn any further than the various Help commands, which you can use while logged into the device through the CLI:

- ✔ ?: Lists all the valid entries at any point of the command line.

- ✔ Help topic *command_name*: Displays configuration guidelines for any command entered as the command_name.

- ✔ Help syslog *syslog_message*: Displays the meaning of specific syslog_messages.

Using Juniper Networks Technical Publications

www.juniper.net/techpubs

Juniper Networks technical documentation includes everything you need to understand and configure all aspects of Junos and all Juniper Networks devices. The documentation set is comprehensive and thoroughly reviewed by Juniper engineering. And, for the best part, all Juniper-developed product documentation is freely accessible at this site, in convenient task-based topics or in traditional books and references.

Joining J-Net Forums

http://forums.juniper.net/jnet

J-Net is an interactive community for users to share information, best practices, and questions about Juniper products and solutions. Registration is free, and you also get access to premium content such as its free Day One books, a series written with a singular focus: to help you quickly deploy a new Junos device or feature set. You can post questions and collaborate in the community forums and subscribe to content via RSS and e-mail. In addition, there are regular promotional events in the community open only to members. J-Net is one of the best places to be if you work with the Junos OS.

Finding Videos and Webcasts

www.juniper.net/junos

Find frequently produced videos, webcasts, and other media presenting relevant topics of Junos OS at the central site for Junos.

Finding Books

`www.juniper.net/books`

Juniper Networks Books works with reputable book publishers around the world, such as the *For Dummies* publisher, to help publish networking tracts for use in the field or classroom. All the books are either written, edited, or reviewed by Juniper Networks subject-matter experts and engineers. Because this program matches the right book with the right publisher, you'll find these books refreshingly realistic and singularly focused on architecting and deploying new networks. All Juniper Networks Books support open standards, while showcasing new ideas and emerging technologies, and are available at technical bookstores and book outlets around the world. Check out other *For Dummies* titles about Juniper Networks technology, including Junos Pulse.

Using the Knowledge Base

`http://kb.juniper.net`

Search through the entire Juniper Networks Knowledge Base (KB) and find answers, solutions, and tips on your specific issues, troubleshooting, or network maintenance. You can install a KB search engine plug-in on your laptop or computer's browser, or get the mobile edition for your smartphone. The KB is constantly updated.

Taking Certification Courses

`www.juniper.net/training/fasttrack`

Take certification courses online, on location, or at one of the partner training centers around the world. The Juniper Networks Technical Certification Program (JNTCP) allows you to earn certifications by demonstrating competence in configuration and troubleshooting Juniper products. Juniper's certification courses provide the fast track to earning your certifications in enterprise routing, switching, and/or security through online courses, student guides, and lab guides.

Getting Support

Do you have a question or an issue that requires assistance from technical support? Perhaps you want to upgrade your software. For quick-and-easy problem resolution, Juniper Networks offers an online self-service portal: the Customer Support Center (CSC) at `www.juniper.net/support`.

Contacting Customer Care

For nontechnical customer assistance issues:

✔ **Phone (toll free, United States and Canada):** Call 1-800-638-8296 and select Option 2 for Customer Care.

✔ **Phone (outside the United States):** Call 1-408-745-9500 and select Option 2 for Customer Care.

✔ **Web:** Open a "Customer Care Case" via the CSC Case Manager at `www.juniper.net/cm/case_create_customer_care.jsp`.

Contacting JTAC

For technical assistance issues:

✔ **Phone (toll free, United States, Canada, and Mexico):** Call 1-888-314-JTAC (1-888-314-5822).

✔ **Phone (outside the United States):** Call 1-408-745-9500.

✔ **Web:** For Case Manager, visit `www.juniper.net/cm` (requires login).

Juniper doesn't permit opening JTAC cases via e-mail. For a listing of local telephone numbers, visit www.juniper.net/support/requesting-support.html.

Index

• B •

• C •

• D •

• N •

• *T* •

Apple & Macs

iPad For Dummies
978-0-470-58027-1

iPhone For Dummies,
4th Edition
978-0-470-87870-5

MacBook For Dummies, 3rd
Edition
978-0-470-76918-8

Mac OS X Snow Leopard For
Dummies
978-0-470-43543-4

Business

Bookkeeping For Dummies
978-0-7645-9848-7

Job Interviews
For Dummies,
3rd Edition
978-0-470-17748-8

Resumes For Dummies,
5th Edition
978-0-470-08037-5

Starting an
Online Business
For Dummies,
6th Edition
978-0-470-60210-2

Stock Investing
For Dummies,
3rd Edition
978-0-470-40114-9

Successful
Time Management
For Dummies
978-0-470-29034-7

Computer Hardware

BlackBerry
For Dummies,
4th Edition
978-0-470-60700-8

Computers For Seniors
For Dummies,
2nd Edition
978-0-470-53483-0

PCs For Dummies,
Windows
7 Edition
978-0-470-46542-4

Laptops For Dummies,
4th Edition
978-0-470-57829-2

Cooking & Entertaining

Cooking Basics
For Dummies,
3rd Edition
978-0-7645-7206-7

Wine For Dummies,
4th Edition
978-0-470-04579-4

Diet & Nutrition

Dieting For Dummies,
2nd Edition
978-0-7645-4149-0

Nutrition For Dummies,
4th Edition
978-0-471-79868-2

Weight Training
For Dummies,
3rd Edition
978-0-471-76845-6

Digital Photography

Digital SLR Cameras &
Photography For Dummies,
3rd Edition
978-0-470-46606-3

Photoshop Elements 8
For Dummies
978-0-470-52967-6

Gardening

Gardening Basics
For Dummies
978-0-470-03749-2

Organic Gardening
For Dummies,
2nd Edition
978-0-470-43067-5

Green/Sustainable

Raising Chickens
For Dummies
978-0-470-46544-8

Green Cleaning
For Dummies
978-0-470-39106-8

Health

Diabetes For Dummies,
3rd Edition
978-0-470-27086-8

Food Allergies
For Dummies
978-0-470-09584-3

Living Gluten-Free
For Dummies,
2nd Edition
978-0-470-58589-4

Hobbies/General

Chess For Dummies,
2nd Edition
978-0-7645-8404-6

Drawing
Cartoons & Comics
For Dummies
978-0-470-42683-8

Knitting For Dummies,
2nd Edition
978-0-470-28747-7

Organizing
For Dummies
978-0-7645-5300-4

Su Doku For Dummies
978-0-470-01892-7

Home Improvement

Home Maintenance
For Dummies,
2nd Edition
978-0-470-43063-7

Home Theater
For Dummies,
3rd Edition
978-0-470-41189-6

Living the
Country Lifestyle
All-in-One
For Dummies
978-0-470-43061-3

Solar Power Your Home
For Dummies,
2nd Edition
978-0-470-59678-4

Internet

Blogging For Dummies,
3rd Edition
978-0-470-61996-4

eBay For Dummies,
6th Edition
978-0-470-49741-8

Facebook For Dummies,
3rd Edition
978-0-470-87804-0

Web Marketing
For Dummies,
2nd Edition
978-0-470-37181-7

WordPress
For Dummies,
3rd Edition
978-0-470-59274-8

Language & Foreign Language

French For Dummies
978-0-7645-5193-2

Italian Phrases
For Dummies
978-0-7645-7203-6

Spanish For Dummies,
2nd Edition
978-0-470-87855-2

Spanish
For Dummies,
Audio Set
978-0-470-09585-0

Math & Science

Algebra I
For Dummies,
2nd Edition
978-0-470-55964-2

Biology For Dummies,
2nd Edition
978-0-470-59875-7

Calculus For Dummies
978-0-7645-2498-1

Chemistry For Dummies
978-0-7645-5430-8

Microsoft Office

Excel 2010 For Dummies
978-0-470-48953-6

Office 2010 All-in-One
For Dummies
978-0-470-49748-7

Office 2010 For Dummies,
Book + DVD Bundle
978-0-470-62698-6

Word 2010 For Dummies
978-0-470-48772-3

Music

Guitar For Dummies,
2nd Edition
978-0-7645-9904-0

iPod & iTunes For
Dummies, 8th Edition
978-0-470-87871-2

Piano Exercises
For Dummies
978-0-470-38765-8

Parenting & Education

Parenting For Dummies,
2nd Edition
978-0-7645-5418-6

Type 1 Diabetes
For Dummies
978-0-470-17811-9

Pets

Cats For Dummies,
2nd Edition
978-0-7645-5275-5

Dog Training For Dummies,
3rd Edition
978-0-470-60029-0

Puppies For Dummies,
2nd Edition
978-0-470-03717-1

Religion & Inspiration

The Bible For Dummies
978-0-7645-5296-0

Catholicism For Dummies
978-0-7645-5391-2

Women in the Bible
For Dummies
978-0-7645-8475-6

Self-Help & Relationship

Anger Management
For Dummies
978-0-470-03715-7

Overcoming Anxiety
For Dummies,
2nd Edition
978-0-470-57441-6

Sports

Baseball
For Dummies,
3rd Edition
978-0-7645-7537-2

Basketball
For Dummies,
2nd Edition
978-0-7645-5248-9

Golf For Dummies,
3rd Edition
978-0-471-76871-5

Web Development

Web Design
All-in-One
For Dummies
978-0-470-41796-6

Web Sites
Do-It-Yourself
For Dummies,
2nd Edition
978-0-470-56520-9

Windows 7

Windows 7
For Dummies
978-0-470-49743-2

Windows 7
For Dummies,
Book + DVD Bundle
978-0-470-52398-8

Windows 7 All-in-One
For Dummies
978-0-470-48763-1

Available wherever books are sold. For more information or to order direct: U.S. customers visit www.dummies.com or call 1-877-762-
U.K. customers visit www.wileyeurope.com or call (0) 1243 843291. Canadian customers visit www.wiley.ca or call 1-800-567-4797.

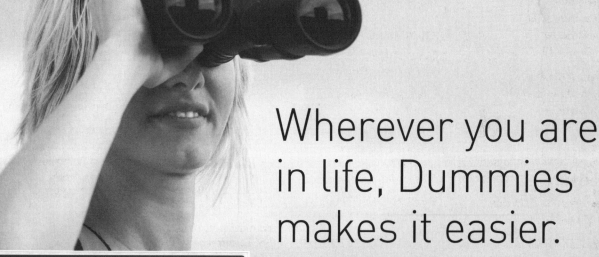

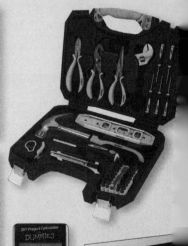